Sustainability Made Simple

Sustainability Made Simple

Small Changes for Big Impact

Rosaly Byrd and Laurèn DeMates

ROWMAN & LITTLEFIELD
Lanham • Boulder • New York • London

Published by Rowman & Littlefield
A wholly owned subsidiary of The Rowman & Littlefield Publishing Group, Inc.
4501 Forbes Boulevard, Suite 200, Lanham, Maryland 20706
www.rowman.com

Unit A, Whitacre Mews, 26-34 Stannary Street, London SE11 4AB

British Library Cataloguing in Publication Information Available

Library of Congress Cataloging-in-Publication Data

Names: Byrd, Rosaly, 1988– author. | DeMates, Laur?en, 1985– author.
Title: Sustainability made simple : small changes for big impact / Rosaly Byrd and Laurèn DeMates.
Description: Lanham, Maryland : Rowman & Littlefield, [2017] | Includes bliographical references and index.
Identifiers: LCCN 2016032731 | ISBN 9781442269095 (cloth : alk. paper)
Subjects: LCSH: Sustainability. | Sustainable living.
Classification: LCC GE196 .B97 2017 | DDC 338.9/27—dc23
LC record available at https://lccn.loc.gov/2016032731

∞™ The paper used in this publication meets the minimum requirements of American National Standard for Information Sciences—Permanence of Paper for Printed Library Materials, ANSI/NISO Z39.48-1992.

Printed in the United States of America

Contents

Acknowledgments

We would like to thank our partners, family, and friends for their support in writing this book as well as their willingness to try new sustainability tips themselves in solidarity. Sustainability and writing can both be intimidating, but through their support and the inspiration we received along the way, *Sustainability Made Simple* is here today. This book not only reflects what we set out to write, but was shaped by the stories of those impacted by environmental issues and those dedicated to making improvements in their communities and the world. We are more inspired than ever.

We would also like to acknowledge the University of California, San Diego's School of Global Policy and Strategy (formerly known as IR/PS) for bringing us together in the first place and enabling us to take on the important issues explored in this book.

Introduction

Sustainability Made Simple provides a helpful approach to understanding sustainability by linking how everyday activities relate to the big-picture environmental issues that sustainability is seeking to address: air and water pollution, deforestation, and climate change. Our approach acknowledges that although society is facing unprecedented environmental challenges, working toward sustainability is an opportunity to do things differently and do things better, enhancing aspects of life such as health and community.

Motivated by the polarized and overwhelming information that exists related to sustainability and sustainable living, this book offers an optimistic, yet realistic, perspective on our relationship with the environment. By translating science-based evidence into easy-to-understand language and applications, we hope to inform and engage everyone on sustainability. This book is designed for those who are interested in learning what sustainability is about and picking up habits to be more sustainable. We don't seek to scare, guilt, or pressure our readers into "going off the grid" or making drastic life changes. Instead, we offer guidance to those who are interested in finding new and relatively easy ways to incorporate sustainability into daily life.

Because the environmental challenges that our world is currently experiencing are complex issues that affect everyone, it'll take everyone to fix them. Governments, companies, and other organizations that shape our lives are beginning to acknowledge the consequences that our actions have on natural resources, and are deploying exciting new strategies to repair flawed systems. As individuals, we can support this shift toward sustainability in a number of ways, creating a new and better norm for people and the environment.

SUSTAINABILITY MADE SIMPLE CONSISTS OF TWO PARTS

Part 1 introduces the concept of sustainability and explores environmental issues that impact our lives. Also covered in Part 1 are examples of how society is already transitioning toward sustainability and why individual action is essential to this process.

Part 2 provides tips on how to incorporate sustainability into daily life and reduce the negative impact our actions have on the environment. The tips are organized by common activities and outline how we and the environment benefit from incorporating these habits into daily routines. We encourage readers to use part 2 as a reference guide, referring back to specific chapters when taking part in related activities to remember how to make them more sustainable.

Part 1

AN INTRODUCTION TO SUSTAINABILITY

When one tugs at a single thing in nature, he finds it attached to the rest of the world.

—John Muir

1

A Brief Overview

In the past 50 years, we have altered our environment more than in the previous thousands of years of human history. Since 1960, we have multiplied our population by more than three, and consumption of oil has grown by a factor of 3.5.[1] The number of motor vehicles has risen from 40 million after World War II to more than 1 billion in 2010.[2] Current levels of carbon dioxide are higher than they have been in at least 800,000 years.[3] Changes in the biodiversity of flora and fauna and the ecosystems in which they live have occurred more quickly in the past 50 years than at any time in human history, and more natural land has been converted to cropland since 1950 than in the 150 years between 1700 and 1850.[4] But in this same time period, we have also mapped the human genome and identified all of the 20,000 genes in human DNA.[5] We developed and deployed the computer, the Internet, and the smartphone on a remarkable scale. We have also experienced several cultural shifts that have altered how we interact with each other and with the environment.[6]

Building on the advancements made in the last 50 years, we now find ourselves in the midst of a shift in how we see ourselves in the world. It is a decisive moment where we are optimistic about the future that technology can bring us, but where we are also looking beyond technology to solve our problems. In this moment, we realize that the actions of individuals and communities can shape the future of our society and we accept that we have the chance to determine if our future will reflect our values.

It is in this context that we see more attention in the United States being given to the environmental challenges that surround us, as well as the economic and health impacts connected to these challenges. It is also in this context that a plethora of strategies are arising on how to safeguard our lives from the impacts of environmental issues such as climate change. Most of these strategies fall under the umbrella of sustainability. Sustainability is frequently defined along the lines of "maintaining the conditions which humans and nature can exist in productive harmony to support present and future generations"[7]: a straightforward description, but also an abstract one that doesn't exactly guide us in how we are supposed to achieve it. Sustainability is dynamic, but it's also pretty simple when you take a step back and think about where the goods and services we consume come from and where they go after we are done with them. By understanding why environmental problems exist, we understand what sustainability is trying to address.

Sustainability is understanding causes and effects; it's long-term thinking rather than short-term; it's a global and local perspective; it's about conserving rather than exploiting; it's realizing that humans are a part of nature, not separate from it; and it's an opportunity to transform our society for the better.

A sustainable society is one that embraces this evolved perspective towards the environment and works with it, not against it. To achieve a sustainable society, we will need to recognize how dependent we are on the environment and what is at risk if we continue to put significant stress on natural resources. This in particular means acknowledging the value of natural resources and what they provide us, and integrating this value into decision-making at all levels.

ECOSYSTEM SERVICES

The environment is made up of natural resources and systems that work together in perfect balance and provide humans with all types of benefits. These benefits that we receive from the environment are generally called "ecosystem services" and can take the form of a wide range of processes, including, among many others, providing us clean drinking water through water purification. This process of purifying water involves several environmental factors, including forests, wetlands, soil, and microbes, all of which play a role in removing metals, oils, sediment, and nitrogen from rainwater so it's not harmful to drink. Forests and wetlands act as a sponge, intercepting the rain, absorbing and storing pollutants from the water in their soil for microbes to break them down, and then letting clean rainwater move on to streams and lakes. Wetlands can remove 20 to 60 percent of metals, 80 to 90 percent of sediments, and 70 to 90 percent of nitrogen from the water. Forests can reduce nitrogen concentration from the water by up to 90 percent, keeping our water clean and drinkable.[8]

Ecosystem services are the basis not only of the things we buy and services we use, but also of our quality of life. They provide us with our drinking water, food to eat, materials to build with, and beaches to enjoy. However, ecosystems must be healthy to function properly, and putting them under too much stress limits their ability to provide such benefits. For instance, in the case of water purification, many factors can inhibit the environment from providing this service, including deforestation and the paving of natural green spaces. Without sufficient plants and soil, there is no sponge to soak up polluting substances from the water. In understanding this connection, we begin to gain insight into how our lives are tied to the health of the environment. We begin to see how the actions of current generations determine the health of natural resources and ecosystem services for future generations.

Air and water pollution, deforestation, and climate change are the results of human activity; they also threaten many of the ecosystem services we depend on. When we look around, it becomes obvious that we have not done a great job at maintaining the environment's ability to provide us with these benefits and that they have not been distributed equally. Millions of people still lack access to basic rights such as clean drinking water. From the Amazon rainforest in South America to the Appalachian Mountains in the United States,[10] communities have had their land and water contaminated from the industrial activities that create the electricity we use and the products we buy. We know that the environment is tied to our future and that situations could be improved for people and the environment, so how did it get to this point?

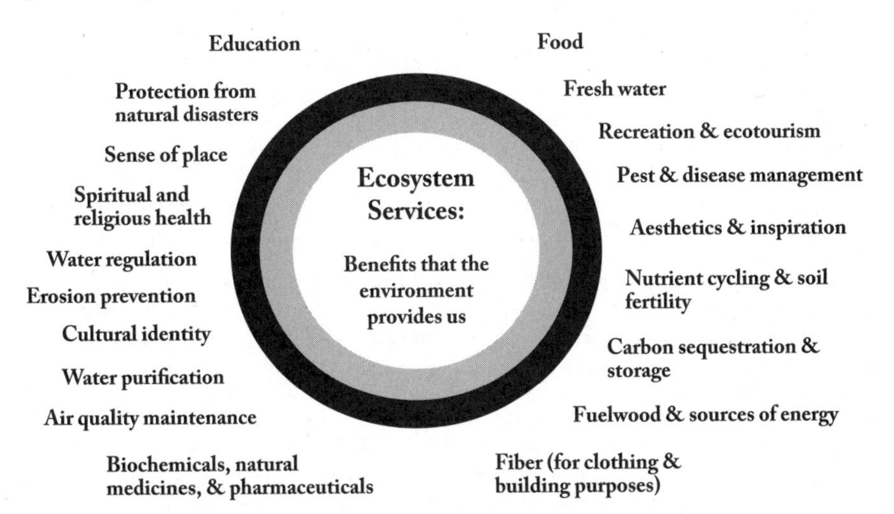

Figure 1.1 Ecosystem Services: Benefits that the Environment Provides Us. Millennium Ecosystem Assessment, *Ecosystems and Human Well-Being: A Framework for Assessment* (2005), accessed February 28, 2016, http://www.millenniumassessment.org/en/Framework.html#download.

Box 1.1 Tragedy of the Atlantic Cod in New England, United States

Fishing cod has been a prominent source of pride and income in New England since the 1600s. As early as the mid-1700s, fear that the fish stocks would be depleted incited local government to limit fishing. However, these efforts were not successful, and by the 1980s, the cod population in New England was completely overfished. The local fishing industry collapsed, with cod populations diminishing to 1 percent of what they once were. For many years it was thought that the cod population could rebound, but that no longer seems likely, particularly due to a warming ocean and ineffective fishing regulations. This problem has been observed around the world as global fisheries have dwindled. In response to this overfishing, in May 2016 the international community came together and signed the Port State Measures Agreement, the first ever binding international accord focusing on illegal, unregulated, and unreported fishing.[1]

Note

1. Food and Agricultural Organization (FAO), "Ground-breaking Illegal Fishing Accord Soon to Enter into Force," May 16, 2016, accessed May 17, 2016, http://www.fao.org/news/story/en/item/414494/icode/?utm_source=twitter&utm_medium=social+media&utm_campaign=faoknowledge.

PROPERLY VALUING THE ENVIRONMENT

Several reasons can be used to explain why environmental degradation occurs, yet the lack of proper valuation of ecosystem services is a key factor and has cascading impacts. More specifically, the cost of environmental impact has largely been missing from how goods are priced, and thus, from decision-making in general. When prices reflect the true value of natural resources, it can be a strong incentive to deter actions that have negative environmental impacts. Think about plastic bags. In most parts of the United States, plastic bags are offered free of charge when we purchase groceries or other items from the store. Yet the production and disposal of plastic bags are associated with various environmental effects, including natural resource extraction, extensive energy use, water pollution that can kill wildlife, and even climate change. Since these negative environmental impacts are not factored into the price they are sold for, plastic bags seem cheap and disposable. Their low market price has created incentives for frequent use and, without convenient avenues for disposal, has led to the pollution of our land and waterways.

Unfortunately, the failure to integrate environmental impacts into price is not unique to plastic; it is the norm. The proper valuation of the environment is generally not reflected in the price we pay for goods and services, resulting in unsustainable outcomes and even billions of dollars spent on services that healthy ecosystems could be doing for free.[11] Think back to the drinking water example. Because the services rendered by forests, wetlands, soil, and microbes (which include, but are not limited to, water purification) are not properly valued, companies and governments are not incentivized to protect them. Instead, they engage in actions that limit the environment's ability to provide clean water in the future, although it can be less expensive to prevent pollution in the first place than to clean contaminated water. For example, according to the Union of Concerned Scientists and the Ecological Society of America, New York State opted to spend $1 billion to restore the watershed that provided New York City's drinking water rather than spend $8 billion on water treatment. However, taking this type of holistic perspective to see and

Box 1.2 The Disappearing Bees

Certain pesticides used in conventional agriculture called neonicotinoids cause severe harm to bees, including to honey bee queens, and can bring down entire colonies.[1] Unfortunately, the combination of pesticides, habitat loss, climate change, and disease is collapsing honey bee colonies at an alarming rate and with dire consequences. Beekeepers in the United States lost 40 percent of their bees in 2015 alone.[2] This is very bad news because bees are pollinators, making it possible to grow around 30 percent of the world's food crops and 90 percent of wild plants. In the United States, bees pollinate over $15 billion worth of crops including apples, berries, cantaloupes, cucumbers, broccoli, onions, carrots, avocados, and almonds. California almond growers even import bees to pollinate their crops.[3] We have essentially been enjoying these pollination services for free, but when quantified they are very valuable and would be extremely costly to lose.

Notes

1. Geoffrey Williams et al. "Neonicotinoid Pesticides Severely Affect Honey Bee Queens," *Scientific Reports* 5 (2015), accessed April 30, 2016, doi:10.1038/srep14621.
2. University of Maryland, "U.S. Beekeepers Lost 40 Percent of Bees in 2014–15," *ScienceDaily* (May 13, 2015), accessed April 30, 2016, www.sciencedaily.com/releases/2015/05/150513093605.htm.
3. Natural Resources Defense Council (NRDC), "Why We Need Bees," accessed April 30, 2016, https://www.nrdc.org/sites/default/files/bees.pdf.

quantify the value of protecting the environment is not the default process. As a result, instead of specifically taking measures to protect watersheds, forests, and waterways as New York State did, the United States spends billions annually for clean water initiatives to provide us with drinking water.[12]

We have a lot of work to do as a society to break past this norm and encourage sustainable decisions. This entails actions by individuals, businesses, governments, the international community, and others. That may sound overwhelming, but being faced with seemingly insurmountable challenges brings people together and spurs innovation, which can create a slew of other positive benefits. This is what we are seeing right now all over the world: Despite the difficulty, we are coming together to change the status quo. For instance, thanks to the hard work and dedication of people around the world, over 190 countries agreed on the first comprehensive international climate change agreement in 2015, the Paris Agreement.

As we will see throughout the remainder of this book, the urgency of climate change in particular is prompting society to act. All types of environmental problems such as water pollution and food waste, issues that have been known for years, are now gaining recognition as the world comes together to act on climate. The United Nations Sustainable Development Goals, agreed upon by world leaders in 2015, demonstrate this momentum toward sustainability and present a guiding framework for all countries to work toward a healthy and sustainable planet.[13]

Such international agreements mark a shift in the way we see our society and present a way for us to be a part of a global movement. However, they are only the first step. To successfully address climate change and meet the goals set forth will require the efforts of everyone. Individuals are integral to providing the support for the structural changes needed to move toward a sustainable society. By deciding to be more sustainability-minded, you are not only reducing your contribution to the big issues explored in more detail in chapter 2, but you are also supporting a shift toward a new norm in which the benefits are exponential.

· 2 ·

The Big Issues

The way humans have been doing things has been unsustainable. We have lost touch with the fact that we are a part of nature and that we rely on ecosystem services for all the activities in our daily lives, and the result has been a system that doesn't adequately value these services. It is possible to do things differently, but understanding what went wrong is key to changing our behaviors and actions. Looking at some of the big environmental issues we see today, including water and air pollution, deforestation, and climate change, it becomes clear that they have large consequences not only on the environment but on human livelihoods too.

By examining these challenges, we can also observe how environmental threats are connected to major social problems that our society faces, such as poverty, epidemics, and the basic survival of humans. It's estimated that nearly one in four deaths in the world is the result of living in unhealthy environments and being exposed to environmental risk factors, such as pollution, chemicals, and climate change impacts.[1] Out of 133 global diseases and illnesses studied by the World Health Organization (WHO) in 2016, 101 had significant links to the environment.[2] Exposure to these risks isn't distributed fairly either; people who are already vulnerable to disease, illness, and poverty often feel environmental problems more than others.

Some human actions have only local impacts on the environment, while others can affect people all over the world. Furthermore, while most of the big environmental issues are caused by an aggregation of many individual actions, sometimes the effect of one single action, such as by a company or a power plant, can be just as damaging (or even worse). Despite whether the unsustainable action is done by one or is the aggregate of many, we need to, and can do, something about it. Being informed and understanding how everything is connected are important first steps.

Air and water pollution, deforestation, and climate change are four dominant environmental challenges of our time. These challenges have both direct and indirect consequences on our lives and are much closer to us than we might imagine. The impact of big environmental problems do not only occur in faraway places, but can often be felt and seen in our own states and communities. We may already be familiar with these issues from news reports or even from our own experiences, but may not be aware of the exact causes. By diving into these four interconnected issues and unpacking the human causes associated with each one, we can better conceptualize our relationship with the environment and why sustainability is important.

AIR POLLUTION

Media images of people wearing facemasks to protect themselves from pollution are often captured in Beijing, China. In December 2015, air pollution in Beijing reached record levels, causing the government to issue its first "red alert," which forced vehicles off the road, and factories, construction sites, and schools to close for three days. One week later, a second red alert was issued, again for three consecutive days, as some areas throughout the city were exposed to air pollutants almost 30 times the maximum level recommended by the WHO. Beijing, however, doesn't even make the list of the world's most polluted cities, which is dominated by cities in India where public air quality alert systems are not as reliable. Air pollution is not limited to Asia or developing countries either, as half of the world's population – more than 3.5 billion people – live in areas with unsafe levels of air pollution.[3] Although in the United States overall air quality has improved, there are still improvements to be made. In some U.S. cities, air quality has actually gotten worse, and over 50 percent of Americans still live in places with unhealthy levels of air pollution.[4]

THINKING ABOUT IMPACT

Although everyone can be affected, children, the elderly, and individuals who already have asthma, diabetes, or other cardiovascular diseases are particularly vulnerable to the health risks of air pollution. There is also evidence that people living in poverty are particularly at risk, as they are more likely to live closer to the sources of air pollution (these sources will be examined in more depth in the second part of this chapter).[5] Plants, water, and wildlife also suffer due to air pollution. There are various types of air pollutants, yet one of the major culprits is ground-level ozone (or smog), which causes low visibility.

Human Health and Healthcare Costs

Exposure to high levels of air pollution has significant negative impacts on human health, such as causing various respiratory problems (including aggravated asthma, lung cancer, heart disease, and stroke).[6] It can even result in death; it is estimated that air pollution accounts for 10 percent of all deaths in the world today.[7] Roughly 30 percent of childhood asthma is a result of environmental exposures, costing the United States $2 billion per year and also keeping kids from going to school: Approximately 10 million school days are lost each year due to asthma.[8] Air pollution in the United States is also estimated to cause 16,000 premature births per year, making up 3 percent of all premature births. According to a 2016 study by NYU Langone Medical Center, the cost of premature births linked to air pollution (which includes prolonged hospital stays, long-term use of medications, and lost economic productivity due to physical and mental disabilities) is $4.33 billion per year.[9] In addition, a study published in February 2016 found that chronic exposure to air pollution was associated with weight gain, increasing the risk of obesity and other illnesses such as heart disease and diabetes.[10] If that wasn't enough, it's also been found that air pollution can cause wrinkles and premature aging.[11]

The economy is hit by air pollution directly through healthcare costs and also through a decrease in productivity. Studies have found that the productivity of agricultural, factory, and even office workers is significantly affected by smog levels.[12]

Plant Health

Similar to human health, air pollution negatively impacts plant health and damages a plant's ability to grow by disrupting photosynthesis processes. The worst pollutants for plants are ground-level ozone (smog) and sulfur dioxide, which can impact their ability to blossom and increase susceptibility to pests and disease. Evidence of air pollution can be observed through a discoloration of leaves.

Agricultural Productivity and Costs

Limits on a plant's ability to grow translates into lower agricultural yields (i.e., the amount of food produced), and since ground-level ozone can impact plants' health, this means that it also impacts food production. Studies have found that ground-level ozone and black carbon had reduced wheat crop yields in India by up to 36 percent, with some areas of the country experiencing yield losses of up to 50 percent.[13] With a growing population, growing less with the same amount of land costs more and threatens overall food security.

Acid Rain

Air pollution can impact more than just air quality. In a phenomenon called acid rain, pollutants such as sulfur dioxide (SO_2) and nitrogen oxides (NOx) react with oxygen and water molecules in the atmosphere. The water becomes acidic and causes long-term damage to plants, soil, and bodies of water when it returns back to earth in the form of rain. Acid rain turns rivers and lakes acidic, damaging and killing fish and other marine species. Plants also lose essential nutrients when acidic rain sinks into the soil. Large parts of the United States and Canada have been plagued by acid rain. For instance, streams and rivers in the Great Smoky Mountains National Park have become acidic from this process and may take decades to recover, despite effective regional measures to combat acid rain.[14]

Box 2.1 Ozone Damage in the Great Smoky Mountains

Air pollution has even left its mark on protected U.S. National Parks, particularly the Great Smoky Mountains. Since 1948, average visibility in the southern Appalachians has decreased 40 percent in winter and 80 percent in summer.[1] Due to coal-fired power plants and cars in the region, for decades smog has replaced the natural fog or mist that usually hangs over the Great Smoky Mountains, and after which the park is named. Ozone levels were injuring trees and plants, with plants at higher elevations experiencing more ozone exposure and damage. Air pollution monitoring found that "up to 90 percent of black cherry trees and milkweed plants in numerous park locations (showed) symptoms of ozone damage" while other plants including the tulip tree, sassafras winged sumac, blackberry, and cutleaf coneflower showed symptoms as well.[2] Fortunately, the park has seen improved air quality in the past ten years thanks to more regional and federal regulations, but many plants are still impacted by the air pollution that afflicted the park for years.

Notes

1. U.S. National Park Service, "Great Smoky Mountains Air Quality," accessed April 10, 2016, https://www.nps.gov/grsm/learn/nature/air-quality.htm.
2. Ibid.

WATER POLLUTION

The 2010 Deepwater Horizon spill in the Gulf of Mexico was the biggest oil spill in the United States' history, with attempts to cap the spill unsuccessful for 87 days. A total of 171 million gallons of oil poured into the Gulf, followed by 1.8 million gallons of toxic chemical dispersant as a response effort, which was largely ineffective.[15] The water pollution killed fish and other marine life and impacted coral reefs up to 150 miles away from the spill.[16] The damage wasn't only environmental either; the local fishing and tourism industries collapsed. Long-term impacts from the spill span industries, communities, and ecosystems. Although the Deepwater Horizon oil spill was a disaster of historic proportion, water contamination is unfortunately more common than one would think.

Some water pollution occurs naturally from sediments and soil entering waterways, but most pollution, including the Deepwater Horizon spill, is caused by humans. Water becomes polluted when pollutants enter lakes, rivers, oceans, groundwater/aquifers, and other bodies of water, and although water is considered a renewable resource, the amount of water humans can access and use is limited.

In addition to being essential for the human body to function, water is needed to grow the food we eat, generate electricity, make clothes and plastics, and refine the gasoline that runs our cars. Water makes up the rivers, lakes, streams, and oceans that we enjoy for recreational activities, and is the backbone to ecosystems that provide us with many more services on which we depend.

THINKING ABOUT IMPACT

Increased demand, overuse, droughts related to climate change, and water pollution all threaten our water supply. Similar to air pollution, water pollution doesn't know boundaries. Pollution moves as the waterways move, transporting negative impacts from one area to another, even to places that don't play a direct role in contaminating the water.

Human Health

In low-income and lower-middle-income countries (such as Haiti and Cameroon, respectively), consumption of contaminated water is one of the top ten causes of death (especially in children).[17] Although for different reasons, there are also cases of contaminated drinking water in the

United States. In 2004, illegal levels of arsenic, known to cause cancer, were found in the drinking water of cities in New Jersey.[18] In West Virginia in 2014, a chemical spill polluted the waterways, affecting 300,000 residents within nine counties.[19] Unsafe levels of lead in drinking water have plagued various cities from Flint, Michigan, and Columbia, South Carolina, to Sebring, Ohio, and Washington D.C., due to corroded water pipes, all within the last 15 years.[20] One can also feel the effects of water pollution without it contaminating the drinking water: a study in Santa Monica Bay, California, found that swimming near areas where storm drainage enters the ocean

Box 2.2 Contaminated Drinking Water in Flint, Michigan

In January 2016, a drinking water crisis in Flint, Michigan, led President Obama to issue an emergency declaration for the State of Michigan, which allowed the Federal Emergency Management Agency (FEMA) to step in, distributing clean water and providing other support to residents.[1] Although numbers documenting the extent of the damage to human health are still unfolding, Genesee County alone experienced a spike of 90 cases of legionnaires' disease (a lung infection caused by bacteria) and 10 deaths due to the contamination.[2] The problem started in 2014 when the local government switched water sources from Detroit's water system to the Flint River (which has been polluted since the 1970s), in order to cut costs. Soon after, fecal coliform bacteria appeared in the drinking water and was treated with chloride. But since the treatment was not accompanied by the normally obligatory corrosion control, the lead pipes leaked lead into the water. The local government was slow to act, and even though the drinking water is once again sourced from the Detroit system, the damage has been done and the corroded lead pipes continue to leak into the water. Four government officials resigned and several lawsuits and investigations have ensued since the story broke.[3]

Notes

1. White House, "FACT SHEET: Federal Support for the Flint Water Crisis Response and Recovery," May 3, 2016, accessed September 10, 2016, https://www.whitehouse.gov/the-press-office/2016/05/03/fact-sheet-federal-support-flint-water-crisis-response-and-recovery.
2. Daniel Bethencourt, "Snyder: Flint Has Seen Spike in Legionnaires' Disease," *Detroit Free Press*, January 15, 2016, accessed September 10, 2016, http://www.freep.com/story/news/local/michigan/2016/01/13/snyder-flint-area-has-seen-spike-legionnaires/78750610/.
3. CNN, "Flint Water Crisis Fast Facts," accessed September 10, 2016, http://www.cnn.com/2016/03/04/us/flint-water-crisis-fast-facts/.

increased swimmers' risk of health effects, including respiratory disease and gastrointestinal illness.[21]

Plant and Animal Health

There are many different pollutants that are detrimental and can kill aquatic plants and animals. When oil and chemicals make it into the waterways, animals are poisoned from ingesting or inhaling the pollutants, or from skin and eye irritation. Chemicals that contain nitrogen or phosphate can cause algal blooms, which reduce the amount of oxygen available for other aquatic life to survive, in a process called eutrophication. Eutrophication can collapse ecosystems, creating dead zones. If the waterways are connected to the ocean, the negative effects continue there. According to the United Nations Educational, Scientific, and Cultural Organization (UNESCO), close to 500 dead zones exist, covering more than 95,000 sq. miles globally, or about the size of the United Kingdom.[22]

Seafood and Fishing

Commercial and recreational fishing can be affected by water pollution. The Gulf of Mexico, which accounts for 40 percent of commercial seafood caught

Box 2.3 Great Pacific Garbage Patch

The Great Pacific Garbage Patch is a huge congregation of trash floating in the ocean between California and Japan that was discovered in 1997. It's estimated to be about the size of Texas, but size is debated as it is constantly changing. Although its composition changes as well, we do know that the patch is made up mostly of microplastics, the product that results when plastic breaks into smaller and smaller pieces. About 80 percent of the Great Pacific Garbage Patch debris originated in North America and Asia, brought there via wind and waves. It takes about six years for North American trash to get there and about a year for trash coming from Asian countries.[1] Unfortunately, the Great Pacific Garbage Patch isn't the only congregation of trash in our oceans; additional patches have been observed in other parts of the Pacific, as well as the Atlantic and Indian oceans.

Note

1. National Geographic, "Great Pacific Garbage Patch," accessed March 5, 2016, http://education.nationalgeographic.org/encyclopedia/great-pacific-garbage-patch/.

in the continental United States and 41 percent of all fish caught recreationally, is threatened by various human-caused pollutants.[23] Water pollution can kill fish, and also poison them, which means the seafood you eat can contain toxic pollutants. Mercury contamination in fish has attracted the most attention, but fish ingest and absorb many other pollutants into their tissue, especially chemicals from the plastic debris that ends up in the ocean (see the case study on the Great Pacific Garbage Patch).[24]

Recreation and Tourism

Can you imagine your favorite beach, river, or lake contaminated with water pollution? No one wants to swim with oil, chemicals, or plastic. Many communities also rely on tourism as their main source of income so local impacts are social and economic.

DEFORESTATION

Alaska's Tongass National Forest is one of the last old-growth temperate rainforests standing on earth. It covers 17 million acres of southeast Alaska and contains rich ecosystems and critical wildlife.[25] It is also the only U.S. national forest where subsidized, large-scale old-growth commercial logging continues. In 2015, the U.S. Forest Service sold off 6,000 acres of Tongass' old-growth forests (and 2,000 acres of new-growth forest), to be clear-cut for logging purposes and to make roads. Since the 1950s, southeastern Alaska has lost almost one million acres of old-growth forest due to logging, harming ecosystems and threatening local animals like the Alexander Archipelago wolf.[26]

The rate of global forest loss has increased in the past 15 years. The world has lost an average of 180,749 km^2 (18.1 million hectares) of forest annually since 2000,[27] or a little more than the size of Florida lost every year. Although most of the stories you hear about deforestation today are in tropical places like Indonesia or the Amazon rainforest, there is a long history of deforestation in the United States, one that has only begun to reverse. Fortunately, the Alaskan clear-cut case is not common in the United States today, where forest cover is actually increasing overall.[28] As demonstrated in the second part of this chapter, although factors contributing to deforestation can be locally fueled (such as for subsistence farming and fuel production), it is largely a global economic issue driven by demand for specific goods in both developed and developing countries. Moreover, forests are usually threatened by a combination of factors (not one sole factor) and the most prevalent threat often varies by forest.

THINKING ABOUT IMPACT

The effects of deforestation reverberate throughout the ecosystem as well as in our own lives. Since there are many ecosystem services that are connected to and depend on the health of trees, forests are a major lifeline to other natural resources. Moreover, trees are the source of our own existence, taking in carbon and releasing the oxygen we need to breathe. As we saw in chapter 1, trees and forests also maintain healthy water quality by acting as a filter, preventing sediments and other particles from entering waterways and the ocean in coastal areas (which can lead to the destruction of coral reefs).[29] They also support a host of other ecosystem services on which we as humans depend, including fertile soil, habitat for biodiversity, carbon sinks, flood prevention, and regulation of precipitation.

Loss of Biodiversity

Ecosystems can only function properly when all the related parts are healthy, so a loss of biodiversity can have serious impacts on other ecosystem services the environment provides us. Not only does deforestation result in a loss of habitat for flora and fauna, but it can also lead to desertification or the transformation of fertile land into desert. Deforestation and biodiversity loss also have negative impacts on human health,[30] since when parts of the ecosystem are missing, insects that normally wouldn't play a large role in the system can thrive. Deforestation is linked to diseases such as Lyme disease from ticks and malaria from mosquitoes. [31]

Loss of Carbon Sinks

Carbon sinks are natural systems that absorb and store carbon dioxide from the atmosphere. Forests and trees are one type of carbon sink, and as such are very valuable in mitigating climate change. As long as these trees and plants are not cut down, they keep a large amount of CO_2 out of the atmosphere.

Flooding

Without trees and their ability to retain water and topsoil, erosion often results, causing flooding, mudslides, and landslides when it rains. This can disrupt roads, power lines, and water pipes, destroy property, and even cause injuries and death when rapidly moving water pushes around debris. Individuals, businesses, and governments all incur economic costs when

Box 2.4 Plants and Deforestation in the Amazon Rainforest

The Amazon rainforest in South America is home to at least 10 percent of the world's known biodiversity, including 15,000 different species of trees.[1] [2] Yet the rapid rate of deforestation in the Amazon threatens these ecosystems; a 2015 study suggests that at least 36 percent and up to 57 percent of all Amazon tree species are likely at risk of extinction, if future deforestation rates do not slow.[3] These threatened trees and plants have not been sufficiently explored, and if lost forever, we will never know what benefits they offered. In the quest to find plants that may have medicinal properties or cures for known diseases, a group of Brazilian researchers brought back 2,200 samples of plant extracts from the Amazon rainforest. Over 70 were demonstrated to have some effect against tumors, while over 50 showed results against bacterial infections.[4] And there's much more that the Amazon could potentially contain in regards to medicinal properties: researchers have only just begun identifying and discovering the estimated 80,000 species of flower-bearing plants in the Amazon.

Notes

1. World Wildlife Fund (WWF), "Inside the Amazon," accessed January 25, 2016, http://wwf.panda.org/what_we_do/where_we_work/amazon/about_the_amazon/.
2. Hans ter Steege et al. "Estimating the Global Conservation Status of More than 15,000 Amazonian Tree Species," *Science Advances* 1 (2015), accessed January 25, 2016, doi:10.1126/sciadv.1500936.
3. Ibid.
4. Tom Phillips, "Brazilian Explorers Search 'medicine factory' to save Lives and Rainforest," *The Guardian*, April 27, 2009, accessed June 8, 2016, http://www.theguardian.com/environment/2009/apr/27/amazon-rainforest-medicine.

public and private properties are damaged and infrastructure reparations are required.

Drought

Another essential role forests play in the ecosystem is to increase the amount of water that gets back into the atmosphere. Through a process called evapotranspiration, trees and forests increase the rates at which precipitation (rainfall and snow) is put back into the atmosphere (think evaporation). Thus, deforestation "diminishes the recycling of water vapor in the atmosphere," leading to increased likelihoods and extent of drought.[32] For instance, deforestation in Brazil has been connected with longer dry seasons, as well as a severe drought in 2014-2015. The drought was recorded as the country's worst since the early 1900s, drying up Sao Paulo's Cantareira reservoir, the largest and most important reservoir in the state.[33]

Loss of Aesthetic Value

The beauty of natural and pristine landscapes is captivating. The feeling of finding ourselves surrounded by wilderness, escaping urban life to enjoy majestic trees and wild terrain is often a strong force that attracts many of us. Not only does nature provide us with aesthetic value, in 2015 researchers discovered that in an increasingly urbanized world it can be beneficial to our mental health. The study found that people who took a 90-minute walk through a natural environment had lower levels of the specific brain activity that is linked to mental illness risks, compared to those who did not have the natural environment experience.[34] With deforestation, the aesthetic value and other benefits disappear.

CLIMATE CHANGE

In 2016, a Native American tribe in Louisiana became the first people to be displaced by climate change in the United States. The Isle de Jean Charles, where the Biloxi-Chitimacha-Choctaw tribe have called home for centuries, has lost more than 1,900 square miles of land in the past 80 years – equivalent to the size of a football field lost every 45 minutes.[35] The low-lying coastal area has been plagued by sinking land and oil extraction, and now climate change will cause sea levels to rise. Climate change also increases the likelihood of extreme weather events that cause further flooding, such as the rains that brought devastating and historic flooding in August 2016.[36] The tribe was awarded $48 million from the federal government to relocate, but the story doesn't end there; many more communities in low-lying Louisiana and elsewhere in the United States are poised to feel the effects of climate change.

Climate change, or sometimes referred to as global warming, is a phenomenon caused by the release of GHG emissions. When GHGs are emitted into the atmosphere, they trap in the heat from the sun, instead of letting this heat radiate back into space. As a result, our planet becomes warmer, disrupting the planet's stability and thus changing how our climate works. GHG emissions are usually discussed in terms of carbon dioxide (CO_2), the most common GHG, or carbon equivalent (CO_2e), which standardizes all GHGs into the same unit.

Scientists have warned of catastrophic, irreversible impacts if the world-sees 2 degrees Celsius (3.6 degrees Fahrenheit) of warming. For this reason, staying below 2 degrees has become the unifying goal within the United Nations climate change negotiations.[37] However, there is some debate about the use of this threshold as it might not be enough. Many scientists and policymakers alike recommend setting the official goal at 1.5 degrees Celsius.[38] The 2015 Paris Agreement commits countries to holding temperatures well below 2 degrees, while encouraging them to pursue efforts to keep below 1.5 degrees. Since 2007, China has been the world's largest emitter of GHGs, but before that it was the United States, the world's second largest emitter and number one in total historic emissions.

THINKING ABOUT IMPACT

The severity of climate change is due to the international nature of the problem and also to its multitude of impacts that permeate ecological systems, transforming and unbalancing delicate natural processes. Both developed and developing countries feel the impacts of climate change, yet it affects people around the world unequally, most severely impacting vulnerable populations that are not responsible for causing it. Depending on where you live, you will experience different effects of climate change. Pennsylvania, for instance, is projected to see increased extreme heat threats and inland flooding, while Utah will see more drought and wildfires.[39]

Warming

According to the National Oceanic and Atmospheric Administration (NOAA) and the National Aeronautics and Space Administration (NASA), every month since October 2015 has broken the temperature record for each month, and as of August 2016, July broke the absolute record for the hottest month since records began in 1880.[40] Although 2016 is said to break new records, 2015 was 0.23 degrees Fahrenheit (0.13 degree Celsius) hotter than the previous record

Table 2.1 Five Cities Most Impacted By Climate Change

City	*Climate Impacts*
New Orleans, Louisiana	Sea level rise and vulnerability to hurricanes and typhoons
Minneapolis, Minnesota	Drought
Las Vegas, Nevada	Temperature rise and drought
New York, New York	Sea level rise, increase in extreme precipitation, and vulnerability to hurricanes
Kansas City, Missouri	Temperature rise and drought

Source: The Weather Channel, "Climate Disruption Index," accessed April 16, 2016, http://stories.weather.com/disruptionindex.

set in 2014.[41] The planet's average surface temperature has risen by about 1.8 degrees Fahrenheit (1.0 degree Celsius) since the late nineteenth century. NASA stated that this change was largely driven by increased CO_2 and other human-made emissions into the atmosphere.[42] This increase in temperature is the major cause of all the other climate change impacts.

Sea Level Rise

Sea level rise is the result of melting glaciers and thermal expansion (when warm water takes up more space than cold water). Low-elevation coastal areas (areas that are less than 30 feet above sea level) are home to 634 million people in the world, or roughly one in ten people.[43] Sea level rise is projected to displace millions of people, as homes on low-lying islands and coastal areas become reclaimed by the sea. Sea levels are also rising faster than expected. Research published in 2016 revealed that, if GHG emissions aren't abated, by 2100 sea levels will rise almost twice as much as previously thought. More specifically, the previous models put potential sea level rise at under three feet by 2100, but these estimates underestimated the melting of the Antarctic ice sheet. The 2016 study says that Antarctica on its own has the potential to contribute a little more than three feet of sea level rise by 2100, bringing the estimate closer to six feet.[44] About 70 percent of the coastlines worldwide is projected to experience sea level change with the actual amount of sea level rise varying by location.[45]

Extreme Weather

Different areas will experience different types of extreme weather such as stronger hurricanes, tropical storms, monsoons, and drought. We are already seeing evidence of extreme weather all over the world. The Western Hemisphere experienced the most powerful hurricane ever measured in October 2015 with Hurricane Patricia. Typhoon Haiyan, also one of the most powerful typhoons ever recorded, devastated the Philippines in November 2013, displacing four million people and leaving more than 6,000 dead.[46] In the United States, in 2015 South Carolina saw flooding that had the chance of occurring once every 1,000 years, and was thus called the "1,000-year flood." We have also not forgotten 2012's Hurricane Sandy that hit North Eastern states hard.

Some places will struggle with lack of water rather than too much. East Africa is already facing disastrous droughts. In the United States, the West Coast has already suffered through five years of extreme drought. Pakistan and Europe are experiencing deadly heat waves, and India has seen a 61 percent increase in the number of deaths attributable to heat stroke across the country between 2004 and 2013.[47] Extreme weather occurrences become the new norm in a world transformed by climate change.

Wildfires

Areas that will experience drought due to climate change will also be faced with the perfect conditions for wildfires. Wildfires bring their own set of problems for the environment, ecosystems, and human health. A Yale-led study shows that in the Western United States droughts are becoming more frequent and intense with climate change, exposing "tens of millions of Americans to high levels of air pollution in the coming decades." Individuals in Northern California, Western Oregon, and the Great Plains will fare particularly badly when it comes to wildfires.[48]

Water Scarcity and Conflict

Through high temperatures and drought, climate change will decrease the amount of water available for people's daily activities, growing food, and

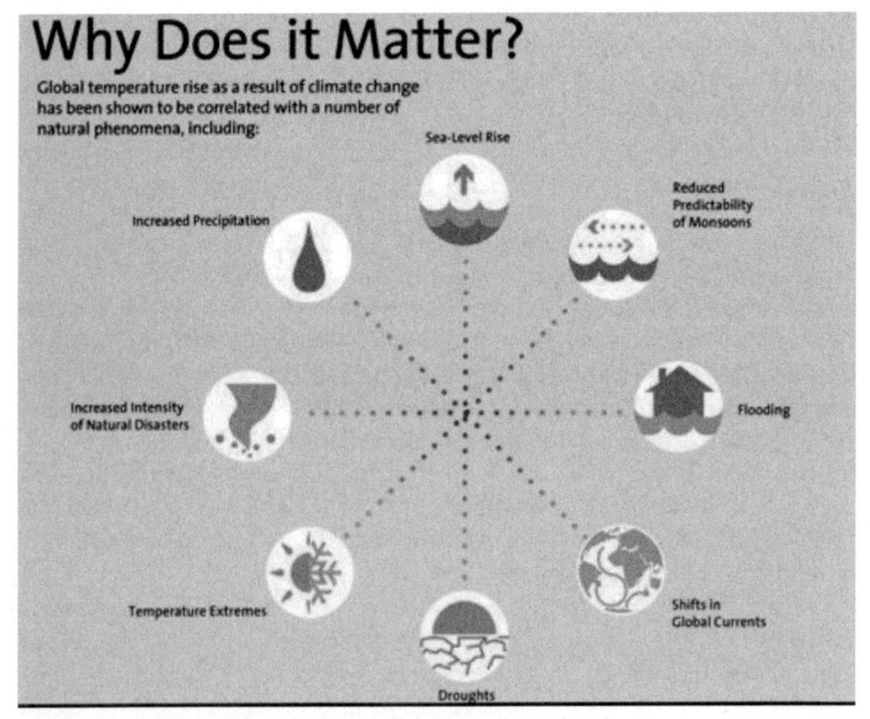

Figure 2.1 Climate Change: Why Does It Matter?
Source: Yale Environmental Performance Index 2016, "Climate and Energy," accessed February 12, 2016, http://epi.yale.edu/chapter/climate-and-energy.

producing goods. The less water available (water scarcity), the more often shortages will occur. In addition, less water means it will become more competitive and expensive to get water, raising the price of food. According to a World Bank report, where economic growth is impacted by rainfall, episodes of droughts and floods have generated waves of migration and spikes in violence within countries.[49] Climate change will impact areas that currently have an abundant supply of water and make situations even worse in areas that already suffer from water scarcity.

Exacerbated Poverty

The poor are already vulnerable to volatile food prices, natural disasters, and tropical diseases such as malaria, which are all expected to get worse with climate change. A 2015 study by the World Bank found that climate change could push more than 100 million people into extreme poverty by 2030.[50] The decline in agricultural yields from extreme weather and the resulting increase in food prices will be one of the main drivers pushing people toward extreme poverty. The poor are also more vulnerable to heat-related illness, disease, and death due to climate change because they are less likely to get the care they need. All the improvement from decades of social and economic development and aid programs are threatened to be undone by climate change.

Displacement

Many individuals will lose their homes due to rising sea levels and extreme weather, and small island nations are among the first to feel the effects. The former president of Kiribati, Anote Tong, already accepted that a proportion of the island's 102,000 inhabitants will need to relocate, a realization that prompted the purchase of land in nearby Fiji for Kiribati people. The Maldives, the world's lowest-lying country, is also worried about its future, and was one of the first countries to ratify the Paris Agreement. It's not only the small island states, but coastal areas all over the world that will see land taken back by the sea. In addition to sea level rise, extreme weather also threatens to displace people from their homes as houses and livelihoods are destroyed in storms or by droughts that limit the amount of food or water available, forcing people to leave and find other places to live.

Biodiversity Loss

Many plants and animals will be threatened and lost as the climate changes. Coral reefs are deteriorating due to warmer and more acidic oceans, while polar bears are having difficulties hunting seals and fish as ice melts.

Thousands of murres, a penguin-like seabird, washed up dead on Alaska's coast in January 2016, starved from not being able to find food in a warming ocean.[51] One-fourth of the Earth's species could face extinction by 2050 due to climate change.[52]

Mosquitoes, Pests, and Disease

With a warming planet, mosquitoes that carry illnesses like malaria will be able to live in areas that were once too cold for them to survive. The 2016 outbreak of the Zika virus, which can cause birth defects, is a glimpse into what new mosquito-borne illnesses can bring. In mountains in the Western United States, the mountain pine and bark beetles are also enjoying warmer temperatures and killing trees at alarming rates. Pine beetles have been around to chow down on different types of pine, spruce, and fir for a long time, but with a warming world, their eggs can survive through the winter.[53] Pests like cockroaches, termites, wasps, fleas, and ticks will also find new opportunities.

Landscape Change

Rising temperatures and changing patterns of rain and snow are forcing vegetation shifts. Many forests and vegetations are moving northward or higher in altitude to find cooler temperatures, and woodlands are "giving way to grasslands in the African Sahel" while shrublands are "encroaching onto tundra in the Arctic," according to a study done by the University of California, Berkeley in coordination with the U.S. Department of Agriculture Forest Service.[54] Other species are dueling in Darwin's survival of the fittest, in a new evolution favoring species of plants and trees that can survive warmer temperatures.

Economic Loss

There are different models estimating how much the loss and damage from climate change will cost the global economy, but we do know it will be very costly. In terms of economic productivity, incomes in most countries around the world will fall 23 percent by the year 2100 if GHG emissions and climate change continue unmitigated, according to a 2015 study by researchers at Stanford.[55] The study demonstrates that the major factors that run the economy (workers, agriculture) will suffer with higher temperatures. And that's likely to be an underestimation because the study doesn't take into consideration other damages due to climate change like flooding, sea level rise, or more intense storms. In the United States specifically, the U.S. Environmental Protection Agency estimates that if global emissions are not reduced by the end of the century climate change will cost up to $180 billion due to drought and water shortages alone.[56] In addition, by 2100, road maintenance and adaptation will cost the United States between $4.2 and $7.4 billion including another $170 billion in lost wages, since over 1.8 billion labor hours are projected to be lost.[57]

Human Health

As previously mentioned, ground-level ozone pollution (smog) is detrimental to human health, causing respiratory problems and exacerbating asthma and lung disease. This is projected to get worse with climate change, as ozone pollution increases as temperature increases. In 2011, the Union of Concerned Scientists published a paper estimating that in 2020 the United States could pay an estimated $5.4 billion extra in health costs associated with increased ozone levels due to climate change.[58]

Allergies

Climate change also means more favorable growing conditions for allergy-inducing weeds. Because the first frost episodes in the fall have been occurring later and later in the season, ragweed's pollen season has been lengthening.[59] In general, more CO_2 and warmer temperatures means that plants are active and shedding pollen more months out of the year. This translates to more misery for allergy sufferers.

Food Supply and Prices

From seafood to fruits and vegetables, food sources all over the world are threatened by climate change due to droughts, floods, and extreme temperatures. It isn't only our basic crops and staple foods that are at risk either: Climate change is altering the growing conditions in wine-producing areas, while also threatening the quality and quantity of coffee beans in various regions. In 2014, a drought in Brazil resulted in poor coffee bean harvests and the fastest rise of coffee prices in more than 13 years.[60] Oranges and citrus, fruits that depend on mild winters and springs, could also see decreased yields, resulting in higher prices.

Developed countries aren't shielded from the effects of climate change on food supplies either. In a 2016 study that looked at cereal production loss due to extreme heat and drought, damage was actually 8–11 percent worse in developed countries than in developing ones.[61] This is most likely a result of a difference in farmers' priorities: While farmers in developing countries may prioritize resilience over risk and high yields and use intercropping systems

Box 2.5 Ocean Acidification and Seafood Loss

Oceans are forms of carbon sinks, capturing carbon dioxide from the atmosphere, turning it into carbonic acid, and increasing the acidity of the water. Although this is a natural process, too much carbon dioxide in the air means the ocean turns too much of it into carbonic acid, and a highly acidic ocean is bad for all types of marine life as well as individuals and companies that rely on seafood for food and income. In 2014, a shellfish producer on Vancouver Island in British Columbia lost three years' worth of scallops, $10 million, and had to lay off 30 percent of its workforce due to high levels of carbon dioxide in the Georgia Strait.[1] The scallops in the company's hatchery were unable to survive in the acidic water caused by the uptake of carbon dioxide from the atmosphere. As GHG emissions continue to be emitted and increase the acidity of oceans, marine life and thus seafood operations will be impacted.

Note

1. John Harding, "10 Million Scallops Are Dead; Qualicum Company Lays off Staff," *The Parksville Qualicum Beach News,* February 25, 2014, accessed March 2, 2016, http://www.pqbnews.com/news/247092381.html.

such as agroforestry, in developed countries, agriculture tends to focus on maximizing profits and uses non-resilient monocropping systems. However, developing countries are also feeling the impacts of decreased yields, especially as harvests often serve as the main source of food and income for individual households.

Sports and Activities

Hikers and climbers may lose that big payoff of the gorgeous lake or waterfall at the end of their treks, as vital water sources dry up in areas experiencing drought. In 2014, Yosemite Falls in California was dry for much longer than usual, drying up two months earlier than expected, and only starting to flow again a month later than normal.[62] Other areas will see heavy rainfall and severe storms, more erosion, and path obstructions that may prevent hiking. Various plant and animal species will also be compromised due to climate change, but burdensome plants like poison ivy actually thrive in an atmosphere with high levels of CO_2; the oil that causes the poison ivy rash is expected to become more "powerful and supercharged" if we continue on our current path of GHG emissions.[63]

Climate change is putting winter sports in danger as well. This past decade has been the warmest on record, and lack of snow and shortened winters may be the new norm. Less snow means less than ideal conditions and less time on the slopes. The United Nations Environment Programme has even indicated that the ski industry will be highly impacted by climate change.[64]

Divers and snorkelers should pay particular attention, as climate change is the biggest threat to coral reefs. Our world's coral reefs are already being negatively affected by infectious disease, bleaching, and decreased growth due to rising ocean temperatures and ocean acidification, which will only get worse with climate change. Coral bleaching of the Great Barrier Reef off the coast of Australia reached extremely high levels in 2016.[65] Coral reefs support much marine life, so their demise has a domino effect on ocean ecosystems.

Surfers and other ocean sports aren't immune to the impacts of climate change either. Researchers have concluded that some surf breaks will change significantly or even disappear, particularly if they are on coral reefs.[66] In addition, ocean currents like the Gulf Stream may be transformed by melted glaciers, changing the storm patterns that bring waves.[67]

Beachgoers who prefer the sand to the ocean will also see their leisurely activities affected. Beaches will shrink with increased sea level rise and coastal erosion from intensified storms. More dredging of sand to replenish beaches will be a common occurrence in the coastal cities that want to retain their beaches.

LEADING CAUSES OF THESE ENVIRONMENTAL CHALLENGES

Now that we have a brief overview of the various impacts that air and water pollution, deforestation, and climate change have on ecosystems and on our own lives, we can explore the causes of these environmental challenges. Many of the same air pollutants that cause harm to our health and other aspects of the environment are also GHGs that cause climate change. In addition, many sources of pollution or degradation contribute to more than one environmental problem. Take conventional agriculture for instance, which can cause deforestation, destroy soil health, release GHGs, and pollute waterways. Although the following section does not exhaust all sources of environmental destruction, a general idea of what got us in this situation can help shape the way we view sustainability and how to be more sustainable.

Electrical power generation (power plants). Most of our electricity comes from power plants, which are powered by the burning of fossil fuels (coal, oil, and natural gas). Electricity contributed to 31 percent of the total GHG emissions in the United States in 2013[68] and 35 percent on a global scale

Table 2.2 Key Pollutants - What You Need to Know

Air Pollutant	*Source*	*Impact*
Carbon dioxide (CO_2)	Combustion of fossil fuels, mainly from electricity generation, transportation (cars, trucks, air travel, marine travel, rail), industry (production and consumption of minerals and metals such as cement, iron, and steel). Also emitted as a result of deforestation and land conversion.	Contributes to climate change: Makes up most of the GHGs that are emitted (in 2013 CO_2 accounted for about 82 percent of all U.S. GHG emissions from human activities) and stays in the atmosphere for decades to centuries (depending on the agents that can remove or absorb them, such as oceans).
Nitrogen oxides (NOx)	Combustion of fossil fuels mainly from oil and gas industry; electricity generation (coal-fired power plants), transportation (cars, trucks, air travel, marine travel); synthetic fertilizer.	Causes smog (O_3) through its interaction with sunlight and VOCs; causes acid rain; causes $PM_{2.5}$; causes eutrophication and dead zones in bodies of water through algal blooms.
Nitrous oxide (N_2O)	A form of nitrogen oxides (NOx); synthetic fertilizers in agriculture; combustion of fossil fuels mainly from transportation (cars, trucks, air travel, marine travel); industry (manufacturing of nylon and other synthetic products).	Contributes to climate change: Impact of one pound of N_2O on warming the atmosphere is almost 300 times that of one pound of CO_2; causes eutrophication and dead zones in bodies of water through algal blooms.
Sulfur dioxide (SO_2)	Combustion of fossil fuels, mainly from electricity generation (coal-fired power plants) and industry; 99% of SO_2 comes from human activities.	Causes acid rain; causes smog (O_3) through reaction with NOx; harmful to human health.
Methane (CH_4)	Natural gas extraction and production; livestock enteric fermentation; landfills.	Contributes to climate change: Stays in the atmosphere for 12 years, but has 25 times more GWP than CO_2.
Volatile organic compounds (VOCs)	Indoor and outdoor pollution; emitted as gases and include a variety of chemicals; released from household products such as paints, varnishes, wax, cosmetics, cleaning products, aerosols, building materials, office equipment; diesel and gasoline-fueled cars' exhaust.	Causes smog (O_3) through its interaction with sunlight and NO_x; harmful to human health.

Particle pollution $PM_{2.5}$ and PM_{10}	Indoor and outdoor pollution in the form of small particles in the air. Can be directly emitted or can be formed in the atmosphere when the pollutants from fossil fuel combustion mix (for instance, sulfates (SO_2) and nitrates (NOx) from power plants, smoke, industrial soot, diesel exhaust) . $PM_{2.5}$ and PM_{10} are different-sized particles with the numbers referring to particle diameter in micrometers.	Causes smog (O_3); harmful to human health.
Black carbon	A component of particulate matter formed by the incomplete combustion of fossil fuels, biofuels, and biomass. Emitted directly into the atmosphere in the form of fine particles ($PM_{2.5}$).	Harmful to human health; contributes to climate change.
Hydrofluorocarbons (HFCs)	Gases inside refrigerators, air conditioners, foams, aerosol cans; HFCs are emitted as a result of leaks in these products. No natural source, simply anthropogenic. Type of a VOC.	Contributes to climate change: high GWP.
Chlorofluorocarbons (CFCs)	Gases inside refrigerators, air conditioners, foams, aerosol cans; largely have been phased out due to the Montreal Protocol.	Ozone depletion; contributes to climate change: high GWP.

in 2010.[69] Unfortunately, the burning of fossil fuels releases a mix of CO_2, a GHG, as well as SO_2, NOx, and particle pollution ($PM_{2.5}$), which are notorious for causing smog and health problems.

Of all electrical power generation, coal-fired power plants are the most harmful to human health and the most carbon intensive (contributing the most to climate change by releasing CO_2), and also require great amounts of water. In a report released in 2016, the current coal-fired power plants being used globally consumed enough water to supply the needs of one billion people.[70]

Unfortunately, we burn a lot of coal all over the world. In 2013, coal provided approximately 41 percent of the world's electricity needs,[71] and in 2016 there were 8,359 existing coal power plant units around the world.[72] About half of the world's coal consumption is in China, and while the consumption and production of coal has been decreasing in the United States due to the production of natural gas, coal still made up 33 percent of total U.S. electricity generation in 2015.[73] Coal production and coal-fired power plants are not evenly distributed across the United States, however. Most coal production occurs in Wyoming, West Virginia, Kentucky, Pennsylvania, and Illinois.[74]

Transportation (especially motor vehicles). Most forms of transportation, including via air, land, or sea, have negative effects on the environment, most notably causing smog and climate change. The fuel that is burned in conventional, gas-fueled cars and trucks releases pollutants such as CO_2 and N_2O, as well as SO_2, $PM_{2.5}$, and volatile organic compounds (VOCs), which cause smog.

In 2010, the transportation of goods and passengers made up 23 percent of total global GHG emissions,[75] while it made up 27 percent of total emissions in the United States in 2013.[76] In the United States, motor vehicles made up almost 60 percent of total transport emissions in 2013. Freight trucks contributed around 23 percent of transport emissions, while other activities such as rail, commercial airlines, and boats contributed significantly less.[77]

Globally, emissions from motor vehicles are not expected to decrease significantly because as countries develop and middle classes emerge, more people drive. And while emerging economies like India, Brazil, and China are currently facing this problem, emissions from motor vehicles in the United States are not decreasing either. Although fuel efficiency standards in the United States continue to improve and more people are driving hybrid and alternative-fuel cars, Americans drive a lot, emitting GHGs. In 2015, Americans drove more than ever due to cheap gas prices and a growing population and economy.[78] Miles driven by Americans are expected to be even higher in 2016, as June 2016 saw a 3-percent increase compared to the year before.[79] Globally, the number of cars worldwide is set to double by 2040.[80]

Overview of Greenhouse Gases

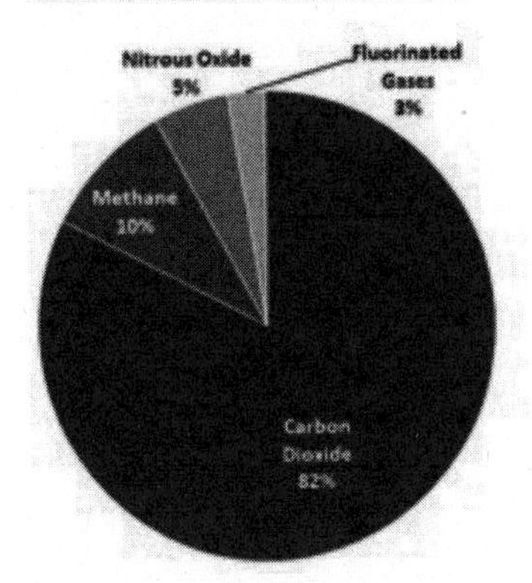

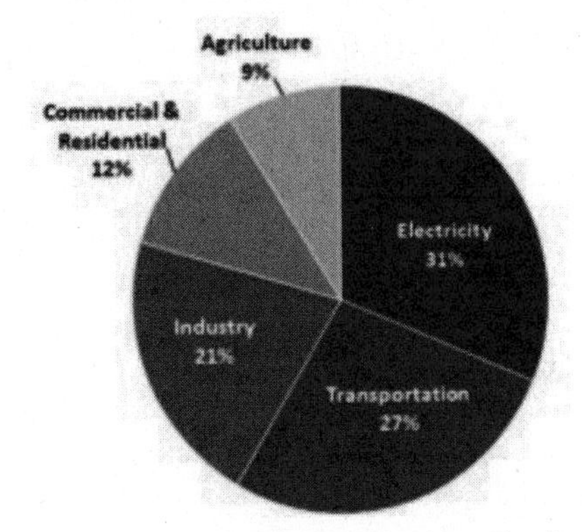

Figure 2.2 Total U.S. Greenhouse Gas Emissions by Economic Sector in 2013 (land use change and forestry not included).
Source: U.S. Environmental Protection Agency, "Inventory of U.S. Greenhouse Gas Emissions and Sinks," 2015, accessed January 27, 2016, https://www3.epa.gov/climatechange/Downloads/ghgemissions/US-GHG-Inventory-2015-Main-Text.pdf.

Chemical and manufacturing industries. The most polluting companies (both in terms of air and water pollution) are usually in the chemical, oil and gas, and manufacturing industries, which supply everything we consume. In regard to climate change, emissions from industry accounted for 30 percent of global GHG emissions in 2010[81] (more than the transportation sector) and 21 percent in the United States in 2013.[82] These emissions come from manufacturing anything made from plastics, cement, steel, aluminum, iron ore, and so on and take into account the process of extracting natural resources and the actual manufacturing of products from these materials. In addition to emitting CO_2, VOCs, NOx, and SO_2, industrial processes used to create goods can pollute local waterways. Industrial waste, such as chemicals and metals, can end up in waterways when industries aren't sufficiently regulated or held accountable. This is extremely dangerous to human health when it contaminates drinking water.

Agriculture. Agriculture provides us with the food we eat, but it plays a large role in air and water pollution, deforestation, and climate change. Commonly used agricultural products such as fertilizer and pesticides are often made from synthetic (man-made) chemicals, which contain high levels of nitrogen to help plants grow. These chemicals easily make their way into streams and rivers when crops are watered and when it rains, in a process called agricultural runoff. As a result, agricultural runoff pollutes waterways, potentially contaminating drinking water with arsenic (a known carcinogen) and jump-starting algal blooms that cause dead zones through eutrophication.

Box 2.6 Chemical Spill in Charleston, West Virginia

In 2014, a chemical spill in the Elk River prompted the governor of West Virginia to issue a ban on drinking, bathing, or cooking with tap water in Charleston and nine other counties in West Virginia. The ban was lifted five days later, but subsequent research shows that chemical concentrations persisted longer than expected and even made their way into neighboring Kentucky.[1] The drinking water became contaminated when a local chemical plant leaked chemicals into the river, about a mile from one of the state's largest water treatment facilities. The spill was one of American history's most serious incidents of chemical contamination due to the large size of the spill and type of chemicals that went into the waterway.

One of the leaked chemicals was 4-methylcyclohexane methanol (MCHM), which is used by the mining industry to wash clay and rock from coal before it is burned. Symptoms of MCHM exposure include nausea, vomiting, dizziness, headaches, diarrhea, reddened skin, itching, and rashes.[2] According to the U.S. Chemical Safety Board, an independent federal agency charged with investigating serious chemical accidents, 369 patients were treated for nausea, skin rashes, and vomiting following possible exposure to MCHM in water, and 13 were hospitalized.[3] The West Virginia Poison Center received almost 2,000 calls reporting exposure in the days following the spill. Most schools, restaurants, and hotels closed during the ban; the city ceased normal operations.

The aspect that makes the spill deplorable is that the leak, which was caused by small holes in huge chemical tanks, could have been prevented with adequate environmental regulation and enforcement. Investigation by the U.S. Chemical Safety Board showed that Freedom Industries, that owned and operated the plant, did not conduct sufficient inspection. Although environmental regulation exists to prevent such spills, the incentive to conduct strict inspections is weak and punishment for noncompliance is minimal. In one five-year span, West Virginia recorded 25,000 violations of the Clean Water Act by coal companies, of which none were ever issued a fine.[4] The case of West Virginia is particularly devastating and worrisome, but is not unique.

Notes

1. William Foreman et al. "Determination of (4-methylcyclohexyl)methanol isomers by heated purge-and-trap GC/MS in Water Samples from the 2014 Elk River, West Virginia, Chemical Spill," *Chemosphere* 131 (2015) accessed May 29, 2016, doi:10.1016/j.chemosphere.2014.11.006.

2. Toxnet Toxicology Data Network, "4-Methylcyclohexanemethanol," accessed May 29, 2016, https://toxnet.nlm.nih.gov/cgi-bin/sis/search/a?dbs+hsdb:@term+@DOCNO+8182.

3. Rebecca Trager, "Investigators find cause of West Virginia chemical spill" Chemistry World, July 24, 2014, accessed May 29, 2016, http://www.rsc.org/chemistryworld/2014/07/investigators-find-cause-west-virginia-chemical-spill.

4. Evan Osnos, "The Crisis in Flint Goes Deeper Than the Water," *The New Yorker*, January 20, 2016, accessed June 9, 2016, http://www.newyorker.com/news/news-desk/the-crisis-in-flint-goes-deeper-than-the-water.

In 2010, the agricultural sector comprised about 10–12 percent of global GHG emissions and about 9 percent of U.S. emissions.[83,84] In the United States, GHG emissions from agriculture are mainly attributed to the application of synthetic fertilizers that emit N_2O, and livestock, which includes cattle and other domesticated animals such as pigs and sheep. Beef and dairy cattle are one of the main livestock culprits due to their enteric fermentation process (i.e., burps), which emits large amounts of N_2O and methane. Methane is a GHG with a global warming potential (GWP or relative measure of how much heat a GHG traps in the atmosphere) 25 times greater than that of CO_2.[85]

Agriculture is also a major cause of deforestation, as forests are often cut down to make room for plantations (particularly to produce soy beans and palm oil) and cattle ranching (to produce beef). In Latin America, commercial agriculture and livestock farming is the largest cause of deforestation, accounting for two-thirds of total deforestation in the region.[86] Agriculture, both for commercial and subsistence purposes, was reported as being the direct driver of 80 percent of global deforestation in 2012.[87]

As briefly mentioned in the beginning of the chapter, because trees take in CO_2, they are a valuable factor in keeping emissions out of the atmosphere. But when trees are cut down, they release the CO_2 that they had once absorbed. So while trees and forests prevent CO_2 from entering the atmosphere when they are standing, when cut down, they can actually add to climate change. As a result, determining the net effect of forests and trees on climate change is not as simple as tracking other sources. For example, although it is estimated that forestry accounted for 12 percent of all global anthropogenic (man-made) CO_2 emissions between 2000 and 2009, the regrowth of forests during this time absorbed the amount of CO_2 equivalent to 60 percent of the emissions due to deforestation.[89]

Slash-and-burn, where land is burned after being deforested in order to convert land for agricultural use, often occurs in both subsistence and commercial farming. In this process, more GHGs are added to the atmosphere than if the land were just deforested because the burning emits CO_2, methane,

Box 2.7 Deforestation and Palm Oil Demand

The demand for palm oil, which comes from the oil palm tree grown in the tropics, has increased greatly over the last decade and is not going to slow down in the near future. Palm oil is highly versatile and it can be found in all types of products we consume, from chocolate, ice cream, and chips, to paper, soaps, and biodiesel. Its high yields and competitive price make palm oil the most consumed oilseed in today's market (compared to soybean and sunflower oil), and almost all of the well-known international brands sell products that contain palm oil. For these reasons, Indonesia, a tropical country with 47 percent of the population living in rural areas and agriculture being their main source of income, finds palm oil an attractive option for cultivation.[1] It's become so attractive that rainforest cover in Southeast Asia is now being cut down at alarming rates to make room for palm oil plantations. Researchers at the University of Maryland found that Indonesia had the highest rates of deforestation in the world in 2014, topping that of Brazil.[2] This deforestation has been disastrous for local endangered wildlife, destroying the habitat of orangutans and the Sumatran tiger, while also polluting local rivers and aquifers. In the summer of 2016, the Bornean orangutan was officially listed by the International Union for the Conservation of Nature (IUCN) as being critically endangered (only one step from being extinct), alongside the Sumatran orangutan.[3] According to International Animal Rescue (IAR), an animal rescue charity, it is predicted that orangutans will be extinct from the planet within ten years unless action is taken to preserve forests in Indonesia and Malaysia.[4]

Notes

1. World Bank, "Rural Population (Percent of total)," accessed March 3, 2016, http://data.worldbank.org/indicator/SP.RUR.TOTL.ZS.
2. Belinda Arunarwati Margono, et al. "Primary Forest Cover Loss in Indonesia over 2000–2012," *Nature Climate Change* 4 (2014), accessed March 3, 2016, doi:10.1038/nclimate2277.
3. International Union for Conservation of Nature (IUCN). "Whale Sharks, Winghead Sharks and Bornean Orangutans Slide Towards Extinction," July 8, 2016, accessed September 5, 2016, https://www.iucn.org/news/whale-sharks-winghead-sharks-and-bornean-orangutans-slide-towards-extinction.
4. Ian Johnston, "Orangutans Face Complete Extinction Within 10 Years, Animal Rescue Charity Warns," The Independent, August 19, 2016, accessed September 5, 2016, http://www.independent.co.uk/environment/orangutans-extinction-population-borneo-reasons-palm-oil-hunting-deforestation-rainforest-a7199366.html.

and black carbon. Southeast Asia has been plagued by haze from the smoke of forest fires due to slash-and-burn practices taking place in Indonesia to make room for palm oil plantations.

Mining and drilling. The excavation, drilling, and mining processes involved in extracting minerals, metals (aluminum, gold, tin, copper, etc.) and fossil fuels (natural gas, oil, and coal) have harsh implications on our water systems, forests, and on our climate. Mercury and other toxins used to mine for metals easily enter waterways as part of the normal process of mining and drilling. Coal ash, or the industrial waste from mining coal which is largely unregulated in the United States, contains harmful metals such as lead, mercury, chromium, and cadmium, that can end up in groundwater since it is often stored close to waterways. Vegetation and trees are also cleared from the areas before excavation.

Mining occurs all over the world, from South America, and Africa, to Australia and the United States. Land-use change in the Appalachian Mountains in the United States is dominated by mountaintop coal mining. Mountaintop mining is a mining technique where the tops of mountains are stripped of trees and topsoil, and then explosives are used to access coal underneath. This process not only removes forests, releasing carbon into the atmosphere, but it destroys mountains and nearby creeks and waterways, upsetting balanced ecosystems and contributing to runoff and flooding. Scientists have even concluded that the impacts of mountaintop mining are "pervasive and irreversible" and that mitigation cannot compensate for the losses.[89]

Attention is also increasingly being paid to a process called hydraulic fracturing (also known as fracking). Fracking is a relatively inexpensive and easy process to extract natural gas from rock formations underground, which is then used for electricity needs. As a part of the drilling process, a chemical mix is injected underground into the rock formation to force out previously inaccessible natural gas reserves. This chemical mix has been known to enter local aquifers and groundwater, contaminating the drinking water of residents in the area.

Oil spills are not technically part of the extraction process, but they are all too common and have long-lasting environmental and economic effects.[90] Spills from the process of drilling and transporting oil contaminate land, oceans, and rivers with visible impacts that are expensive to clean and often irreversible. Spills can happen over time too as in the case of the Chevron-Texaco oil leak in the Ecuadorian Amazon that wreaked havoc on the environment and hurt local communities over decades.

Refrigerants, propellants in aerosol applications, and solvents. The compressed gases used in products that keep air conditioners and refrigerators

Box 2.8 Natural Gas and Methane in the United States

Carbon dioxide overshadows other GHGs because of its prevalence, yet in the United States methane, a short-lived climate pollutant, plays a large but often overlooked role in contributing to climate change. The main source of methane emissions is natural gas. The United States has become the largest producer of natural gas in the world, thanks to fracking. The infrastructure and equipment used to extract and produce natural gas often leaks, releasing methane into the air. Even the storage of natural gas can have disastrous impacts: a massive leak at the Aliso Canyon natural gas storage facility in Southern California spewed out 97,100 metric tons of methane from October 2015 to February 2016. The leak at its peak is said to be the single largest contributor to climate change in California, equal to the daily emissions of seven million cars or six coal-fired power plants.[1] It is also the second largest natural gas leak in U.S. history and will have the largest climate impact. Fortunately, the contribution of methane to climate change and the need to prevent leaks is gaining more attention. In 2016, the U.S. Environmental Protection Agency released the first standards to reduce methane emissions from the oil and gas sector. The United States and Canada also issued a joint statement committing to reduce methane emissions 40 to 45 percent below 2012 levels by 2025.

Notes

1. Suzanne Goldenberg, "A Single Gas Well Leak Is California's Biggest Contributor to Climate Change," The Guardian, January 5, 2016, accessed March 5, 2016. http://www.theguardian.com/environment/2016/jan/05/aliso-canyon-leak-california-climate-change.
2. S. Conley, et al. "Methane Emissions from the 2015 Aliso Canyon Blowout in Los Angeles, CA," *Science* (2016), accessed March 5, 2016, doi: 10.1126/science.aaf2348.

cold, as well as in aerosol cans (think spray paint, hair spray, and shaving cream cans), are sources of air pollutants that include N_2O, hydrofluorocarbons (HFCs), and chlorofluorocarbons (CFCs). In the 1980s, scientists discovered there was a hole in the atmosphere's protective ozone layer. Atmospheric ozone, which must be differentiated from the smog-causing ground-level ozone, is beneficial because it keeps us from being beamed by the sun's harmful ultraviolet (UV) rays.[91] The international community was able to come together and phase out the use of CFCs through an agreement called the Montreal Protocol, due to their role in depleting the ozone layer. Ironically enough, the use of CFCs in aerosols and coolants was substituted with HFCs, which was later found out to be one of the most potent GHGs.

Waste. Trash that can't be recycled or reused usually ends up in landfills that emit methane. Waste in landfills can also contaminate our drinking water when rainwater leaks into aquifers below the landfill, bringing with it many of the chemicals from our trash. According to the World Bank, the amount of waste created globally continues to increase: in 2012, 3 billion residents generated 1.3 billion tons. This is projected to increase to 2.2 billion by 2025, with waste generation in developing countries contributing most to this increase. The United States generates the most waste out of any country, creating 642,700 metric tons per day. Other countries that make the list of top waste generators include China, Brazil, Japan, and Germany.[92]

Trash also ends up in waterways, which is especially detrimental when it's material that doesn't biodegrade. As observed in the Great Pacific Garbage Patch case, plastic is the big culprit here as it's cheap, is used every day around

Box 2.9 Garbage Dump Outside in Mumbai, India

The Deonar garbage dump in Mumbai, India, is the city's oldest garbage dump. With heaps of trash reaching up to the size of a nine-story tall building and half of Mumbai's 10,000 tons of daily waste ending up there, the Deonar garbage dump contains approximately 16 million tons of trash.[1] In early 2016, the garbage dump caught fire twice, likely due to a self-combustion of the methane emitted from the rotting trash. The result was a massive fire that could be seen from space.[2] One hundred firemen, 12 fire engines, and 8 tankers were needed to control the flames. The smoke from the fire was said to have cloaked the surrounding area, where local inhabitants had to inhale the toxic fumes. Garbage in other countries is related to us because our waste (especially our electronic waste) is sometimes shipped to developing countries for disposal. It's also related to us because it is likely that developing countries will follow in the footsteps of developed countries once they reach certain income levels. By changing unsustainable habits in the United States and other developed countries, we can instill a sustainable culture that can be adopted by other countries.

Notes

1. Gabriele Parussini, "Mumbai's Vast Garbage Dump Catches Fire Again, Covering City in Smog," *The Wall Street Journal*, March 22, 2016, accessed September 5, 2016, http://blogs.wsj.com/indiarealtime/2016/03/22/mumbais-vast-garbage-dump-catches-fire-again-covering-city-in-smog/.
2. Euan McKirdy and Mallika Kapur, "Poor Suffer as Mumbai Chokes on Garbage Dump Haze," CNN, February 5, 2016, accessed March 7, 2016, http://edition.cnn.com/2016/02/05/asia/mumbai-giant-garbage-dump-fire/.

the world, and takes hundreds of years to decompose. A plastic bottle, for instance, will take 450 years to decompose in the ocean.[93] These plastics can kill sea animals such as sea turtles that eat plastic bags when they mistake them for jellyfish, and can poison sea life and the fish that we eat.

Stormwater. Stormwater is the result of rainwater landing on pavement and then being ushered into a storm drain, collecting all the substances that are on streets and parking lots on the way. This includes motor oil, detergents from car washing, pesticides, and fertilizers, all of which end up in the storm drain and ultimately get discharged into our waterways. This pollution is harmful to marine life and also pollutes our local rivers and oceans, making them unsuitable for swimming. As will be explored in part 2, there are various ways we as individuals can combat this to ensure the health of our waterways.

Logging. Commercial logging (both legal and illegal) usually occurs to produce and sell lumber and paper products. Although much of the logging that takes place globally is not in the United States, the deforestation of the old-growth forest in Tongass National Park for logging purposes will result in CO_2 emissions equivalent to over four million vehicles annually on Alaska roads for the next 100 years, according to a recent study.[94] In Madagascar, the international demand for unique woods such as ebony and rosewood has resulted in high rates of illegal logging. The pulp and paper industry has been the major culprit of exploitation of natural, virgin forests (along with the palm oil industry), although more companies are committing to sustainable practices. The pulp and paper industry also contributes to water pollution by dumping effluents into waterways.

FINDING SOLUTIONS: RENEWABLE ENERGY

We've seen that many of our environmental problems stem from how we extract, produce, and use energy. Fortunately, there are alternatives to fossil fuels (natural gas, coal, and petroleum), most notably renewable energy. Renewable energy is generated by sources that can be replaced rapidly by a natural process, including from the sun (solar power); wind; tides and waves (tidal power); geothermal heat; water (hydropower); and biological processes (biomass). These types of energy generate electricity with little pollution or GHGs, and are often referred to as "clean energy." The price of renewable power is falling and becoming competitive with (and thus replacing) fossil fuels but we have a long way to go.[95] As will be described in chapter 3, there are many inspiring initiatives working to bring renewable energy to every house and every business.

By exploring the most notable environmental problems the world is facing, we can see that we're connected to and dependent on natural resources and systems. Our actions, and those of previous generations, have had a tremendous effect on the environment. But the tide is turning and meaningful efforts are being made to help bring human action into balance with the environment. The following chapter outlines select initiatives that are redefining the way we interact with the environment.

3

Who's Doing What

The causes of water and air pollution, deforestation, and climate change are linked to the way we live our lives, the way that organizations operate, and the infrastructure that supports our economy. With the extent of our environmental problems coming to light, more support is being given to efforts to make our society into one that protects environmental health and human well-being. However, the transformative change away from unsustainable actions will need to be accomplished as a joint effort. Making real progress toward sustainability will require coordination and cooperation, holding companies and governments accountable, and aligning incentives for sustainability. Many have already begun the process of transformation toward sustainability, inspiring others to find new, innovative ways to do things. Governments, companies, and many other types of organizations are using new and existing mechanisms to take on environmental issues and catalyze change.

INTERNATIONAL COMMUNITY

As explored in chapter 2, many environmental issues are international in scope, affecting people in countries that may not have contributed to the problem in the first place. For this reason, the international stage is a relevant place for global environmental challenges to be addressed. The international community, including the United Nations and multilateral institutions such as the World Bank, are working in various ways to address these global environmental problems. From facilitating commitments and funding, to providing information, tools, and technical assistance, international institutions empower individual countries and others in tackling environmental challenges.

Multilateral Environmental Agreements

Over the years, nations have convened to address many of the big environmental issues to some extent, and many of these meetings have resulted in international agreements. However, producing effective international agreements is often a slow and challenging process because it's difficult to achieve global consensus, and because vague language in the agreements can dilute their significance. Despite their challenges, international agreements can deeply influence if and how issues are dealt with at home, and we have seen successful multilateral environmental agreements take form. One example is the Montreal Protocol, which committed countries to phasing out ozone-layer-depleting pollutants that went into effect in 1989, and has successfully helped in shrinking the hole in the ozone layer. In 2016, an amendment was added to the Montreal Protocol to start phasing down HFCs (the potent GHG that replaced ozone-depleting substances).

The United Nations Framework Convention on Climate Change (UNFCCC) is the international body that has been in charge of creating a global climate change agreement for the past two decades. Yet getting the world to come together on climate change is not an easy task and gridlock ensued, preventing many strong agreements from going forward. For instance, the 1997 Kyoto Protocol, which committed developed countries to reducing greenhouse gas (GHG) emissions, was the UNFCCC's first product and entered into effect in 2005. However, its effectiveness was limited in part because the United States, the largest emitter of GHGs at the time, did not ratify the agreement. The Kyoto Protocol expired at the end of 2012, presenting the opportunity to shift approaches, expand the scope, and further integrate considerations of equity and flexibility into a new international agreement. In 2015, at the UNFCCC's 21st Conference of the Parties (COP21) in Paris, the world's leaders finally delivered the Paris Agreement, a historic international agreement on climate change.

Sustainable Development

Over the past decades, the international community has increasingly acknowledged that ecosystem services are essential to economic and social development and that climate change threatens to undo decades of work to reduce poverty around the world. In an effort to integrate environmental issues into the development platform, sustainable development has emerged. First introduced in 1987 in the Brundtland Commission, the concept of

Box 3.1 The Paris Climate Change Agreement

In the months leading up to the 2015 UNFCCC conference in Paris, each country quantified their national GHG reduction goal, called an Intended Nationally Determined Contribution (INDC), and submitted it to the international community. A total of 162 INDCs were submitted, representing 189 countries and 99 percent of global emissions.[1] Each INDC includes contextual information on how the country will be affected by climate change, as well as strategies for climate mitigation and adaptation. The conference resulted in the Paris Agreement, an international climate change agreement to reduce GHG emissions and limit warming to below 2°C. The agreement included a mechanism for INDCs (called NDCS after the agreement is in effect) to be reviewed and strengthened over time. It also broke records for the agreement with most signatories ever on the first official day of signing. The Paris Agreement went into effect in November 2016, not even one full year after it was agreed upon in Paris, after more than 80 countries representing 60% of global emissions formally ratified it.

Although there is debate about whether the aggregated INDCs are enough to keep the world from seeing a 2°C increase and whether a 2°C warming will even avoid the most disastrous effects of climate change, the Paris Agreement was unprecedented in the overwhelming acknowledgment that human activities contribute to climate change and that climate change poses serious threats that demand international action. The Paris Agreement set the stage for how climate change will be addressed at the national level and beyond for the coming years.

Note

1. World Resources Institute (WRI), "CAIT Climate Data Explorer: Paris Agreement Tracker," accessed September 4, 2016, https://cait.wri.org/indc/#/ratification.

sustainable development has now turned into a global agenda, and in 2015, the world's leaders agreed on the United Nations Sustainable Development Goals (SDGs). The goals, which are part of a new development framework, outline what we want to achieve as a global society by 2030. There are 17 SDGs including goals to tackle climate change, fight inequality, and end poverty. National, subnational, and local governments will work to achieve these goals, in partnership with civil society and the private sector. What makes the SDGs relevant and exciting is that they are the first to incorporate environmental goals into the desired objectives of our society, along with social and economic objectives. The environmental goals include:

- Ensuring sustainable consumption and production patterns
- Taking urgent action to combat climate change and its impacts
- Conserving and sustainably using the oceans, seas, and marine resources for sustainable development
- Protecting, restoring, and promoting sustainable use of terrestrial ecosystem

Financing

The international community has played a key role in financing projects and providing technical assistance to help developing countries prevent and cope with environmental problems. Funds administered by institutions such as the UNFCCC and the World Bank are enabling sustainable projects, especially related to climate change mitigation (reducing GHGs to slow climate change) and adaptation (making the world more resilient to the impacts of climate change). The UNFCCC's Green Climate Fund committed to its first investments in 2015, which includes supporting vulnerable communities to manage climate change-induced water shortages in Maldives and

Box 3.2 REDD+

The Reducing Emissions from Deforestation and Forest Degradation (REDD+) program designed by the international community offers financial incentives for developing countries to reduce global emissions by eliminating deforestation, reforesting, and engaging in sustainable land use practices. Through REDD+, communities in developing countries can receive payments for preserving their forested areas. Developed countries, namely Denmark, Japan, Luxembourg, Norway, Spain, and Switzerland, have financed REDD+, to a total of $215.2 million, to date.[1] The program is designed to take a holistic look at sustainable management and conservation of forests, helping countries find financial value for the carbon stored in these landscapes, but also ensuring that the co-benefits (such as ecosystem services and livelihoods) associated with a forested area are also valued correctly. REDD+ is still new, but has been gaining more attention and prominence, particularly as the role of forests in combating climate change was of particular interest and importance in the Paris Agreement.

Note

1. United Nations Reducing Emissions from Deforestation and Degradation (REDD+) Programme, "UN-REDD Programme Donors," accessed June 4, 2016, http://www.un-redd.org/Donors_and_Partners/tabid/102612/Default.Aspx.

improving urban water supply and wastewater management in Fiji. Since 2008, the World Bank has issued $9 billion dollars in green bonds, bonds that when purchased by private investors provide the organization with funds for clean energy and climate-smart infrastructure projects.[1] The active role that international institutions have taken in the use of green bonds has also helped develop the market and boost investor confidence in this financial instrument.

FEDERAL GOVERNMENT

The U.S. federal government's role in addressing environmental issues takes many forms. One form is committing to international agreements on the national level, while another is harmonizing policies across states and prompting action at the state level. In 2015, the Obama administration set a goal of reducing GHG emissions 26–28 percent below 2005 level by 2025. This was the official goal submitted by the United States as part of the Paris Agreement and applies to all states. Through regulation, such as standards and reporting requirements, and financial incentives, such as rebates for the purchase of electric vehicles or installing solar panels, the federal government has the ability to support (or hinder) the changes needed to meet this goal. The federal government can also influence what is being done by others.

Regulation and the U.S. Environmental Protection Agency

Much of the environmental regulation in the United States has its base in the Clean Air Act and the Clean Water Act, laws passed by Congress in the early 1970s that have been amended over time to address a wide range of environmental issues such as air pollution, GHG emissions, pesticides, toxic substances, water, and wetlands restoration. The U.S. Environmental Protection Agency (EPA) is in charge of implementing and enforcing these laws. However, a common concern when it comes to environmental policy in the United States is the lack of funding for monitoring and enforcing existing environmental regulations, loopholes that limit effectiveness, and the power of corporate interests that benefit from these weaknesses. Interests groups often politicize efforts to address environmental issues, making progress difficult to achieve. One example of this reality is the delayed Clean Power Plan, which seeks to allow the EPA to regulate GHG emissions from coal-fired power plants, reducing emissions 32 percent below 2005 levels by 2030. With the help of interest groups, many states sued the EPA, taking the case to the U.S. Court of Appeals Court in February 2016.

Comprehensive Plans and Executive Orders

Plans and executive orders (EOs), which are rules issued by the president that have the force of law, play a very valuable role when it comes to complex issues, such as sustainability. President Obama utilized these avenues to address climate change. The President's Climate Action Plan released in June 2013 set the tone for the federal government to play a more active role in climate change mitigation and adaptation as well as the environmental issues tied to it. The comprehensive plan has been followed by further EOs such as November 2013's EO 13653 "Preparing the United States for the Impacts of Climate Change" that directs federal agencies to take a series of steps to make it easier for communities in the United States to increase their resiliency against climate change, as well as 2014's EO 13677 "Climate-Resilient International Development" that requires federal agencies to systematically incorporate considerations of climate-resilience considerations into development work. Several federal agencies are also acknowledging the threats that

Box 3.3 Reducing the Federal Government's Own Footprint

Executive Order (EO) 13693, signed March 2015, supersedes and builds on previous executive orders (13514 and 13423) that commit the federal government to reducing GHG emissions from federal operations 40 percent by 2025. The executive order also outlines requirements and strategies for how federal agencies are to reduce emissions, which include increasing energy efficiency in federal buildings and fleets, sourcing renewable energy, water efficiency, and purchasing sustainable products.

In October of the same year, the Obama administration also signed a memorandum directing federal agencies to factor the value of ecosystem services into federal planning and decision-making.[1] The memorandum provides guidance for federal agencies on integrating ecosystem-service assessments into relevant programs to ensure sustainable use of natural resources. It is a significant measure that demonstrates and institutionalizes the importance of correctly valuing ecosystem services. Because the federal government is one of the largest consumers of energy and other natural resources in the world, efforts to make federal operations more sustainable will have a cascading effect.

Note

1. Tamara Dickinson, Timothy Male, and Ali Zaidi, "Incorporating Natural Infrastructure and Ecosystem Services in Federal Decision-Making," The White House, October 7, 2015, accessed September 5, 2016, https://www.whitehouse.gov/blog/2015/10/07/incorporating-natural-infrastructure-and-ecosystem-services-federal-decision-making.

climate change poses to their own objectives and operations, such as the Department of Defense, which is already making great efforts to confront the effects climate change will have on the military.

Clean Energy Research and Development (R&D)

Under President Obama, the federal government focused its sustainability efforts on shifting from an economy based on fossil fuels to one that utilizes renewable energy. In 2016, the U.S. government budgeted over $6 billion for clean energy R&D such as for technologies that improve energy efficiency or reduce energy consumption.[2] The United States joined the Mission Innovation initiative, which commits its members to doubling their clean energy R&D funding by 2021. Mission Innovation was launched by 20 countries in December 2015 at the conference that resulted in the Paris Agreement.

STATE AND LOCAL GOVERNMENTS

Environmental policy can also be set at the state or local level. While the federal government can often influence state governments to implement environmental policies, it is also common for states and local governments to take on issues that the federal government hasn't addressed yet and/or adopt policies that are stricter than federal mandates. Because many environmental issues have local causes and impacts, state and local governments are often in the best position to address them. However, efforts to address environmental problems can also be polarized at this level as well, posing challenges to implementing effective policy.

Clean Energy Commitments

State and local governments are looking to the future by committing to becoming more sustainable and making their communities stronger. Setting goals is a simple, yet powerful approach that catalyzes regulation needed to meet such goals. For example, Burlington, Vermont, is already running off of 100 percent renewable energy and San Diego, California, the eighth largest city in the United States has committed to go 100 percent renewable by 2035.[3, 4] These local governments aren't alone. As of October 2016, 136 cities, states, regions, and provinces from around the world have signed the Memorandum of Understanding (MOU) on Subnational Global Climate Leadership (known as Under 2 MOU). Each signatory commits to limit their emissions to 80–95 percent below 1990 levels, or below two metric tons per

Box 3.4 Carbon Pricing

Putting a price tag on each ton of carbon emitted can be done through a carbon tax or through a cap and trade system. In 2015, about 40 national jurisdictions and over 20 cities, states, and regions – representing almost a quarter of global GHG emissions – were putting a price on carbon through either a tax or a cap and trade system. With a tax, the government determines the price per ton of carbon pollution and companies have to pay that price. With cap and trade, the government decides an amount of emissions to be cut, and then releases a certain number of permits or allowances representing the ability to pollute. The amount of allowances released by the government and the demand for these allowances is what determines the price. The main idea behind carbon pricing is that it costs some companies more than others to reduce pollution and that companies should be able to choose the option that works best for them to reduce, which is usually the most cost-efficient option. With carbon pricing, the government is not directly telling companies how to reduce emissions, but leaving it up to the market to encourage innovation.

capita, by 2050. There aren't legal repercussions if governments don't meet the goal, but signing the MOU demonstrates a commitment to reducing GHGs.

Bans

Similar to the federal government, state and local governments have a number of policy options available to help them address environmental concerns. One such instrument is a ban, which some jurisdictions are using to target serious environmental issues. Combatting the use of plastic bags is an excellent example of where state and local bans are effective measures in changing behaviors and addressing the negative environmental impact associated with their use. Over 150 cities including Chicago and Seattle have banned the provision of plastic bags by stores. Through the combination of county bans, Hawaii has implemented the first statewide ban on plastic bags, while California formalized a state ban in 2016.[5]

UTILITIES

The increasing amount of renewable energy feeding into the grid has power utilities and other stakeholders working hard to make sure the grid and

Box 3.5 New York Fracking Ban

In 2015, New York State used one of the strongest types of regulation available to policymakers in order to address the detrimental environmental and health effects of hydraulic fracturing (fracking): a ban. Before the ban, a moratorium (short-term ban) on fracking had been in place for seven years. New York has significant oil and gas supplies, but made a move to protect their natural resources and communities after seeing the extensive damage from fracking in Pennsylvania, New York's neighboring state and the second largest natural gas producer in the United States (Texas is number one).[1] Many cities have bans on fracking, but New York is the first to put a stop to the process at the state level.

Note

1. U.S. Energy Information Administration, "Which States Consume and Produce the Most Natural Gas?" accessed January 9, 2016, https://www.eia.gov/tools/faqs/faq.cfm?id=46&t=8.

related infrastructure can handle the job. Many states have passed laws requiring that all utilities in the state generate a certain percentage of their electricity from renewables, while also requiring that a certain percentage of funds be spent on programs that support energy efficiency and renewables. As a result, it's common for utilities to offer rebates, technical assistance, information, and other incentives to its residential and business customers to encourage energy efficiency and renewable energy. For instance, customers can receive rebates for purchasing energy-efficient appliances or installing solar panels on their roofs. Many utilities are also offering the option for customers to pay a premium on their bill for renewable energy or be part of programs that fund community renewable energy projects.

PRIVATE SECTOR

Due to pressure from engaged consumers, investors, nonprofits, and other stakeholders, companies are beginning to take a more comprehensive and long-term view (vs. narrow and short term), and sustainability is starting to take root. Such a shift is possible and is moving forward with support from industry organizations that unite and guide companies. However, these companies make and distribute all the goods we consume using complex and often nontransparent supply chains that are riddled with negative environmental impacts and social concerns. There is a lot of progress to be made. When acknowledging their corporate social responsibility (CSR) to people and the environment, companies usually start by donating funds to nonprofits or hosting volunteer days where employees give back to the community in which they work. Other companies have integrated sustainability into its core such as Patagonia, who even discourages their customers from buying goods they don't really need. Most companies are somewhere in the middle, making charitable donations, but also making changes to their buildings and operations toward sustainability. Efforts range from resource-efficient buildings (i.e., LEED certification by the U.S. Green Building Council), to engaging with suppliers to meet minimum standards for working conditions, to reducing GHG emissions from the transport of products.

Corporate Social Responsibility Goals and Reporting

Most multinational corporations release sustainability or CSR reports, which outline the ways the company is becoming more sustainable and set goals for the future in regard to sourcing renewable energy or reducing energy, waste, and water use. Although more quantitative and comparable reporting is needed, companies continue to strengthen the goals they set and disclose more in CSR reports and elsewhere. The process of creating a sustainability report is also valuable in its own right to help the company analyze the risks that environmental problems pose and the opportunities that sustainability

Box 3.6 Levi Strauss

Levi Strauss or Levi's is taking on environmental and social issues within the apparel industry, an industry which has been in the spotlight for environmental concerns as well as unjust working conditions for a long time. Levi Strauss conducted comprehensive research to understand the environmental impacts of jeans throughout the supply chain and the entire life of the product, and uncovered the main concern: water. A pair of 501® jeans uses 3,781 liters of water during its full life. However, Levi's is taking steps to be more sustainable and move the industry by co-founding The Better Cotton Initiative which seeks to improve environmental impacts, labor standards, and livelihoods of individuals producing cotton. The company also encourages their customers to limit washing after purchase and has partnered with a number of nonprofits such as the World Wildlife Fund and Natural Resources Defense Council to further sustainability efforts, including an innovative design to embed sustainability into products from the very beginning.

Table 3.1 PUMA's Environmental Profit and Loss Account

In 2011, PUMA, a German multinational apparel and shoe corporation partnered with Trucost, a company that quantifies and puts a price tag on the value of natural resources, to create the first Environmental Profit and Loss (EP&L) account. The EP&L shows how valuable resources such as water is to PUMA and how much it would cost the company if they had to pay for the real cost of resource use and environmental degradation. The EP&L is comparable to the traditional Profit and Loss (P&L) account that documents a company's income and gains, and expenses and losses. Although the practice of quantifying and monetizing impact (a process generally called natural capital accounting) is complex and based on many assumptions, it continues to become more refined and common. The EP&L is a great example of how insight of environmental impact can help companies make more informed decisions about their operations, contributing to enhanced risk management and to the long-term health of the company.

Environmental P&L	
Water use	$Million
Greenhouse gas emissions	$Million
Land use	$Million
Other air pollution	$Million
Waste	$Million
Total	$Million

Source: Trucost, "EP&L," accessed April 9, 2016, http://www.trucost.com/environmental-profit-and-loss-accounting.

offers related to direct operations and the supply chain. Many companies then submit their environmental data to transparency initiatives such as the Carbon Disclosure Project, which facilitates benchmarking and motivates improvement. New and better tools and best practices continue to be released helping companies better understand their impacts and identifying innovative ways to reduce impact.

Start-ups and Tech Companies

Sustainability is getting a boost from innovative start-ups and tech companies of all sizes. Small, flexible, start-up companies with big ideas continue to emerge and are quickly moving from the idea-stage to the market, often with support from forward-thinking investors and accelerator programs. With a focus on mobility, cost, and the ability to leverage open-source resources and data, existing environmental problems are being approached in new ways. Some examples of the products coming out of start-ups based around the world include devices that monitor fertilizer and irrigated water in agriculture to ensure optimal use in the United States; water leak sensors in Europe; the provision of off-grid power to rural areas in Africa; and apps that track and reward prizes for individual activities to promote sustainability in Chile. All around the world we are seeing creative solutions to sustainability being developed.

Box 3.7 Innovation: Turning Old Phones into Forest Guardians

One example of the innovative work being done in the tech industry comes from Rainforest Connection, a start-up that transforms used and unwanted cell phones into autonomous, solar-powered listening devices that can monitor and pinpoint deforestation as it occurs. The phones pinpoint deforestation by detecting chainsaw activity and can be used by local authorities and other stakeholders for real time interventions to stop illegal logging and poaching. Rainforest Connection makes the data available in real-time to anyone, anywhere. Old cell phones get new lives and rainforests, as well as those working to protect them, receive some help.

Leading tech companies are also approaching sustainability in new ways in order to reduce direct impact, guide companies, and spur change beyond the tech industry. One focal point of sustainability efforts is on using energy and water more efficiently, since these are key inputs in running data centers, the backbone to their operations. Large tech companies are also leading the way when it comes to renewable energy. Almost all of Apple's facilities worldwide run on renewable energy. Facebook aims to power 50 percent of its infrastructure from renewable energy by the end of 2018. Microsoft's direct operations have been powered by 100 percent renewable energy since 2014 and it is working to run its data centers on at least 50 percent renewable energy by the end of 2018. Microsoft also priced carbon internally, which facilitates climate-smart decision-making.[6] In 2016, Facebook and Microsoft, along with 60 other companies, joined environmental groups to push for the development of 60 GW (enough to power 15 million homes) of renewable energy in the United States by 2025. This push, through The Renewable Energy Buyers Alliance, works with utilities and regulators to make it easier for companies to source renewable energy.

FINANCIAL INSTITUTIONS AND SHAREHOLDERS

Prominent financial institutions are evolving to support sustainability both in the financing of sustainable projects and considering environmental, social, and governance (ESG) factors in different types of investments. Many firms and other organizations are moving away from investments that are tied to big environmental issues such as oil and gas operations: in 2015, global investment in renewable power capacity was $265.8 billion, more than double the allocation to new coal and gas generation.[7] And as data on sustainability becomes more standardized and comparable, incorporating the relevant data into financial analysis and investment decisions will only become easier, furthering sustainability initiatives in the financial industry. For instance, stock exchanges around the world are putting in place sustainability reporting requirements for companies to be publicly listed on the exchange. In addition, ESG data are available and increasingly accessed on the Bloomberg Terminal, the computer system that financial professionals use for market data. There is also a push to integrate sustainability information into existing reporting required by the U.S. Securities and Exchange Commission (SEC) and factored into company valuations and investment ratings.

The integration of sustainability into finance is also being advanced through investor demand and shareholder resolutions, which are proposals that are introduced and voted on by a company's investors. Sometimes resolutions receive a majority vote and pass, other times not, but just the introduction of such resolutions prompts discussions on the issues. The Investor Network on Climate Risk (INCR), a project facilitated by the nonprofit Ceres, leverages the commitment of investors representing $14 trillion in assets to integrate sustainability into finance, shareholder resolutions, and company dialogues. INCR helped spur over a hundred corporate commitments in 2014 and 2015 to address critical sustainability challenges including reducing GHG emissions, limiting fossil fuel industry risks, and protecting forests.[8]

Shareholder resolutions have been filed on a range of sustainable topics at companies in many different industries; for example, in 2016, a resolution was filed at Amazon calling for the company to issue a sustainability report including GHG reduction goals, while at Antero Resources, an oil and gas company, a resolution was filed to push the company to monitor and disclose methane emissions.[9] Exxon Mobil, the world's largest private oil company with at least $8 trillion under management, is under increasing scrutiny for its unwillingness to acknowledge climate change and the risk it imposes on company operations. A shareholder resolution was filed in 2016 asking Exxon to support the goal of limiting warming to below 2 degrees, in line with the Paris Agreement, or to disclose how resilient investments would be if policy measures to restrict warming to 2 degrees were implemented.[10]

UNIVERSITIES AND OTHER ACADEMIC INSTITUTIONS

Universities and other academic institutions were some of the first to address sustainability, mainly through engagement and pressure from student groups. These institutions responded and embraced sustainability through actions such as operational changes and goals to reduce overall environmental footprint; contribution of research and coursework on sustainability-related topics; as well as understanding the impact of their investments. Universities

Box 3.8 Sustainability at Stanford, California

In 2016, it was estimated that Stanford reduced its emissions 68 percent from its 2011 peak, achieved a 36 percent reduction in water use compared to 2000, and sourced 50 percent of their electricity from solar, years ahead of their goals.[1] The deployment of exciting new energy systems and other technologies is making these huge strides possible, but the support for sustainability is seen throughout the campus. Students and employees are collaborating on innovative programs that cover areas such as sustainable products, food, waste, and transportation. Building-level dashboards that display energy and water consumption data almost in real time are also available online.

Although Stanford is not one of the universities to divest from fossil fuels, their Board of Trustees points out the many other ways the university is supporting a shift toward sustainability in their own operations (and beyond) such as through extensive funding for sustainability-related projects and research centers.[2] The university's President and Chair of the Board of Trustees even sent an official letter to the President of the UNFCCC COP21 conference in Paris discussing Stanford's accomplishments and reminding world leaders of the valuable role that universities play in taking on climate change.

Notes

1. Stanford University Office of the President, Letter to Laurent Fabius, President, COP21 Conference, October 28, 2015, http://news.stanford.edu/news/2015/october/climate1_statement_102815.pdf.
2. "Stanford and Climate Change: A Statement of the Board of Trustees," *Stanford News*, April 25, 2016, accessed June 7, 2016, https://news.stanford.edu/2016/04/25/stanford-climate-change-statement-board-trustees/.

invest in order to generate income, and historically these investments have included shares in oil, coal, and gas companies, which are the main source of GHG emissions. However, over 15 U.S. universities, alongside a number of governments, faith-based groups, and foundations, have committed to partially or fully divesting from the fossil fuel industry. One example is the University of California, which pulled $200 million from coal and tar sands investments. Georgetown University and Yale University both committed to partial divestment, and University of Hawaii committed to a full divestment.[11] Divestment is a tool to signal to the market that investments that significantly contribute to climate change are risky. However, although the divestment movement has garnered much needed attention to climate change and the need to invest smarter, some think it's too simple of a response. Many universities have rejected students' demands for divestment on claims that it's just as valuable (or more) to work with these companies as shareholders in order to integrate climate considerations and advance alternative energy sources.[12]

CIVIL SOCIETY AND ACTIVISM

Civil society organizations, which include nonprofits, community organizations, and foundations, are important to sustainability as they take on the environmental and social issues that are not sufficiently addressed by the public and private sector. Civil society organizations vary widely in their approach, but these approaches can include research initiatives, providing assistance to those most impacted, educating the general public, and engagement (or pressure) with companies and governments. We also see organizations leveraging technology and establishing creative partnerships to support their work, as is the case with World Resources Institute's (WRI) Global Forest Watch, an initiative powered by Google to provide accurate and up-to-date mapping on forest cover and deforestation. Many nonprofits such as Rainforest Alliance and Fair Trade use their expertise to develop standards on environmental and social impact and then certify private sector products and services based on these standards, supporting sustainability and helping customers make informed decisions.

Box 3.9 350.org

The grassroots activist group and website 350.org was one of the main organizers of the People's Climate March that took place for the first time in 2014. The march united 400,000 people in New York City to demand action on climate change with coordinated events taking place in cities all over the world. 350.org has had various campaigns to hold leaders accountable in keeping the amount of CO_2 in the atmosphere below 350 parts per million, the designated threshold or safe amount of CO_2 that should ever be in the atmosphere to avoid the most destructive climate change impacts. Unfortunately, there is now over 400 parts per million CO_2, but 350.org's momentum to act on climate change continues to grow. 350.org has a presence in 188 countries, and several campaigns including divestment from fossil fuels, zero offshore drilling for oil, and stopping the Keystone XL Pipeline, a pipeline that would have transported crude oil from the tar sands of Canada to the Texas gulf coast (which President Obama rejected in 2015 after several years of debate).

Box 3.10 Helping the Community and the Environment in Oakland, California

Urban Releaf is a nonprofit organization that was formed in 1998 with three goals: plant trees, sponsor youth, and enrich the community. Since then, Urban Releaf has engaged local residents to plant over 15,000 trees in low-income communities around the San Francisco Bay Area in California. Urban Releaf was formed by a local resident who not only wanted to plant trees to make neighborhoods more aesthetically pleasing and improve air quality, but also felt that it was a way for the community to come together and create a sense of positive self-identity. A local resident can put in a request for a tree to be planted on their property and then Urban Releaf conducts weekly tree planting events fulfilling the requests. Community members, schools, businesses, and other organizations volunteer to plant trees that are well suited for the area. At tree planting events, volunteers learn about trees including the benefits they provide and how they should be maintained. Urban Releaf also mentors and employs at-risk and hard-to-hire youth and adults.

Some civil society organizations address big, global issues such as sustainable development, protecting biodiversity, or reducing food waste. Other civil society organizations are founded by community members to address a local environmental concern such as protecting a specific watershed, restoring habitats with native plants, or promoting the consumption of healthy, sustainable foods in local schools. These community-based organizations often have the co-benefit of bringing people together and supporting a sense of community.

RELIGION

Faiths of all kinds are taking a more active and progressive stance on human's responsibility as stewards of the earth. This makes sense as big issues such as climate change bring up some real questions about how we interact with the environment. One of the most visible and vocal religious leaders on climate change has been Pope Francis, head of the Catholic Church. In May 2015, Pope Francis released an encyclical stressing the responsibility we as humans have to guard the environment, and in 2016 he reinforced and built on this message. In the encyclical, titled "On the Care of Our Common Home," Pope Francis acknowledges that climate change is a "global problem with grave implications," and that human life is "grounded in three fundamental and closely intertwined relationships," one being "the earth itself." In addition,

Pope Francis addressed his concern that "people may well have a growing ecological sensitivity but it has not succeeded in changing their harmful habits of consumption, which appear to be growing all the more."[13]

Other religions are also calling for humanity to act on climate. The Dalai Lama was the first to sign the Buddhist Declaration on Climate Change, which came out in 2009 and includes statements such as "instead of an economy that emphasizes profit and requires perpetual growth, to avoid collapse, we need to move together towards an economy that provides a satisfactory standard of living for everyone while allowing us to develop our full (including spiritual) potential in harmony with the biosphere that sustains and nurtures all beings, including future generations."[14] In August 2015, Muslim leaders including faith leaders, senior international development policymakers, academics, and other experts issued an official Islamic Declaration on Climate that acknowledges climate change is occurring and that the earth's balance is being disrupted as a result of human actions. The declaration calls for the world's Muslims to not "strut arrogantly on the earth," and for countries around the world to reduce their GHG emissions.[15]

In April 2016, over 120 faith groups from many different faiths signed and sent a letter to the members of the U.S. Congress requesting that they approve President Obama's proposed $750 million contribution to the Green Climate Fund to help support those hit hard by the effects of climate change. Faith-based organizations are also taking action through divesting from fossil fuels; in the United States, more religious organizations than universities have divested from fossil fuels.[16] Support for sustainability is being strengthened through religious leaders who are communicating the need for change.

LEARNING FROM OTHERS

Countries around the world are designing and implementing policies that reflect a shift in thinking about the way we use natural resources. We can and should learn from these experiences to improve our society and transform the way we do things. For instance, in 2016, France became the first country to ban food waste by supermarkets, prohibiting stores from throwing away or destroying unsold food, and forcing them instead to donate it to charities and food banks. In 2016, Italy also passed a law committing funds to reduce food waste in the country: Supermarkets and other businesses can receive a reduction in their trash tax when donating unsold food to charities. British Columbia, Canada, has a carbon tax where revenue goes to individuals living in the area. Germany, the country with the most installed solar capacity, continues to lead the way when it comes to solar and integrating solar into the grid. On July 11, 2016, in an effort to achieve a pledge made at the Paris 2015 climate negotiations, 800,000 volunteers in the Indian state of Uttar Pradesh came together to plant 50 million trees, and broke the record of trees planted in one day.[17]

Chilean president Michelle Bachelet announced in 2016 that metros in Santiago, Chile, will be powered by 60 percent renewable energy sources by 2018, an impressive feat considering Chile's metro system ranks as the second largest in Latin America.[18] Paris is also revolutionizing its streets and public squares by removing some of the traffic lanes and making room for pedestrians and cyclists.[19] These types of infrastructure changes are signaling a shift toward a society that prioritizes modes of transportation other than cars. And this is just the beginning. There are many examples of policies and projects taking place around the world that we can learn from in establishing a culture of sustainability in the United States.

NEW LENSES

Sustainability is about changing the way things are done for the better, and in some cases that requires a whole new way of looking at an issue. Using new lenses to look at existing problems can provide an expanded or holistic view of the relationships that exist within society and with nature, showing us the potential of sustainability. We see new lenses being used by many of the different organizations and institutions outlined in this chapter, as well as in the new partnerships sprouting between governments, nonprofits, and private sector companies. One example of such a lens, developed by Harvard Business School professors, shows that companies can generate economic value in a way that also produces value for society by helping to address society's challenges. Presented as the future of CSR, the Creating Shared Value approach asserts that by rethinking products and markets, redefining productivity in the value chain, and building supportive industry clusters at the company's locations, companies can contribute to their bottom line and to the good of society.[20]

Another new lens that continues to evolve is the idea and value of purchasing services instead of things. The Sharing Economy is one result of this new approach, and is shaping the way companies and individuals see value and consumption. In the Sharing Economy, individuals can rent and share products such as cars, apartments, and tools. In general, this is a cost-effective option for individuals to gain access to products they don't frequently need access to, reducing the need to buy unnecessary things.

Taking the value of sustainability to another level is the Social Progress Index, which redefines how we as a society think about progress and well-being.[21] The Social Progress Index is an alternative to Gross Domestic Product (GDP), which, instead of looking at the well-being of a country through measuring the goods and services produced there, measures progress by factoring in social and environmental considerations. Some of the factors included in the index are water and sanitation, ecosystem sustainability, and the health and wellness of people's lives.

New lenses are redefining business models, well-being, how we consume products, and expectations for the systems that shape our lives. These new ways of looking at and doing things are emerging from all over the world and are helping individuals, companies, and governments be more sustainable, catalyzing the shift toward sustainability.

· 4 ·

The Role of Individuals

Chapter 2 showed us how environmental challenges are impacting our lives, while chapter 3 provided insight into how the institutions that shape our society are shifting toward sustainability. Now it's time to examine how we as individuals fit in and why our actions matter. We know it can be overwhelming to think about big-picture environmental issues such as climate change, and sometimes it feels like individual actions don't have an impact, but they do. If they didn't, we wouldn't need to write this book.

Through the consumption of natural resources such as water and energy, household consumption contributes to more than 60 percent of global greenhouse gas (GHG) emissions. It also makes up 70 percent of total global land use and more than 80 percent of global water use.[1] But there's a lot of potential for us to easily scale this back, contributing to a healthier planet and society, without having to make drastic changes to our lives.

Incorporating sustainability into daily life isn't an all-or-nothing approach. You don't have to put solar panels on your house or produce zero waste in order to make a difference. Instead of trying to go 100 percent green overnight, we suggest focusing instead on sustainable habits that are the most practical for your life and that you can envision yourself integrating for the long term. Why and how we integrate environmental considerations into our lives is intrinsically tied to what we value: our health, combating climate change, saving money, creating a sense of community, preserving green spaces, etc. There are many ways and co-benefits of integrating sustainability so it's a classic win-win.

By thinking about sustainability and integrating it into daily life, we not only reduce our own direct footprint, but we also support a change in what is acceptable and expected of governments and companies – we support a shift toward a culture of sustainability. Even if companies want to make operational changes or politicians want to implement policy in the direction of sustainability, they need our support to do so. Public support for sustainability, which can be fueled by the power of community groups, social media, and networking, encourages governments, companies, and other organizations to be more sustainable. As we saw in chapter 3, the shift has already begun. Prompted by the increasing evidence of climate change and its impact on people all over the world, everyone, from international leaders to Hollywood stars, is starting to think and talk about the environmental challenges we face. They are also exploring the possible solutions to these concerns. Your neighbors, coworkers, friends, and family members are too: Americans are acknowledging sustainability and more. Americans are now worried a "great deal" or a "fair amount" about climate change (more than at any time since 2008), and in 2014, 400,000 people participated in the People's Climate March in New York City.[2]

Supporting a culture of sustainability in the United States is particularly necessary because we have one of the biggest environmental footprints on the planet.[3] We would need almost five Earths if the rest of the world lived like Americans do.[4] And other countries are catching up to our levels of consumption. When household income levels rise and spending increases, environmental footprint increases as well.[5] Consumption at rates seen in the United States is not sustainable in a world with limited resources and the impacts are global. Our footprint is not completely our fault as systems have been set up over the last 50 years to make unsustainable actions the norm. Yet, being aware of environmental problems and our contribution to them is the foundation of sustainable living. Sustainability starts with us. We're ready to do things a bit differently and we hope you are too.

Box 4.1 Earth Overshoot Day

Every year the Global Footprint Network calculates the day on which humans consume more than the earth can produce that year, in what is called "Earth Overshoot Day." Earth Overshoot Day is coming only eight months into the year. In 2016, humanity officially used up the amount of resources needed to live sustainably for the year on August 8. In 2015, the day came on August 13 and in 2014 on August 19. Global Footprint Network calculates Earth Overshoot Day by dividing the amount of natural resources available (the planet's biocapacity) by how much of the planet's resources we use up (humanity's ecological footprint), and then multiplying it by the days in a year.

CONSUMING LESS, MORE SUSTAINABLY

Most of our environmental footprint as individuals comes down to consumption. Using and purchasing less, whether it's energy, water, gasoline, and so on offers the greatest opportunity to reduce our footprint and also save money. Another way to reduce our negative impact on the earth is to look for companies that are becoming more responsible and accountable in order to make it easier for us to consume more sustainably. By supporting companies and products that are making efforts to reduce their own footprint and shunning companies that are not taking responsibility for environmental damage, we assist in the transition to a new era, one in which companies are accountable and responsible for all their actions.

One of the first steps in being a conscious and sustainable consumer is to learn about how the products you buy are made and where they come from. Certain certification labels such as Certified Organic, Fair Trade Certified, and Rainforest Alliance Certified can help you make informed choices. Certification standards continue to be refined and expanded to cover more products and services.

There are a number of product labels and statements that sound environmentally friendly, but unfortunately aren't reliable enough for us to endorse wholeheartedly, either because a standardized definition doesn't exist or because manufacturer statements are not verified or regulated. This is true for cage-free, pasture-raised, and all-natural. This isn't to say that these statements aren't true or that the companies that use them are not trying to reduce their environmental impact. It's simply that the systems aren't in place to be as confident that the statements are credible as there are with the third-party verified statements in Table 4.1.

Thinking beyond labels, websites and apps like GoodGuide[6] and those offered by the Environmental Working Group (EWG)[7] can also help us to make informed decisions regarding the products we use. Both databases rate a wide array of products from popular brands on their health, environment, and social impact. EWG's Skin Deep Cosmetics Database[8] and ThinkDirty[9] are two such tools that focus specifically on personal care products (e.g., makeup, shampoo, and soap).

EDUCATION

Becoming knowledgeable about your specific impact on the environment can help guide you to the best place to focus efforts in being more sustainable. For instance, looking at your electricity and water bills is a great way to see how much you are using and see the impacts of any changes you make. Look back

Table 4.1 Key Certification Labels - What You Need to Know

Certification Label	*Certification Requirements*	*Who Sets U.S. Standards*	*Related to*
Certified Organic	Certified Organic Principles: – Preserve natural resources and biodiversity – Support animal health and welfare – Provide access to the outdoors so that animals can exercise their natural behaviors – Only use approved materials – Do not use genetically modified ingredients – Receive annual onsite inspections – Separate organic food from nonorganic food	United States Department of Agriculture (USDA)	Food and other agricultural products For example, meat, vegetables, fruit, and cotton
Fair Trade Certified	The Fair Trade model is designed and audited to ensure equitable trade practices at every level of the supply chain. Principles: – Fair prices and credit – Fair labor conditions – Direct trade – Democratic and transparent organizations – Community development – Environmental sustainability	Fair Trade USA	Food and other agricultural products For example, coffee, chocolate, and fruit
Certified Humane	The Certified Humane Raised and Handled label assures consumers that animals were raised and slaughtered in a responsible way. Standards for the different products include the requirement that animals have enough room to move around and a diet of quality feed, without animal by-products, antibiotics or growth hormones.	Humane Farm Animal Care	Eggs, dairy, meat, and poultry
Rainforest Alliance Certified or Verified	The Rainforest Alliance Certified seal assures consumers that the product has been grown and harvested using environmentally and socially responsible practices. Farms and forestlands that meet the rigorous, third-party standards of the Sustainable Agriculture Network or the Forest Stewardship Council are awarded the Rainforest Alliance Certified seal.	Agricultural products: Sustainable Agriculture Network (SAN) Forestry: Forest Stewardship Council (FSC)	Agricultural and forest products, tourism

	For forestry products, businesses or projects that have reached appropriate milestones as set forth and verified by specific Rainforest Alliance programs may apply for the Rainforest Alliance Verified mark.	Tourism: Rainforest Alliance	
FSC Certified	FSC-certified products are coming from responsibly managed sources. Principles: – Compliance with laws and FSC principles – Tenure and use rights and responsibilities – Indigenous Peoples' Rights – Community Relations and Worker's rights – Benefits from the forests – Environmental impact – Management plan – Monitoring and assessment – Maintenance of high conservation value forests – Plantations	Forest Stewardship Council (FSC)	Forest products For example, printer paper, paper cups, and wood
Certified Compostable	BPI-certified products are materials and products that have been scientifically proven to completely biodegrade in approved composting facilities.	Biodegradable Products Institute (BPI)	Foodservice products, resins, and packaging including bags and films
Green Seal	Green Seal standards consider the total environmental impact of a product and reduce that impact while maintaining performance and quality.	Green Seal	Cleaning and laundry products and services, personal care and cosmetic products (soap, shampoo), paper, hotels, restaurants, and home products (paints, coatings, stains, sealers, recycled latex paint, windows, CFLs)
ENERGY STAR Certified	ENERGY STAR is the simple choice for energy efficiency.	U.S. Environmental Protection Agency	Appliances, electronics, heating and cooling, office equipment, lighting, water heaters, commercial food equipment, building products For example, televisions, washers, and dryers

and see a spike in your bill? Try and figure out why that was and avoid it in the future. Many utilities offer online services or apps to help you visualize and track your energy use.

Bills provide insight into your direct use of resources, but as we have learned so far, environmental impact goes far beyond energy and water use at home. There are a number of more holistic online tools to help estimate individual environmental footprint. The main variables determining overall environmental impact across these online tools are semi-fixed, such as where we live, where our energy comes from (electricity, natural gas, renewables, etc.), and our home's type, size, and number of occupants. However, there are a number of variables that we do have more control over including:

- How often meat and dairy is consumed
- How often meals are eaten at home and are made from local, seasonal foods
- How frequently goods (clothing, shoes, health and beauty products, etc.) are purchased
- The amount of trash sent to landfill rather than composted or recycled
- How and how often we use transportation (including driving and taking flights)

These are factors we can address in our everyday lives and will be explored in more detail in part 2.

DISCUSSION

The majority of people around the world have accepted that climate change is happening and that it is a serious issue, but a social phenomenon has been observed in which many people still think that others don't share the same opinion, so are inclined to avoid the subject.[10, 11] The phenomenon is not unique to climate change and has been observed in other cultural shifts and situations in the United States and elsewhere. We think it's important to overcome any tendency to not talk about climate change for fear that other people might not feel the same way. If you agree that changes need to happen to address climate change, you are not on the fringe of society, but in line with the 97 percent of scientists that agree climate change is happening.[12]

Talking about climate change and environmental concerns can be a prompt to working together with others. Incorporating sustainable habits into our lives can be the most fun when we are doing it with the people that surround us. By sharing interesting facts or strategies with family, friends, neighbors, or coworkers on how to live more sustainably, we can also spread the impetus for change. Suggest some healthy competition on waste or energy reduction efforts to get your close network involved in reducing their impact as well. Overall, discussions about climate change help Americans get up to speed with the rest of the world when it comes to acknowledging climate change, and can act as a domino effect.

GETTING INVOLVED

A key aspect of being sustainable is being knowledgeable of what is going on in your community and supporting efforts that you believe in. We have discussed a number of environmental issues that are likely having impacts where you live, so it is worth making sure you are in the loop. Talk to people and look online to see what the key environmental issues are in your area. Check out what your town or city is doing to reduce pressure on local resources, or find local groups that may be trying to make sure that sustainability is considered in city planning and processes. Find volunteer opportunities that you are interested in; maybe there is one specific thing that you are most motivated about in your efforts to live a more sustainable life such as environmentally friendly food systems or protecting your local rivers or beaches from pollution. Find organizations or groups that are addressing this issue and see how you can help (e.g., volunteer with a community garden for healthy vegetables or a beach clean-up).

VOTING POWER

We can also participate in making our world more sustainable through our voting power. More specifically, we can support politicians and legislation that protect or improve the health of people, communities, and the environment, and block unsustainable legislation. It's not always straightforward what a vote for or against a specific legislation (or an elected official) actually means, but a little bit of research can help you in understanding the potential outcomes. Using your vote to have a say in the issues that will affect you and the people you know and care about (as well as future generations) is a powerful tool we all should use. Voting in local elections is also just as important as at the national level. Mayors and governors are pushing forward projects that make U.S. cities and states more sustainable, but they can only continue to break down the barriers to sustainability if we elect those that champion these causes.

By empowering others, especially individuals in key positions, the structural and cultural changes needed for sustainability are put in motion. Through being conscious of the products we buy, talking to people we know, getting involved, and voting, we as individuals can support a shift toward sustainability. There are also many easy, cheap, and fun ways to make our own lives more sustainable, which will be explored in part 2.

Part 2

SMALL CHANGES TOWARD SUSTAINABILITY

Problems cannot be solved at the same level of awareness that created them.

—Albert Einstein

5

Household Chores

Whether we rent or own an apartment or a house, there are lots of opportunities to integrate sustainability. We can cut our negative environmental impact at home by adopting habits that reduce energy, water, and chemical use, as well as the amount of waste that goes to the landfill. This often means doing daily tasks in a slightly different way or making one-time changes that also save money on our water or energy bill. By using this chapter as a guide, we can learn more about our footprint and take small steps to improve the places we call home.

WASTE DISPOSAL

Trash is a serious issue in the United States. The average American creates almost five pounds of waste each day, most of which ends up in a landfill where it takes up valuable land and emits methane, contributing to climate change.[1] However, there are a number of ways we can reduce the amount of waste that we send to the landfill.

Find out what's recyclable in your area. Recycling is not a new concept and recycling rates have increased significantly over the years, but since we now create more waste than ever, it's even more important to recycle.[2] Recycling keeps items out of the landfill and gives them a new life as a useful product. It also requires significantly less energy to create items from recycled material than from virgin or raw material. According to the U.S. Environmental Protection Agency (EPA), recycling 10 plastic bottles saves enough energy to power a laptop for over 25 hours.[3] However, knowing if an item is recyclable and what to do with it can sometimes be confusing. The How2Recycle[4] standardized labeling system is becoming more common, helping consumers to make informed decisions on what can be recycled.

Most cities recycle aluminum and metal cans, glass, and rigid plastics, but the recycling of other items varies because what is accepted to be recycled is often dependent on what type of technology and infrastructure for recycling is in place in your city. For this reason, it is a good idea to check with your local waste collection agency to see their full list of acceptable items. Sometimes waste collection agencies will even have a list or sign that can clear up any confusion regarding what can be recycled or not. The website Earth911 also allows you to search for the best way to dispose of a specific item in your area, including retail drop-offs and processing facilities.

There are also a couple of practices to keep in mind in order to keep items as valuable as possible in terms of recyclability. The first is to keep recyclables separate from the waste that goes to the landfill. Paperboard, a common packaging for cereal and crackers, for example, illustrates the importance of separation. Paperboard is often accepted for recycling, but when it's put in trash bins, it can get soiled to the point where it can't be recycled at all. The second is to quickly wipe off or rinse out containers that held food products before putting them in the recycling bin. Once at the recycling facility, items are usually sorted and shipped to buyers that use the material to manufacture new goods, including carpet and toothbrush handles.

Table 5.1 Potential of Key Recyclable Items

Recyclable Item	*Future Life if Recycled*
Magazines	Paperboard (the material that cereal or snacks comes in)
Glass bottles and jars	New bottles and jars
Aluminum cans	New aluminum cans
Plastic bottles (#1 plastics)	Carpet, backpacks, insulation for sleeping bags or jackets, and polar fleece
Plastic milk, juice, and detergent bottles (#2 plastics)	New bottles, plastic lumber, playsets, buckets, containers, Frisbees, and stadium seats
Metal cans	New cans, bike parts, car parts, appliances, steel beams, and rebar
Paper	New paper, tissue, paper towels, toilet paper, and napkins
Cardboard	New cardboard, paperboard, and paper bags

Source: Maine Department of Environmental Protection Sustainability, "What Do Your Recyclables Become?" accessed March 6, 2016, http://www.maine.gov/dep/waste/recycle/whatrecyclablesbecome.html#cardboard.

Don't forget to recycle aluminum cans. The difference between producing one aluminum can from recycled material versus producing the same can from virgin material is quite dramatic. It takes 95 percent less energy to produce the same can from recycled material, and it emits only 5 percent of the CO_2 compared to when making the can from aluminum's virgin material.[5]

Think twice about plastic bags. Plastic bags are made from fossil fuels, which contribute to climate change and often end up contaminating land and waterways, threatening wildlife. They are also around much longer than us: plastic bags can take between 500 and 1,000 years to break down. Although thin plastic bags (e.g., from the grocery store or takeout food) are technically recyclable, not all waste collection agencies are equipped to recycle them. Some grocery stores and other retailers have drop-off boxes for recycling thin plastic bags. However, since plastic bags are reusable, try to use them a few times before offering them up for recycling in order to maximize their use and reduce their footprint.

If you use plastic bags as trash bags, be sure to consolidate trash bins in your house and make sure trash bags are completely full before throwing them out. This way you'll be able to minimize the number of plastic trash bags you send to the landfill.

Box 5.1 What's the Big Deal with Aluminum?

Aluminum foil, cans, and other aluminum products come from an ore called bauxite, which is mined in various countries, including Australia, China, Jamaica, and Guinea. The aluminum extraction and production process, like other mining processes, is energy and resource intensive. It involves open-pit mining that removes all native vegetation and results in the loss of local wildlife habitat, as well as significant soil erosion, water contamination, air pollution, and greenhouse gas emissions from the smelting process. In Jamaica, one of the biggest producers of bauxite, mining has resulted in water wells with high levels of sodium and pH, poor water retention capability in the soil, and the degradation of coral reefs from aluminum spilling into the ocean during ship loading.[1] However, aluminum can be continuously recycled like other types of metals, so the need for more raw material can and should be minimized.

Note

1. Trade and Environment Database (TED), "Jamaica Bauxite Case," accessed May 11, 2016, http://www1.american.edu/TED/bauxite.htm.

Go paperless. To cut down on items that need to be recycled in the first place, sign up to get your bills and other correspondence via email instead of sent in hard copy. Each time you see a bill in your email inbox you'll know you are saving paper, reducing the need to cut down trees, and reducing overall waste.

Unsubscribe from junk mail. Each year approximately 100 million trees are cut down to produce junk mail. The average adult receives 41 pounds of junk mail each year and about half of that goes straight to the landfill.[6] Requesting companies to stop sending unwanted magazines and advertisements will cut down on waste, preserve resources, and save you time in the long run from not having to sort through as much unsolicited mail. You can call or email companies directly to request to be removed from their marketing list, and

Box 5.2 The Zero-Waste Home

The zero-waste home is a minimalist-inspired movement to eliminate the amount of waste homes create with a goal of ultimately sending nothing to the landfill. A visible leader of the zero-waste lifestyle is Bea Johnson, a blogger and author who has gone zero waste since 2008, creating only a quart-size jar of landfill waste each year. In her book and blogs, Bea emphasizes that reducing waste has many benefits for her and her family, and outlines a number of tips including her own personal motto, which is a play on a familiar adage: Refuse, Reduce, Reuse, Recycle, and Rot (and only in that order). Reduce, reuse, and recycle are pretty straightforward, but refuse speaks to not taking unnecessary things such as plastic bags from the store, while rot highlights the value of composting. Although small investments in reusable glass jars and cloth bags are needed, the zero-waste home lifestyle is mostly composed of simple shifts in habits to make them more sustainable, similar to what is discussed here in *Sustainability Made Simple*. Specific aspects of the zero-waste home include fixing things when they are broken instead of buying new, utilizing bulk bins, and buying products that can be recycled or composted.[1] Bea shows through her experience that it is possible for a family to live a zero-waste life, be stylish, and still live comfortably.

Note

1. Bea Johnson, "Zero Waste Home-About," accessed May 15, 2016, zerowaste-home.com.

there are also a number of websites[7] that manage junk mail on your behalf. If you receive a lot of offers for credit cards, visit the OptOutPrescreen website[8] to be removed from the lists used by creditors and insurers.

AIR-CONDITIONING (A/C) AND HEATING

In the United States, about 100 million tons of carbon dioxide are emitted each year from air-conditioning, an average of about two tons for each home with A/C.[9] That's equivalent to the amount of GHGs that would be emitted if a car in each of these households drove 4,350 miles, more than driving from Los Angeles to New York City. Heating and cooling is the largest energy expense, contributing to 48 percent of energy usage in a typical U.S. home.[10] Although summer and winter weather often require the use of A/Cs and heaters, ensuring that they operate efficiently can help minimize energy consumption and GHG emissions. There are various ways to minimize this energy use and related GHG emissions, as well as save money on your energy bill without having to invest a lot of time or money.

Close the shades to keep rooms cool. To keep the house cooler in the summer, close the curtains or blinds in rooms that aren't being used. Blocking direct sunlight from entering through windows will go a long way in keeping rooms cooler, giving your A/C a break.

Be conscious of when you use the oven. During warm summer days, try to use the oven in the evenings or at night in order to prevent extra heat in the house. The same applies to heat-producing machines such as dishwashers and dryers. Summer is also the perfect time to grill or barbecue, keeping the heat outside.

Turn on the fan (or open a window) when it isn't hot enough for A/C. Although fans don't actually cool the air as A/Cs do, they do help by moving air around that cools us down. Check to make sure ceiling fans are programmed to run counterclockwise in the summer for cool downward airflow and open windows at night to bring in cool air and ventilate the house.

Utilize natural heat. Opening the curtains of any south-facing windows during the day and closing them at night will make the temperature in your home more comfortable during the winter. Incoming sunshine will contribute to

Box 5.3 Where Does My Energy Come From?

In the U.S, the energy you use at home is likely to come from the combustion of a fossil fuel (coal, natural gas, and petroleum) at a power plant. However, the mix of energy sources varies depending on where you live and even at different times of the day. Electricity from power plants makes its way to your house through a grid and transmission lines, while natural gas (used by gas stoves and heaters) is transported via underground pipelines. In 2015, the U.S. Energy Administration estimated that about 80 percent of the energy consumed in the United States was from fossil fuels, almost 10 percent from renewable energy, and 8 percent from nuclear power. Although solar, a renewable energy source, still makes up less than 1 percent of energy consumption in the United States, solar installation continues to increase at an impressive rate.[1]

Note

1. U.S. Energy Information Administration, "Total Energy," accessed May 7, 2016, http://www.eia.gov/totalenergy/.

the warmth and closing the curtains at night will keep the house from losing heat. Consider swapping your bedsheets out seasonally, using flannel sheets with down or synthetic down duvets to keep warm in winter and sheets with natural fibers like cotton during summer.

If you have central heat and air, set the temperature or turn the system off during the day when you aren't home. In the winter, reducing inside temperature from 72°F to 68°F in the day and 65°F at night lowers your household energy consumption approximately by 4 percent.[11] During the summer when trying to keep the house cool, maintain the thermostat at around 80°F when you're not home: you can save 7 percent on your cooling costs for each degree set above 78°F.[12] To maximize efficiency in the summer, make sure doors to all rooms are kept open in order to keep air ventilated and to prevent the system from working too hard and using unnecessary energy. If it isn't extremely cold or warm out, simply turn the system off until you get back home.

If you don't have central heat and air, only heat or cool rooms in use. Instead of heating or cooling an entire house or apartment, limit it to the rooms that are most used. When using space heaters, use them sparingly, and make sure doors are closed to avoid heat from escaping.

INDOOR AIR QUALITY

Even though we are less likely to face life-threatening indoor air pollution in the United States compared to developing countries, air quality is still a key issue that we should be aware of, especially since we spend a good amount of time inside our homes. Common household items such as furniture and particle board can release low levels of formaldehyde while plastics, paints, and furniture release benzene. These types of air toxins can lead to health problems such as itchy eyes, drowsiness, respiratory and sinus congestion, headaches, allergies, and even cancer with long-term, high exposures.[13] Letting fresh air in to ventilate and filter out stale, dusty air can go a long way, but there are a few other things that you can do to improve the air quality of your home.

Indoor plants filter toxins. In the late 1980s, NASA conducted a study on the ability of plants to reduce indoor toxins in an effort to learn more about purifying the air in space stations. They discovered that certain plants are very effective at absorbing the harmful gases and toxins that often linger from furniture, paints, and plastics. See table 5.2 for specific plants that help to filter and purify the air.

Nontoxic cleaning supplies. We know some situations call for heavy-duty cleaning supplies, but chemical-based cleaning supplies are often made up of substances such as formaldehyde and benzene that, in addition to being dangerous to your health, pollute the air and contribute to water pollution when poured down the drain or flushed down the toilet. Cleaning instead with environmentally friendly, nontoxic cleaning products will limit the harsh substances you use in your home. There are lots of cleaning supplies made with natural ingredients these days, but check labels closely to make sure that claims of being "natural" are true. Items with the Green Seal label are a safe bet. In general, it is a good idea to avoid products with chlorine or phosphates because of their potential to pollute the air and water as well as their harmful health effects. There are also a number of other chemicals that should be avoided,[14] but as mentioned in chapter 4, websites and apps such as GoodGuide and EWG's Guide to Healthy Cleaning[15] can help in determining exactly which products are safe to use.

Common household items such as baking soda, white vinegar, and lemon can easily replace pricey cleaning products from the store. Baking soda and white vinegar act as natural odor neutralizers and remove dirt, grease, and stains from pots and pans, as well as tough bathroom residues. Hydrogen peroxide is another option for disinfecting and sanitizing as an alternative to bleach.

Table 5.2 Air Filtering Plants

Name	*Description*
Boston fern	These look lovely as hanging plants and do a great job filtering out formaldehyde. Place them by a window, as they prefer bright, indirect sunlight.
Palm trees	There are actually a number of palm trees small enough to place inside the house such as the Areca palm (also called the butterfly palm) which is known for its ability to purify air and usually grows according to the pot it's planted in.
Rubber plants	These plants remove toxins such as trichloroethylene, benzene, and carbon monoxide from the air. Rubber plants don't need a lot of sunlight, so they are great for places in your house that may not receive much natural light.
Craig Dracaena	This indoor plant was shown to remove about 78 percent of benzene from the air within a 24-hour period according to the NASA study. Keep these dark, leafy plants in a place in your house that receives the morning sun. You can keep them a little on the drier side since they don't need much water.
English ivy	English ivy works great as a potted plant and is the perfect size for small apartments. They filter out benzene and formaldehyde and help reduce allergies. In the NASA study, English ivy removed 90 percent of benzene from the air.
Peace lily	In addition to taking toxins out of the air, the peace lily can also help remove mold. These compact plants don't need much, just some indirect, sunlight and water once a week. Be careful with pets though; this plant is toxic when eaten by cats or dogs.
Golden pothos	The golden pothos removes formaldehyde and other VOCs like benzene from the air. Another plant that brightens up a room as a hanging plant, the golden pothos needs bright indirect sunlight, much like the Boston fern.
Flowering plants such as florist's mum, Gerbera daisies, or tulips	Bring some color to the house while filtering chemicals and pollutants from the air with these vibrant and fun flowers.

Sources: B.C Wolverton et al. *Interior Landscape Plants for Indoor Air Pollution Abatement*. National Aeronautics and Space Administration(NASA) Office of Commercial Program-Technology Utilization Division and the Associated Landscape Contractors of America. (1989), accessed March 6, 2016, http://ntrs.nasa.gov/archive/nasa/casi.ntrs.nasa.gov/19930073077.pdf.

Emily Main, "7 Plants That Purify Air," Rodale's Organic Life, April 2, 2015, accessed March 6, 2016, http://www.rodalesorganiclife.com/garden/7-plants-purify-indoor-air.

LIGHTS

Lights made up around 10 percent of total residential electricity consumption according to the U.S. Energy Information Administration.[16] The biggest environmental impact of light bulbs is the energy they consume (compared to manufacturing and disposal), but because they are made out of metals and can contain hazardous chemicals, we should try to replace (and dispose of) them as seldom as possible.[17] Incorporating sustainable habits related to lighting will save energy and money on our electricity bills, and can also help in limiting how often we replace light bulbs, all of which decreases the pressure we put on natural resources.

Turn off the lights. Although we can sometimes get by with natural light, we still turn on lights out of habit. By being mindful of whether turning on a light is necessary, you can conserve the lifespan and energy of your bulb in the long run. When leaving a room, incandescent bulbs and light-emitting diodes (LEDs) should be turned off. Typically, lights in the hallway, closet, or pantry are the ones that are left on unnecessarily. If you use compact fluorescent lamps (CFLs, the ones that take a little longer to warm up and turn on), the general rule is that if you are going to be out of a room for 15 minutes or less, go ahead and leave them on.[18]

Replace burnt-out bulbs with LEDs or CFLs. LEDs are the most efficient light bulbs, followed by CFLs, and then incandescents, but that doesn't mean you should replace all your lights with LEDs in one fell swoop. Extending the

Table 5.3 Lighting - What You Need to Know

Lighting	*Efficiency and Disposal*
LED (light-emitting diode)	Lasts approximately 50,000 hours or about 11 years LEDs should be kept separate from other recyclable items and dropped off at a local waste collection agency or retail store if possible. If LEDs aren't accepted in your area, they can be disposed of in your regular trash bin since they don't contain mercury.
CFL (compact fluorescent lamp)	Lasts approximately 10,000 hours or a little more than one year (417 days) CFLs should be kept separate from other recyclable items and dropped off at a local waste collection agency or retail store if possible. CFLs contain mercury, so are more likely to be accepted by a local waste collection agency or retail store. This also makes it important that they are recycled instead of put in the regular trash bin.
Incandescent	Lasts approximately 1,000 hours or about 42 days Currently being phased out, incandescents are generally not recyclable and don't contain mercury, so can be disposed of in your regular trash bin.

Sources: Nobel Prize, "Blue LEDs – Filling the world with new light," accessed March 8, 2016, https://www.nobelprize.org/nobel_prizes/physics/laureates/2014/popular-physicsprize2014.pdf.

Erica Taub, "How Long Did You Say That Bulb Would Last?" *New York Times Bits*, February 11, 2009, accessed August 30, 2016, http://bits.blogs.nytimes.com/2009/02/11/how-long-did-you-say-that-bulb-will-last/.

life of a light bulb as long as possible (regardless of the type of bulb) is the key to minimizing our impact from sourcing new and disposing of old bulbs. When your lights finally go out, make sure they are disposed of properly and consider LEDs or CFLs as replacements.

Unplug or use a power strip. Some energy consuming products such as electronics and small appliances use electricity when they are plugged in but not turned on. These products, which have been coined "energy vampires," can cost households around $200 each year.[19] Unplugging electronics and small appliances when not in use or plugging them into a power strip and turning the power strip off can eliminate this unnecessary standby power. Power strips are helpful for outlets that are difficult to reach, and for turning on and off multiple items at once.

LAUNDRY

Doing laundry means using quite a bit of water: laundry makes up about 22 percent of the total water used in households.[20] According to ENERGY STAR, the standard front-load washing machine uses 23 gallons of water and top-loading washing machines use around 40 gallons.[21] Doing a load of laundry in top-loading machines uses almost the same amount of water as taking a 20-minute shower.[22] Because doing laundry also means using energy, doing laundry more efficiently reduces your environmental impact and saves money on your bills. Besides ensuring that your washing machine is full before starting a load, here are some other tips to take into account next time you do laundry.

Use cold water instead of hot water. Not only does washing your clothes in cold water prevent them from fading as quickly (and thus reducing the need to replace them), it also helps reduce energy use. The energy it takes to heat water accounts for 90 percent of the energy it takes to operate a washing machine.[23] In addition, heating hot water makes up 12 percent of the typical U.S. household's energy bill, so do your clothes and your wallet a favor by switching to cold water.[24]

Hang dry clothes instead of using a dryer. Hanging clothes outside or inside on a movable rack by a window or heating source eliminates the energy needed to dry clothes. It also makes your clothes last longer by treating them more delicately.

Nontoxic laundry detergent. Similar to other cleaning products, laundry detergents can contain harmful ingredients. At a minimum, check to make sure your detergent doesn't contain sodium lauryl sulfate or phosphates, which have a detrimental effect on marine life.[25] Some big companies are already taking the initiative to cut harmful chemicals from their products,[26] but it's a good idea to double check the ingredients list or refer to GoodGuide or EWG to gain insight into what your laundry detergent contains. If you see the Green Seal label, you can be sure that your product does not contain harmful chemicals.

ADJUSTMENTS, REPAIRS, AND REPLACEMENTS

If you are ready to take on a small home improvement project or you need to make repairs or replace something in your home, take the following tips into account – which are cheap or free – in order to minimize your household's environmental footprint.

Turn your water heater down. The manufacturer's setting for hot water heaters is often at 140°F, but most households only need it to be set at 120°F. Turning down the temperature to 120°F saves $25 to $60 per year and helps the water heater and pipes last longer.[27] It also does not impact the enjoyment of a hot shower.

Clean out your A/C (or furnace) air filter and make sure all vents are open. Air filters that have not been cleaned or replaced in a while mean that free-flowing air is being blocked, making the system work harder to push air out. Similarly, closed vents mean that the system will work harder to maintain a constant temperature. It may sound counterintuitive but keeping vents open actually allows air to circulate, and saves you money on your electricity bill. In addition, make sure that furniture or curtains aren't blocking any vents around the house. The U.S. Department of Energy website provides additional and more specific guidance on maintaining your air conditioner.[28]

Strip and seal up your home. If you live in an older house or apartment, it may not be well insulated, causing you to lose energy and money. Check if your utility or another program offers incentives for residential energy efficiency.[29] Some utilities offer discounted energy audits, which identify where energy is being lost, as well as other types of assistance. Cheap ways to address energy loss include putting weather strips on window and door frames, and sealing up leaky cracks and holes with a caulking gun. Caulking guns can be found at your local hardware store for between $5 and $20 and be sure to ask for low-VOC caulk as well. Covering drafty windows with an old blanket or a piece of plastic can also help if making improvements isn't an option.

Buy used and repair broken items instead of buying new. Although it may seem like a better option to buy new rather than fixing broken things, it is often not the case when the environmental costs are considered. Buying used keeps items out of the landfill and deters the use of natural resources to make new products. The value of buying used items extends to all types of products such as furniture, clothing, and common household items. Craigslist, garage sales, thrift stores, local papers, and putting the word out through your personal network are all cost-effective strategies to finding used versions of the goods you are looking for.

When purchasing new appliances go for models with the ENERGY STAR label and check for rebates. Although the opportunity to purchase new appliances such as refrigerators, washers, and dryers doesn't come often, if it does, look for the ENERGY STAR label, which signals that the product

Box 5.4 Tool Libraries and Repair Cafes

Two new types of spaces are popping up all over the world making it easier to fix things that are broken and to repurpose items instead of buying new. The first initiative is called a tool library, which, as the name suggests, lets people rent out tools instead of books, usually for free or at a minimal charge. Tool libraries are convenient for all sorts of do-it-yourself (DIY) projects; for example, instead of buying new chairs, you can rent a drill and a staple gun to reupholster them. The second initiative is a repair cafe, which similar to a tool library, provides tools and material to help you fix things. Repair cafes also provide an area where you can bring items in to work on and expert volunteers are often available to help. Repair cafes are free of charge but tend to operate on donations. There are now over 1,000 repair cafes registered in countries across the world including the United States, India, and Japan, as well as many within the European Union. The Repair Cafe website (repaircafe.org) provides information on where cafes exist and on setting up one in your community. There may be an informal group or similar offering in your community that isn't registered as a repair cafe so ask around if your city isn't on the list.

is energy efficient. ENERGY STAR covers a wide range of electronics and appliances, and it is common for utilities and local programs to offer rebates for the purchase of these products. Rebates can help offset the upfront cost of purchasing energy-efficient products and make payback time even quicker.

See if your utility offers an online tool or app to visualize energy use. More and more utilities are providing customers with energy use data in accessible and easy-to-understand formats, either through their own platforms or partnering with outside companies. Over 100 utilities have partnered with the technology company Opower, which specializes in providing utility customers with in-depth home energy analyses, as well as information on how their energy use compares to their neighbors.

Sign up to generate renewable energy. Want to support the transition to clean energy but not in a position to install solar panels? Some utilities give individuals the option to contribute a small premium each month toward new wind and solar installation projects, increasing the contribution of renewables to the energy mix. The generation of energy from renewable sources increases its competitiveness with dirty fossil fuels. Ask your utility where your energy comes from and what options you have to support clean energy.

Table 5.4 States with the Best Energy Efficiency Policies

According to the American Council for an Energy-Efficient Economy, these ten states are doing the best when it comes to encouraging energy efficiency. The ranking takes into account various efforts by government and utilities in areas such as transportation and building energy codes.

1. Massachusetts	6. Connecticut
2. California	7. Maryland
3. Vermont	8. Washington
4. Oregon	9. New York
5. Rhode Island	10. Illinois

Source: Annie Gilleo et al. *The 2015 State Energy Efficiency Scorecard.* American Council for an Energy-Efficient Economy. (Washington, D.C.: 2015), accessed June 5, 2016, http://aceee.org/state-policy/scorecard

· 6 ·

In the Kitchen and at the Dinner Table

Food and cooking are integral parts of life that not only provide our bodies with the nutrients we need to function but also bring people together. However, it takes land, energy, and water to raise, grow, process, and transport the food we eat. As explored in chapter 2, agriculture and the production of food are associated with water pollution, deforestation, and climate change.

Food waste is another side of this story. Approximately 1.3 billion tons of food is wasted globally each year. In terms of GHG emissions, wasted food has a devastating effect as it contributes to an estimated 3.3 billion tons of GHGs each year through wasted emissions from the production, transportation, and disposal of food.[1] That means that if food waste was a country, it would be the third largest emitter of GHGs, after China and the United States. Food waste is a serious environmental issue, but one that has a lot of potential to be addressed, particularly in our own kitchens.

We can reduce our environmental footprint by choosing which foods to bring to the table and how efficiently they are used and disposed. In addition, being conscious about the materials we use in the kitchen and how we cook our food can save a little money on the purchases we make, while bringing more sustainability into our lives.

MEAL CHOICES

Although there are various campaigns and movements under way to inform consumers about where their food comes from, a comprehensive understanding of a meal's environmental impact can still be tricky since we don't always have all the information that we need to help us make sustainable decisions.

Minimize your consumption of GHG-intensive foods. One of the most GHG-intensive foods is beef. Producing 2.2 pounds of beef emits the same amount of GHGs as driving 64 miles in the average passenger car. The majority of these emissions come from producing the feed to give to cattle as well as enteric fermentation (i.e., cow burps), which emits methane.

Figure 6.1 Which of our foods contribute the most to climate change?
Source: Kari Hamerschlag and Kumar Venkat, *Meat Eaters Guide to Climate Change + Health Methodology*, Environmental Working Group, (2011) accessed March 8, 2016, http://static.ewg.org/reports/2011/meateaters/pdf/methodology_ewg_meat_eaters_guide_to_health_and_climate_2011.pdf.

Note: Graphic designed by The Sustainability Co-Op, and kg CO2e converted to miles driven with the EPA's Greenhouse Gas Equivalencies Calculator, accessed March 12, 2016, https://www.epa.gov/energy/greenhouse-gas-equivalencies-calculator.

Box 6.1 Beef and Deforestation

Beef takes a large amount of natural resources and other inputs to be produced; lots of energy, land, and water are all required to raise cattle, let them graze, and finally produce the product you see in grocery stores and restaurants. But where do these cattle graze, exactly? Cattle ranching for beef is one of the main drivers of deforestation in the Brazilian Amazon rainforest, which means it contributes not only to biodiversity loss but also to climate change. Beef produced on recently deforested land can result in "up to 25 times more GHG emissions than beef produced on established pastures."

About 60 percent of deforested areas in the Amazon are pastures to feed cattle. Fortunately, the issue has gained attention over the years, and the industry has responded. In 2009, three of Brazil's major meatpacking companies signed a zero-deforestation cattle agreement, stating that they would only purchase from direct ranchers that reduced deforestation to zero, causing many ranchers to register as zero-deforestation ranching in order to be able to sell their cows to these meatpacking companies. Before the agreement in 2008, one of the three meatpacking companies, JBS, had 40 percent of its direct suppliers linked to deforestation, but by 2013, this percentage dropped to just 4 percent. Over the past few years, due in part to international pressure, companies like McDonald's and Dunkin Donuts that buy meat from meatpacking companies have also signed zero-deforestation cattle agreements. Because the supply chain of meat has various levels, and due to loopholes and lack of monitoring, it's difficult to be certain of zero deforestation, yet these moratoriums are a step in the right direction. Consumers should continue to demand zero deforestation in the supply chain from their producers to ensure real, lasting change and transparency.

Notes

1. Zero Deforestation Cattle, accessed May 13, 2016, http://www.zerodeforestationcattle.org/ch1t2.html
2. Embrapa, "Embrapa e Inpe apresentam dados sobre o uso da terra na Amazônia," May 9, 2016, accessed May 13, 2016, https://www.embrapa.br/busca-de-noticias/-/noticia/12355787/embrapa-e-inpe-apresentam-dadossobre-o-uso-da-terra-na-amazonia
3. Allie Wilkinson, "In Brazil, Cattle Industry Begins to Help Fight Deforestation," *Science* (May 15 2015), accessed May 13, 2016, http://www.sciencemag.org/news/2015/05/brazil-cattle-industry-begins-help-fight-deforestation
4. H. K. Gibbs et al. "Did Ranchers and Slaughterhouses Respond to Zero-Deforestation Agreements in the Brazilian Amazon?" *Conservation Letters* 9 (2016), accessed May 13, 2016, doi: 10.1111/conl.12175.

Beef is a big culprit due not only to its large environmental footprint, but also due to its prevalence in the American diet.

Implement "Meatless Monday." We can reduce our environmental impact just by dedicating one day out of the week to not eat meat. If everyone in the United States ate no meat or cheese just one day a week, it would be equivalent to not driving 91 billion miles – or taking 7.6 million cars off the road.[2] Eating less meat and more fruits and vegetables also has health benefits including helping you avoid the problems associated with excess meat consumption, which include heart disease, stroke, type 2 diabetes, obesity, certain cancers, and premature death.[3]

Be aware of water-intensive foods. Foods that require a lot of water to produce can be problematic for water scarcity, especially in drought-prone areas. Almonds, walnuts, cashews, lamb, and lentils make the list of water-intensive foods. The production of beef is also water intensive: around 850 gallons of water produces an eight-ounce steak; that's equivalent to 34 ten-minute showers.[4]

Support organic agriculture. Buying organic food supports a food system that causes less environmental impact and is not dependent on substances that cause pollution such as synthetic fertilizers and pesticides. Conventional (nonorganic) farming damages the land and requires intense processes that degrade soil fertility, release GHGs, and that pollute nearby waterways. Unfortunately, the environmental costs of conventional agriculture are not factored into the prices we see at the store. This is why organic food (e.g., meat and produce) is often more expensive than conventional. However, the markup for organic products is often minimal. As more people support organic farming and as the real price of conventional farming gets factored into its price tag, the price difference between conventional and organic food is expected to go down.

Table 6.1 Fruits and Veggies with the Highest Pesticide Loads (aka The Dirty Dozen)

If you can't buy organic all the time, EWG recommends making the effort to do so when it comes to the following 12 items due to their high levels of pesticide residue.

1. Strawberries	7. Cherries
2. Apples	8. Spinach
3. Nectarines	9. Tomatoes
4. Peaches	10. Sweet bell peppers
5. Celery	11. Cherry tomatoes
6. Grapes	12. Cucumbers

Source: Environmental Working Group. "2016 Shopper's Guide to Pesticides in Produce," accessed April 20, 2016, https://www.ewg.org/foodnews/summary.php

Eat local and seasonal. A commonly cited statistic in the United States is that food travels an average of 1,500 miles from the farm to your table.[5] Even though this statistic can vary depending on where you live, it illustrates that our food often travels a long way to get to us and every mile means energy use and associated GHG emissions. The environmental impact of food transport depends on the mode of transportation (e.g., trains are better than trucks), but, in general, reducing the miles your food travels is a good thing.[6] Nowadays it's likely you can find locally sourced meat and produce where you live, and by buying locally, you support the farmers in your area and your local economy. If you're not sure what foods are in season, there are some great resources online that can help you find out what is currently being grown in your area.[7]

Purchasing produce from your local farmer's markets and participating in community-supported agriculture (CSA) programs are two ways to ensure you are eating local and seasonal. According to the U.S. Department of Agriculture, there were over 8,000 farmer's markets in the United States in 2014.[8] In addition, CSA programs allow you to subscribe to receive a box of produce directly from farmers, while also offering you different options on the frequency and size of produce boxes and options for pickup and delivery. Purchasing from these sources not only provides you healthy and low-impact fruits and veggies, but it also supports local farmers.

Box 6.2 Why Eating In-Season Foods Matters

In most climates, different fruits and vegetables are grown and harvested naturally depending on the season. For instance, winter foods include kale, oranges, and pumpkin, while strawberries, tomatoes, zucchini, and plums are typically summer foods (unless you are lucky enough to live somewhere where they are grown year-round). At the grocery store, we can find foods that aren't in season because they are either transported from faraway regions where they are in season, or they are produced in artificial conditions that require extra assistance such as energy or water (i.e., heated greenhouses). If produce is transported long distances, it is usually picked early before it's fully ripened. This means that chemicals and waxes (such as ripening chemicals, preservatives, and irradiation) are often sprayed onto the produce to protect it during the trip. Eating seasonally means you are likely avoiding the chemicals, food miles, and the extra energy it takes to eat foods that aren't in season. In addition, seasonal foods can be less expensive and taste better. Because it is picked only when it's naturally ripe, seasonal produce retains all of the nutrients and flavor that is lost when food is harvested prematurely.

Choose sustainable seafood. Fish and other seafood are another group of natural resources that is at risk due to unsustainable human practices. According to a study published in the academic journal *Nature* in 2016, we may have been seriously underestimating overfishing. In the 60-year period between 1950 and 2010, it's estimated that the number of global catches were 50 percent higher than originally thought (due to inaccurate accounting of catches).[9] In order to avoid eating fish that may be under threat of being over-exploited or illegally fished, being conscious of where your fish comes from is one way to be supportive of sustainable fishing. Monterey Bay Aquarium's Seafood Watch provides a helpful consumer guide with straightforward information on which types of fish and seafood to avoid eating in your state.[10] There are also a number of certification systems that can help you identify sustainable options such as Marine Stewardship Council, Friends of the Sea, the Aquaculture Stewardship Council, and Best Aquaculture Practice.

FOOD WASTE

Food waste has been receiving an increasing amount of attention from the international community, political leaders, local grassroots organizations, talk show hosts, and gourmet food bloggers alike. These individuals have a common understanding of how unsustainable our collective food production and consumption is in the Unites States. The extent of the problem is illustrated by the fact that 40 percent of the food produced in the Unites States goes to waste.[11] Food waste frequently ends up in a landfill emitting methane, which contributes to climate change. At the same time, even though food waste is a major issue, 14 percent of U.S. households may not have enough to eat and are deemed "food insecure" by the U.S. Department of Agriculture.[12]

The entire food system that brings food from farms to your dinner table is riddled with inefficiencies that cause perfectly good food to be thrown into the trash instead of going to those who need it. Although individual consumers are not completely to blame for the food waste issue, each of us tosses out around 300 pounds of food each year or about 25 pounds per month. That's estimated to be $375 per year or $30 per month.[13] Individuals can (and should) do their part to reduce food waste with a little planning and efficiency.[14]

Keep fruit and vegetables dry and separate. Most produce lasts longer if it's dry, but sometimes fruits and veggies from the grocery store have moisture on them when you get home. By taking a second to dry these products either by airing them out or with a towel, you can help them last longer. Also, store veggies and fruits separately, and keep fruits like apples, bananas, and pears

Table 6.2 Getting to Know Your Refrigerator

Fridge Location	*Items*	*Location Characteristics*
Door	Condiments	Warmest
The upper shelves	Leftovers, drinks, yogurt, dips, and sauces	Warm
The lower shelf	Meat, poultry, and fish	Cold
High humidity drawer, if applicable	Vegetables, especially those that might wilt	Less air flow
Low humidity drawer, if applicable	Fruit as well as vegetables that have a tendency to rot	More air flow

Source: Dana Gunders, *Waste Free Kitchen Handbook* (San Francisco: Chronicle Books, 2015).

away from everything else. These fruits emit ethylene gas that will make other produce get ripe and go bad faster, leading to increased food waste.

Optimize your fridge. By not packing your fridge full, the air circulates more and your refrigerator doesn't have to work as hard, which then minimizes energy use. It's also nice to be able to see all of your food and make sure you don't forget about something in the fridge, just to find it later after it has gone bad. Optimizing your fridge can also include organizing food according to how temperature is distributed to make it last as long as possible.

Stir-frys, smoothies, and casseroles. Don't let the time and money you use for buying food go to waste. Try to make the most of the food you buy by coming up with creative ways to eat it, particularly when you sense that your food is going bad. Fruit and veggies are one of the biggest culprits of food waste due to the relatively short shelf life. Stir-frys, smoothies, and casseroles are great ways to use up food before it goes bad.

Stems and ends. Don't be afraid to use the parts of food that many people throw away such as broccoli stalks or bread ends. Cut up those stalks and throw them in the dish or make vegetable stock out of them. Bread ends make great croutons when toasted or sautéed with olive oil and garlic.

The freezer is your friend. Putting leftover food in the freezer keeps it from going bad and can provide a quick meal when you don't feel like cooking or going to the store. Having a few frozen meals to heat up in a pinch is a great alternative to having food delivered, which often comes with unsustainable materials such as plastic and Styrofoam.

Think again about Best Buy/Sell By/Expires On dates. Did you know that the dates printed on food packages are not associated with any regulated testing of food safety or science? The dates are included by the manufacturer to

Box 6.3 Ugly Fruits and Vegetables

Ugly fruits and vegetables are what they sound like: Vegetables or fruits that don't meet the strict color, size, and shape requirements to be sold at grocery stores. Although the produce is perfectly fine to eat, most of it gets thrown away, adding to the significant issue of food waste our society faces. Yet a movement to prevent these ugly fruits and veggies from going to waste has made significant ground. In 2014, the French supermarket chain Intermarché launched an ugly fruit and vegetable campaign, where the store began carrying and selling ugly fruits and veggies at a discounted price, with a clever marketing campaign featuring the "the grotesque apple," "the failed lemon," "the disfigured eggplant," "the ugly carrot," and the "unfortunate clementine." Since Intermarche's campaign, a number of other campaigns have popped up around the world, such as the California-based start-up and advocacy group Imperfect Produce which connects the 20 percent of produce grown in California that doesn't meet the superficial specifications with individuals and restaurants at a 30–50 percent discount.

convey a subjective level of optimum quality, but the lack of standardization creates confusion and food waste because it makes us think our food has gone bad when it hasn't. Support is growing to standardize these dates, but until then, trust your instinct and think twice before throwing out food that still looks and smells good.

COMPOST

When organic material (not certified organic produce, but rather material produced by the earth) gets sent to the landfill, it takes on a anaerobic process (or one not requiring air) to decompose, which emits methane. Yet when this same material is composted, the material decomposes in the most common and natural biological breakdown, in a process that doesn't emit methane, but rather creates nutrient-rich fertilizer. For these reasons, composting is increasingly becoming utilized. Cities all over the United States are launching programs that pick up organic material from your house, along with your trash and recyclables, and individuals are joining together to develop community-based composting programs. About 3,560 community composting programs were documented in 2013, serving 2.7 million households.[15] Don't get discouraged if your neighborhood or city doesn't have an organic waste collection system yet. You can still separate your organic waste to give to

Box 6.4 What Food and Household Materials Can be Composted?

- Fruit and vegetable scraps (both cooked or uncooked)
- Eggshells
- Coffee grounds and filters
- Peanut shells
- Soiled paper products (paper towels, napkins, to-go food containers)
- Paperboard (toilet paper rolls, clean boxes)
- Tea bags and leaves
- Dryer lint
- Hair and fur
- Shredded newspaper paper
- Cotton balls
- Leaves, weeds, plant trimmings, and grass clippings

a local composting facility or even start your own compost to provide fertilizer to your household garden or plants (chapter 8 provides some tips).[16]

APPLIANCES

Our environmental footprint doesn't only come from what we cook, but also from how we cook it. Most dishes require the use of energy and water, but there are small tweaks we can make to our cooking habits to use these resources more efficiently and not skimp on quality or quantity.

Prep before turning appliances on. Before turning on the stove or oven, make sure you have everything prepped to keep the appliance on only as long as needed. This includes chopping and thawing frozen food before putting it on the stove or in the oven. It can also be efficient to prep while your stove or oven preheats, but be mindful that it's not switched on for longer than necessary.

Use lids and heat efficiently. Using lids when boiling water or cooking food on the stove can help in containing the heat, cooking food faster, and keeping the heat in longer. If multiple dishes need to be cooked in the oven, try to put them in at the same time.

Utilize the microwave or toaster oven. Microwaves and toaster ovens can offer an energy-efficient option to heating up your food, particularly if you're only wanting to warm up leftovers. Microwaves use a third of the energy required by conventional ovens, while small toaster ovens that are quick to preheat use just half.[17] In terms of energy efficiency, electric kettles are the best way to go when heating up water, followed by electric stove tops and then microwaves, if you already have them.[18]

Unplug coffee makers, toasters, and microwaves when not in use. As we saw in chapter 5, some small kitchen appliances use electricity when they are plugged in, even if they are not on. Unplugging all the "energy vampires" in your house can help save you 10 percent (or even more) on your monthly utility bill.[19]

DOING THE DISHES

Should you hand-wash your dishes or use a dishwasher? This is a common discussion point when it comes to sustainability and water use in the kitchen. The verdict: using a dishwasher is generally more water efficient than washing by hand, but isn't always the case since it depends on how efficiently you hand-wash. Here are some tips to ensure that regardless of your method you can save water.

Reuse drinking glasses. Washing fewer dishes means using less water. While you don't have to reuse dirty dishes, keeping one drinking glass for multiple uses is an easy way to reduce water use. When preparing meals, it's also helpful to consider how many dishes are being used in order to cut down on the need to wash them later. This also helps free some time up that would be needed for clean-up.

Wash dishes efficiently. If you are doing dishes by hand, make sure that you turn the water off when soaping. If you are using a dishwasher, don't rinse dishes first and only run it when the dishwasher is full. Although studies show that a dishwasher is more water efficient than washing by hand, rinsing dishes before placing them in the dishwasher defeats the purpose of using a dishwasher for water efficiency's sake, as does running a dishwasher when it's below capacity. In addition, use cold water when you can. Just as is the case with laundry, heating water is a major contributor to your energy bill. If you are using a dishwasher, look to see if there is a setting for a "cold wash" or a similar equivalent.

Ditch the chemical dish soap. There are lots of affordable options for dish soap these days that don't contain toxic chemicals. It's important to avoid chemicals such as phosphates because they end up in waterways, contributing to pollution and harming aquatic life. Sometimes it's difficult to decipher which options are good for the environment, so check GoodGuide or EWG

Box 6.5 Compost versus Garbage Disposal versus Trash

When deciding how to dispose of food waste, prioritizing the reduction of food waste in the first place is always the best option, but we do know it takes time to get the hang of finding the optimal amount of food to buy from the store. Composting and giving food that isn't going to be eaten to someone that may use it are the next best choices. Since composting may not be an easy option depending on where you live, the garbage disposal (if you have one – many older sinks do not) can be used to dispose of food. The least environmentally friendly option and last resort for disposing of food waste is putting food in the trash bin to go to the landfill. If you are using a garbage disposal, the food that you put down it will likely end up in a wastewater treatment plant where food waste can be recycled and used to fertilize crops, which is why it's better than going to the landfill where the same food waste will emit GHG emissions. The following items are known to clog the drain, so should not be put in the garbage disposal: items that are greasy or have high fat content (such as butter or oil), pasta or rice, egg shells, celery, potatoes, orange or banana peels, or seeds.

to see the grade your dish soap receives when it comes to potential impacts on human health and the environment.

ADJUSTMENTS, REPAIRS, AND REPLACEMENTS

Many times the performance and efficiency of our appliances depend on the settings they are programmed at. Take a look at the manual guides as they will help to determine which settings are best for optimal energy and water use. Besides checking the manual, check out these other ideas to make sure you are using your appliances in the most efficient way possible.

Use the "eco" setting. If you have a dishwasher with a "fast," "quick," "economy," or "eco" wash cycle setting, take advantage of it. Don't worry about it not being able to clean as well since machines that have these settings are designed to perform well while also saving energy and water.

Set your refrigerator between 35 and 40 degrees Fahrenheit. Keeping your refrigerator at this range keeps food optimal and also minimizes energy use. If the temperature is too warm, food can go bad faster, while if it's too cold, you could be using unnecessary energy.

KITCHEN MATERIALS

Like many of the products we use in our homes, we may not have a great idea of where our kitchen tools and materials come from or how they are made. Knowing this is useful because it can lead us to a better understanding of how we can put less stress on limited resources.

Minimize the use of paper towels and napkins. Instead of purchasing and throwing away disposable paper towels and napkins, use reusable and washable cloth napkins and towels. The fewer paper products you buy is a direct savings for you and also reduces waste and unnecessary paper use. If you do buy napkins and paper towels, try to purchase recycled and/or chlorine-free bleached to show the paper industry your support for using fewer chemicals. Chlorine is the main bleaching agent used by the paper industry and when released into the waterways as part of industrial wastewater it acts as a harmful pollutant.

Minimize the use of plastic. Instead of plastic plates, forks, and containers that are made from fossil fuels, use items made from stainless steel, glass, ceramic, or wood. If you're looking for a new cutting board, for instance, take a look at bamboo ones with a sustainability certification such as FSC or Rainforest Alliance Certified. Bamboo is considered a renewable resource because it grows so quickly. Reducing plastic may be better for your health as well: Many plastic cups, water bottles, and containers contain bisphenol A (BPA), an additive that leaks a synthetic hormone.

Wash and reuse ziplock bags. Ziplock bags are convenient to keep food items from going bad or stale, but at the end of the day, they are made from plastic and are usually not accepted at local recycling facilities. Even if you're lucky enough to be able to recycle these small bags, the most environmentally friendly thing to do is reuse them multiple times before discarding them. Reusing them also saves money because you won't have to purchase them as frequently. Other small plastic bags such as the ones used to hold produce from the grocery store can be rinsed out and reused as well.

Limit use of and reuse aluminum foil. Limiting the use of aluminum foil and extending the life of the foil you use by reusing it several times reduces your overall environmental footprint in the kitchen. Although aluminum foil is often recycled, as mentioned in chapter 5, the extraction process required to make new aluminum products degrades the environment and can contribute to a wide range of environmental issues including water pollution, deforestation, and soil erosion.

Table 6.3 What Do the Numbers on Plastics Mean?

The small number within a triangle of arrows is the resin identification code, telling us what type of plastic it is. Unfortunately, the numbers don't exactly tell us if it's a plastic that is recyclable or not because different recycling facilities are equipped to process and accept different numbers. Some plastics of the same number can be either rigid or thin plastic film, with rigid plastics being more frequently accepted for recycling at recycling facilities than thin plastic film, even if they have the same number.

Plastic	*Examples*
#1: Polyethylene Terephthalate (PET)	Plastic bottles for soft drinks, water, juice, sports drinks, beer, mouthwash, ketchup, and salad dressing; Food jars for peanut butter, jelly, jam and pickles; Ovenable film and microwavable food trays.
#2: High Density Polyethylene (HDPE)	Bottles for milk, water, juice, cosmetics, shampoo, dish and laundry detergents, and household cleaners; Bags for groceries and retail purchases; Cereal box liners; Reusable shipping containers.
#3: Polyvinyl Chloride (PVC)	Rigid packaging applications include blister packs and clamshells; Flexible packaging uses include bags for bedding and medical, shrink wrap, deli and meat wrap.
#4: Low Density Polyethylene (LDPE)	Bags for dry cleaning, newspapers, bread, frozen foods, fresh produce, and household garbage; Shrink wrap and stretch film; Coatings for paper milk cartons and hot and cold beverage cups; Container lids; Toys; Squeezable bottles (e.g., honey and mustard).
#5: Polypropylene (PP)	Containers for yogurt, margarine, takeout meals, and deli foods; Medicine bottles; Bottle caps and closures; Bottles for ketchup and syrup.
#6: Polystyrene (PS)	Food service items, such as cups, plates, bowls, cutlery, hinged takeout containers (clamshells), meat and poultry trays, and rigid food containers (e.g., yogurt); Protective foam packaging for furniture, electronics and other delicate items; Packing peanuts, known as "loose fill;" Compact disc cases and aspirin bottles.
#7: Other	Three- and five-gallon reusable water bottles, some citrus juice and ketchup bottles; Items made with some plant-based material.

Source: American Chemistry Council, "Plastic Packaging Resins," accessed September 5, 2016, https://plastics.americanchemistry.com/Plastic-Resin-Codes-PDF/

· 7 ·

In the Bathroom

When it comes to integrating sustainability into the bathroom, it's all about water use. The average American uses between 80 and 100 gallons of water per day and the bathroom is an easy place to reduce that footprint.[1] Besides water use, there are a number of other things that you can do to be more sustainable that have co-benefits of protecting your health. Take for instance personal care products (e.g., makeup, shampoo, and soap). A survey of over 2,300 Americans showed that the average adult uses nine personal care products each day, with over 100 unique chemical ingredients.[2] Although most of the chemicals are harmless, some have been linked to serious health problems. Avoiding certain chemicals helps safeguard your health and the environment; if a chemical isn't good for humans, it's probably not good for our waterways either. This chapter provides various strategies and resources to help you purchase sustainable personal care products, reduce water use, and minimize the impact of your bathroom habits.

IN THE SHOWER

A few actions can help cut down on your water use in the shower. Consider these easy ways to use water more sustainably, save money on your water bill, and have more time to do other things.

Be quick and efficient. When it comes to showering, time really is money. The average showerhead uses 2.5 gallons of water per minute causing showering

Box 7.1 Where Does Your Water Come from?

Before it comes out of your faucet, it's likely that your water has made quite a journey, something we don't normally have to think about unless there's an issue with the water such as a shortage or contamination. But it is valuable to understand where your water comes from and how to safeguard this precious resource. Your water may come from an underground aquifer (groundwater source), or a river, lake, or reservoir (surface-water source). Your specific water source depends on where you live and may even be transported from far away. Even though water sources can be replenished when it rains, continued overuse strains the source's ability to provide sufficient water for all commercial, industrial, and residential activities. Drought and high temperatures, weather patterns that are predicted to become more and more common due to climate change, will only put more pressure on water sources. To learn about water risk in your area, including how risk will increase with climate change, see the World Resources Institute's interactive Aqueduct tool.[1]

Note

1. World Resources Institute (WRI), "Aqueduct," accessed May 12, 2016, http://www.wri.org/our-work/project/aqueduct.

to account for about 17 percent of indoor water use.[3] Efficient showerheads still use around two gallons per minute but cutting even 30 seconds off of your shower makes a difference: that's a whole gallon!

Skip the bath. There is no easy way to put this, but as you may have guessed, baths consume a lot of water. The average bath takes about 36 gallons of water to fill up.[4] Limiting the baths you take can really help reduce your water footprint.

Reuse towels. Loads of laundry can quickly get filled up with towels that are not dirty. Try reusing a towel for a week before washing it, hanging it somewhere dry to let it air out in between showers so it doesn't get mildew.

Efficient water showerheads. When it comes to showerheads, look for the EPA's WaterSense label or one that doesn't exceed the WaterSense maximum flow rate of two gallons per minute (GPM). Although buying a toilet or sink doesn't come up very often, if you or your landlord find yourself in that situation, ask for one with the WaterSense label, or one that meets the standard for water efficiency.

AT THE SINK

Of course, the sink is another opportunity to reduce water use. But it's also an opportunity to clear up a common misconception and reduce energy use.

Use cold water instead of hot when you can. When it comes to killing bacteria, it doesn't make a difference if you wash your hands with hot water or cold water; we wouldn't be able to physically handle water hot enough to kill bacteria.[5] Avoid the common misconception that warmer water is better, and use cold water at the sink – it will save energy and money.

Shut off the water when brushing your teeth or shaving. Turning off the water while brushing your teeth or shaving can save about a gallon of water for each activity.[6]

Get leaks fixed. Pay attention to leaky or dripping faucets. If you rent, let your landlord know that you have a leak because it's also in their best interest to reduce water use. If you own or pay for your water use, you'll definitely want to take care of leaks as it will reduce how much you pay on your water bill. Leaky faucets left unfixed can waste up to 100 gallons of water per day.[7] Toilets and showers may leak as well so keep an eye out. If you can't get leaks fixed, or your water takes a long time to heat up, don't let it go down the drain – instead capture it in a bucket or bowl and use it for your plants or garden.

PRODUCTS

Many personal care products contain toxic chemicals or components linked to a number of negative health effects and that pollute our waterways when washed down through our drains. This is because common ingredients in personal care products have been largely unregulated in the United States due to a weak and flawed Toxic Substances Control Act (which first passed in 1976 and was only updated in 2016), as well as U.S. Food and Drug Administration loopholes. The 2016 legislation reformed the Act, providing the U.S. Environmental Protection Agency with significantly more authority and support to regulate chemicals.[8] The U.S. Food and Drug Administration also stepped it up in 2016, banning 19 chemicals from hand and body washes.[9] There seems to be momentum from both the government and private companies to address toxic chemicals in personal care products. However, much can still be done, and making decisions on what products are best for our health and the environment really comes down to us as consumers.

Avoid toxic chemicals in your personal care products. The premium for more sustainable personal care products is usually minimal and worth it to safeguard your health and the environment. However, it's easy for companies to take part in greenwashing to make products seem more natural than they actually are; the research to determine which products and ingredients are "natural," bad for the environment, and/or bad for your health can be complicated. Luckily, there are a number of resources to help you make informed decisions when it comes to choosing personal care products. GoodGuide, ThinkDirty, and the Environmental Working Group's Skin Deep Cosmetics Database have each rated around 100,000 personal care products. Products that don't contain toxic chemicals are increasingly accessible, and supporting the companies that don't use any harsh chemicals shows the industry that consumers care about what we put on our bodies.

Don't use products with plastic microbeads. Some toothpastes, soaps, body washes, and cleaning supplies contain plastic microbeads for exfoliating or extra cleansing purposes that end up in our oceans, lakes, and rivers. Plastic

Table 7.1 Which Ingredients Should I Avoid in Personal Care Products?

EWG has compiled the following information on the chemicals to be avoided when it comes to common personal care products. Chemicals are on this list due to an association with a wide range of negative effects on the environment and the human body. Many of these ingredients are already banned for use in Europe, demonstrating the need for much stronger regulation on personal care products in the United States.

Item	*What to Avoid*
Soap	Triclosan and triclocarban
Skin moisturizer and lip products	Retinyl palmitate, retinyl acetate, retinoic acid, and retinol in daytime products
Sunscreen	SPF above 50, retinyl palmitate, aerosol spray, powder sunscreen, oxybenzone, and added insect repellent
Toothpaste	Triclosan
Nail polish	Formaldehyde, formalin, hardeners, toluene, and dibutyl phthalate (DBP)
Acne products	Triclosan, parabens, PEG, ceteareth, and polyethylene
Baby wipes	Bronopol, DMDM hydantoin, and fragrance
Diaper cream	BHA, boric acid, and fragrance
Shaving cream or aftershave	Oxybenzone, PEG, ceteareth, polyethylene, parabens, DMDM hydantoin, triclosan, and fragrance

Source: Environmental Working Group, "Top Tips for Safer products," accessed May 12, 2016, http://www.ewg.org/skindeep/top-tips-for-safer-products/

Box 7.2 U.S. Ban on Plastic Microbeads

In December 2015, President Barack Obama signed a bill that bans the production and sale of products designed for cleaning or exfoliating that contain plastic microbeads 5 millimeters or smaller. The ban, called the Microbead-Free Waters Act of 2015, prohibits the production (taking effect in 2017) and sale (taking effect in 2018) of microbeads, and was signed into law only a year after the first state-level ban on microbeads was passed in Illinois. The move to ban microbeads was swift due to the conclusive research that began to document the incredible amount of microbeads that ended up in our waterways, how they got there, and the long-term environmental impacts. In 2014, it was estimated that eight trillion microbeads entered waterways each day in the United States; that's enough microbeads to cover more than 300 tennis courts each day.[1] The beads follow the path of our home wastewater after being washed down drains during use. They either end up in septic tanks and seep back into the soil and groundwater or are sent to water treatment plants, but in every scenario they eventually make it into our waterways. Although you may still have products with microbeads at home, this policy makes it easier for us to avoid them for now and soon eliminate them altogether.

Note

1. Rochman et al., "Scientific Evidence Supports a Ban on Microbeads," *Environmental Science & Technology* 49 (2015): 10759–10761, accessed April 23, 2016, doi: 10.1021/acs.est.5b03909.

microbeads don't biodegrade, and because of their small size are eaten by fish and other marine life, which can kill them. To avoid contributing to water pollution, make sure that the products you use with exfoliants don't contain plastic, but are rather made from biodegradable material such as pumice, oatmeal, or walnut husks.

Choose products that minimize packaging. Bar soap is often the environmentally preferable compared to liquid soap because it usually comes in less packaging. There are other opportunities to choose products that minimize packaging so keep that in mind for other personal care products as well.

Recycle. Bathroom items such as plastic shampoo and soap containers, toilet paper rolls, and paperboard containers (e.g., the ones that some toothpastes come in) are often accepted by recycling facilities. Rigid plastic containers are often #2 plastics that can be recycled into new bottles, plastic lumber, playsets, buckets, containers, and stadium seats. Toilet paper rolls can be turned into new cardboard, paperboard, and paper bags. Keeping a separate small recycling bin in the bathroom may be a helpful way to remember to recycle these items.

TOILET

Who knew we had so much to tell you about sustainability habits related to the toilet? You can use less water and reduce your impact just by keeping certain tips in mind.

If it's yellow, let it mellow. Yes, you read that right. You don't need to flush the toilet after every use because the toilet is the biggest consumer of water in your house, using around three gallons (new toilets around 1.6) every time you flush.[10] If you live alone, or can get family members or roommates to do the same, not flushing is a great way to reduce water use.

Don't put these items down the toilet. There are certain items that should not be flushed down the toilet because they may have difficulty passing through the pipes and because they can negatively impact marine life. These items include dental floss, feminine products, disposable diapers, and expired medication.

Put a brick-like item in the tank. Putting a heavy item in the tank of your toilet cuts down the amount of water used per flush by half a gallon. Since bricks break down in water over time, other heavy items are recommended such as a plastic beverage bottle filled with sand or rocks.

Minimize paper product use. We use a lot of paper products including toilet paper, tissue, and paper towels. Making paper takes trees, lots of water, and chlorine (or its derivatives) that bleaches paper products to get that common white color that we're used to seeing. Reducing our use of these paper products ensures that we cut down on our contribution to the paper production process that often results in water pollution and deforestation.

· 8 ·

The Backyard

Backyards or green spaces near our homes are special places that allow us to be a little closer to the natural world around us. Incorporating sustainability into how we use these spaces can go a long way in preserving them and being able to continue to enjoy them for years to come. If you are fortunate to have an outdoor space or backyard at home, it presents an opportunity to not only minimize your environmental impact, but to even give back to the environment. If you don't have a yard of your own, many of these tips can be implemented on a smaller scale, or applied if you have a chance to volunteer outside or help someone you know.

PLANTING

Using your space to plant flowers, trees, or a garden is a great way to make you feel connected to the place you live and with nature in general. Adding more greenery can also help restore soil nutrients, aid in slowing climate change, and provide a place for biodiversity. If you're up for it, you can also supply yourself with your favorite seasonal and local produce.

Learn about soil composition. Soil composition is the basis for plant health and longevity. Some plants require high acidity levels while others prefer more alkaline environments. This is controlled by the composition of organic (peat and compost) and inorganic (sand and lime) material within the soil mix. There are a number of simple tests you can do to better understand the soil that you use.[1]

Plant flowers and native plants. Aside from adding a colorful touch to your yard, flowers provide food for local pollinators such as birds, butterflies, and bees. Native plants are preadapted to your local climate, so they will naturally thrive and should be preferred over other nonnative species. Planting native plants can also help attract native wildlife such as owls and songbirds. The Wildflower Center has an extensive online database that can help you find out what plants are native to your area.[2] If you are adding mulch, try native mulching as well by using pine needles, oak leaves, and green mulch.

Plant a vegetable garden. If you have space or have access to a community garden or plot, growing your own organic vegetables and supplying yourself with your favorites (instead of buying them at the market) can be very rewarding. Heirloom vegetables are ideal because you can save the seeds to replant for next year. Having your own vegetable garden can also help you learn what is easiest to grow in your area, as well as what grows seasonally, and which months are best to plant certain foods.

Box 8.1 Milkweed and the Monarch Butterfly

The monarch butterfly is probably one of the most well-known butterflies, thanks in large part to its beautiful colors and migration pattern. Unfortunately, the monarch is threatened by a range of factors, such as the destruction and degradation of its migration habitats, use of herbicides and pesticides, and climate change. Since 1990, about 970 million monarch butterflies have vanished, and only about 30 million are estimated to remain.[1] Every autumn, monarchs set out on their migration, flying south and west from southern Canada and the northern United States, ending in Mexico on a voyage that takes five generations of butterflies to complete. In order to produce the next generation that will complete this migration, the butterflies need to lay eggs on a specific plant: milkweed. The monarchs also eat milkweed leaves when they hatch. Milkweed plants have been disappearing as a result of herbicide use on agricultural fields. Planting milkweeds in your backyard or garden, especially if they are native to your area, is a great way to provide a habitat for these magnificent creatures and help support the existence of the monarch butterfly.

Note

1. Darryl Fears, "The Monarch Massacre: Nearly a Billion Butterflies Have Vanished." *The Washington Post*, February 9, 2015, accessed May 13, 2016, https://www.washingtonpost.com/news/energy-environment/wp/2015/02/09/the-monarch-massacre-nearly-a-billion-butterflies-have-vanished/.

Compost. Composts are a great addition to the backyard, particularly if you have a garden. Using the household food scraps (as mentioned in chapter 6) and other biodegradable materials, you can create natural fertilizer for your garden. You don't need a garden to compost: Add your composted material to potted plants or your lawn, or look into community or city compost programs.

Consider container planters. Planting in containers is perfect if you don't have a backyard or only have a small space, since they don't take up much room. You can turn a crate, barrel, or any other item you can get your hands on into a mini garden. Container planters like EarthBoxes or GrowBoxes[3] are also an easy way to get started with vegetable gardening. These self-watering container planters make it simple to grow vegetables with minimal input.

Skip the synthetic pesticides, fertilizers, and weed killers. As explored in other chapters, synthetic pesticides and fertilizers often run off into waterways, contributing to water pollution and impacting aquatic life. Compost material is a natural alternative that can be used in place of synthetic pesticides and fertilizers. Instead of using harmful or toxic weed killers, try a homemade mix like vinegar or boiling water. Other options include pulling the weeds out, using mulch to keep invasive species out, or keeping native weeds in the ground and finding a creative way to landscape around them.

Succulents. Adding succulents to your outside area, even if it's only on a window sill, adds some nature to your life and are easy to take care of because they don't require much water. Due to their resilience to drought conditions and ability to grow quickly, low-growing groundcover succulents are a great option for landscaping. As groundcover, succulents help prevent erosion and can be a cost-effective alternative to grass or other thirsty options.

Landscaping for shade. Planting certain trees or bushes in strategic areas around your house can help maintain a moderate temperature inside your house by shading it from the sun during the summer. The U.S. Department of Energy has a great website that can help you decide what type of landscape is best for your climate and yard, helping you save energy and money.[4] For instance, deciduous trees planted south of your home can help shade it from the summer sun while also not blocking the breeze, while trees that are lower to the ground can help shade your home from a low, afternoon sun when planted to the west of your home. According to the site, shading is the "most effective way to reduce solar heat gain in your home and cut air conditioning costs."[5]

Box 8.2 Starting a Compost

Composting is a great way to minimize your environmental impact. You can start your own compost directly on bare earth or in compost tumblers, bins, or large storage containers. What you need to start is simple: an equal amount of *browns* and *greens*. Browns can be thought of as dead organic materials, such as dead leaves, branches, twigs; anything you may find on the ground around bushes and trees. Greens include grass clippings and food scraps, such as banana peels, orange rinds, coffee grounds, tea bags, eggshells, and so on. Avoid putting meat, bones, bread, or lots of cooked food in your compost. You should make sure the compost is covered with either a lid or a tarp so it stays moist and damp, which is the ideal condition for worms and microbes to do their work and break down the material. The contents will also need to be mixed up or shaken every two to four weeks. Your food scraps will soon break down, becoming nutrient-rich fertilizer. Don't have anywhere to put the compost? Don't let that keep you from composting: some cities have compost pickup services like Washington D.C.'s Compost Cab or Chicago's Collective Resource, or get in touch with your community Master Gardener organization to see what options they may have for composting.

Landscaping for windbreaks. Similar to providing shade for your house, trees can act as windbreaks, lowering the wind chill around your home and acting as an insulator, all while reducing the cost of heating your home. One strategy to create a windbreak is to plant evergreen trees and shrubs on the north and northwest sides of your home.[6]

Leave your leaves. Whether they're on the tree or the ground, leave your leaves where they are. During autumn, despite what you may have been taught, don't rake and bag the leaves that are in your yard. The layer of leaves on the ground is part of a natural process that provides a habitat for wildlife like chipmunks and butterflies that spend their winters hibernating in the fallen leaves. Fallen leaves also protect tree roots during winter, and recycle nutrients into the soil as part of a natural fertilization process.

If you live in a place where leaves don't change color and fall off trees, and for instance, palm trees are more common, the same tip still holds true – the best thing you can do for them is to leave them alone. Don't cut, trim, or prune your palm fronds – keeping these leaves on the tree, particularly the brown ones that may look dead, encourages wildlife and aids in the health of the tree as these leaves' nutrients will go toward generating new leaves.

WATER USE

Plants do need water to survive, but it is estimated that as much as 50 percent of water used outdoors for watering is wasted due to evaporation, wind, or runoff caused by inefficient irrigation methods. Knowing how and when to water your plants can reduce the amount of water wasted. Rain barrels and rain gardens are also useful in achieving efficient water use, and they prevent excess stormwater from reaching waterways as well.

Know your plants' water needs. Understanding the water needs of your plants allows you to use water efficiently, and even lower the maintenance involved. When arranging your garden, place plants so that the ones with similar water needs are next to each other, in order to make the most of your water.[7] Talking to an expert at a local nursery, someone you know with a green thumb, or doing a quick Google search can provide insight into watering according to your plants' needs.

Save the water from washing fruit or heating up the shower, and use it to water plants. This is an easy way to reuse water that would have otherwise gone down the drain. It takes some coordination, but it's worth the extra effort to minimize water use.

Check for holes or leaks in water hoses and sprinklers. Water hoses and sprinklers can be a source of wasted water if they have holes or leaks in them. Be sure that your irrigation systems or water hoses are working properly so that the water you do use is used in the most efficient way possible.

Water your plants in the morning or evening. If you have to use sprinklers, make sure they are adjusted to turn on in the morning or evening when it's cooler to avoid evaporation. Adding mulch to your garden can also slow the evaporation process.

Rain barrels and rain gardens. Rain barrels, which are storage tanks situated to collect the rainwater that comes off the roof, are beneficial for several reasons: they provide high-quality water to be used for your garden; they protect the foundation of your house by keeping gutter rainwater from hitting and potentially flooding the ground; and they reduce runoff from stormwater that ends up in sewer systems. Diverting stormwater from storm drains and sewage systems is essential because it reduces the pollutants that would ultimately enter local rivers and streams. It also reduces flooding of sewer systems by limiting the amount of water entering the sewers during peak flows.

Box 8.3 Watering in California

Prompted by a multiyear drought, California proclaimed a state of emergency in 2014 and a subsequent Executive Order requiring cities to achieve a 25 percent reduction in the use of potable drinking water compared to their 2013 use. The West Coast drought brought to light the extensive vulnerabilities related to water rights and use in the state, which produces over a third of the country's vegetables and two-thirds of the country's fruits and nuts.[1] California put in place and extended a number of water use restrictions for individuals and businesses, along with other strategies such as rebates for replacing inefficient appliances, new rate structures, and investment in new technologies, in order to minimize water use. However, water reduction measures are largely managed by local water agencies and actions taken to reduce vary by city. When it comes to water use in the backyard, the State Water Resources Control Board granted local agencies the ability to fine individuals $500 for activities that were commonplace before the drought,[2] including:

- Using water for landscaping that runs off onto adjacent property, the sidewalk, etc.
- Applying water directly to the sidewalk or driveway
- Washing your car at home with a hose that doesn't have a shut-off nozzle
- Watering within 48 hours of rain
- Using a decorative fountain

Notes

1. California Department of Food and Agriculture, "California Agriculture Production Statistics," accessed May 12, 2016, https://www.cdfa.ca.gov/statistics/.
2. California Environmental Protection State Water Resources Control Board, "Adopted text of the Emergency Regulation (adopted 5/18/16)," accessed May 21, 2016,http://www.waterboards.ca.gov/water_issues/programs/conservation_portal/docs/emergency_reg/051816_10_final%20adopted%20regs.pdf.

Rain gardens are shallow depressions in the ground covered with plants that have similar functions as rain barrels by capturing rainwater runoff. If you are thinking about a rain garden, make sure to plant it at least ten feet away from your home to prevent water from seeping into the foundation of the house, and try to place it in a naturally occurring low spot where rain can easily be directed. In addition, make sure your garden is at least six inches deep.[8]

Box 8.4 Stormwater Runoff, Water Pollution, and Green Roofs

Stormwater is a major cause of water pollution, and the main culprit for unswimmable bodies of water. Rainwater itself is relatively clean, yet when this water falls to the ground, it washes down a storm drain or sewer system, taking with it chemicals, garbage, detergents, fertilizers, sediment, motor oil, and so on – basically everything it picks up along the way. Because stormwater drains and sewer systems ultimately end up in oceans, lakes, and rivers, this is also the destination of these pollutants. Waterways and bodies of water around the United States have been declared "impaired" due to stormwater pollution; 40 percent of rivers and streams, 19 percent of lakes, and 31 percent of bays and estuaries carry this classification and are deemed unsafe for swimming and recreational use by the EPA.[1]

For this reason, it is beneficial to prevent rainwater from flowing down to the drains and collecting the chemicals and garbage that pollute waterways. Rain barrels or rain gardens are two strategies. The installation of green roofs, roofs covered with plants, is a third and one that is more common for commercial buildings. In addition to providing the building with insulation that reduces energy costs, green roofs reduce rainfall runoff with remarkable efficiency: just three inches of plant growth on roofs can cut rainfall runoff by 50 percent.[2] Chicago is one place where green roofs have taken off, and with good reason since about 90 percent of the Great Lakes shoreline is considered impaired for recreational use due to urban runoff and stormwater pollution.[3] A 2010 study identified 509 green roofs in Chicago, and over 5 million square feet (or 97 football fields) of green roof coverage, including the roof of City Hall.[4]

Notes

1. U.S. Environmental Protection Agency, "National Summary of State Information," accessed May 19, 2016, https://ofmpub.epa.gov/waters10/attains_nation_cy.control.
2. Berghage, Robert D. et al. *Green Roofs for Stormwater Runoff Control*. U.S. Environmental Protection Agency. Cincinnati: National Risk Management Research Laboratory Office of Research and Development (2009), accessed May 19, 2016. http://nepis.epa.gov/Exe/ZyPDF.cgi/P1003704.PDF?Dockey=P1003704.PDF.
3. U.S. Environmental Protection Agency, "National Summary of State Information," accessed May 19, 2016, https://ofmpub.epa.gov/waters10/attains_nation_cy.control.
4. City of Chicago, "Chicago Green Roofs," accessed May 19, 2016, http://www.cityofchicago.org/city/en/depts/dcd/supp_info/chicago_green_roofs.html.

ADJUSTMENTS, REPAIRS, AND REPLACEMENTS

When making upgrades to your backyard, try to keep these tips in mind to ensure that your special space doesn't have unintended negative consequences on the environment.

Efficient outdoor lighting. If you are in need of new lights for your backyard, look for energy-efficient lighting, such as LEDs or motion-sensing or solar-powered lights. Solar-powered lights are a perfect (and often inexpensive) way to add a sustainable touch (and even a conversation starter) to your yard.

Sustainable outdoor furniture. Buying used furniture is one of the best ways to make sure your backyard furniture has a minimal impact. Check out Craigslist, garage sales, thrift stores, local papers, and putting the word out through your personal network to find something that might fit your yard. If you want to buy something new, consider furniture made from recycled materials or sustainably harvested wood. Consider chairs and tables that are made from recycled plastic or plastic lumber. If buying new furniture made of wood, make sure it is FSC certified.

Box 8.5 Turning Floridian Lawns into Edible Gardens

An innovative program called Fleet Farming was established in 2014 by volunteers in Orlando, Florida, with the goal of making lawns more useful by converting manicured lawns into edible gardens and working farms. Through the Fleet Farming program, homeowners sign up to donate the front lawn of their homes to be converted into vegetable gardens. Fleet Farming volunteers ride bikes to participating homes to plant and maintain the gardens, while also encouraging the hosting participants to engage in the farming process. Participants can keep a portion of the harvest from their lawns for free, and the rest is sold at local markets where 100 percent of the sales go back into the organization to cover costs.[1] More than 300 homeowners in the Orlando area have already offered to donate their yards to the program. The program touches on various aspects of sustainability such as rethinking land use and agricultural practices, and supporting the sense of community and the local economy.

Note

1. Catherine Welch, "An All-Volunteer Squad of Farmers is Turning Florida Lawns into Food," *National Public Radio, All Things Considered.* May 16, 2016, accessed May 31, 2016, http://www.npr.org/sections/thesalt/2016/05/15/477036910/an-all-volunteer-squad-of-farmers-is-turning-florida-lawns-into-food?utm_campaign=storyshare&utm_source=twitter.com&utm_medium=social.

· 9 ·

Out-and-About

Every time we turn the ignition on in our cars, we emit pollutants that contribute to air pollution and climate change. Because Americans tend to drive a lot, our transportation choices are one of the major impacts we have on the environment. Our reliance on cars doesn't seem to be subsiding either: Americans drove more than ever in 2015.[1] Our transportation footprint isn't completely our fault; most cities and towns weren't planned or built to support more sustainable modes of transportation like biking and walking. Times are changing though, as cities around the world are rethinking their street plans to allow for more pedestrians and cyclists. Advancements in fuel efficiency and the adoption of hybrid and electric vehicles continue to help reduce emissions from transportation. However, these advancements only go so far and still don't reduce the number of cars on the road or traffic congestion.

Although it's still the norm to own a car in the United States, it's becoming simpler and easier for individuals to go car-less. Public transportation is becoming smarter and easier. Carsharing programs such as Zipcar, Lyft, and Uber help people get around town to places that may not be accessible by walking or by public transportation. A University of California, Berkeley study of the Car2go carsharing program estimated that the program kept 28,000 private cars off the road in 3 years.[2] But even if you live somewhere where you need a car to get around, or you just aren't ready to give up your car, there are many alternative ways to reduce your environmental footprint.

DRIVING

Since the average passenger vehicle emits around 400 grams of CO_2 per mile and in smaller amounts, methane, nitrous oxide, and hydrofluorocarbons (HFCs),

Box 9.1 Electric Cars: Past, Present, and Future

Electric cars are not a recent phenomenon. Experimental electric cars appeared in 1820 and constituted 38 percent of the U.S. automobile market in 1900.[1] This represents a peak for the electric car, as it was shortly overtaken by the internal combustion engine and other improved production technology introduced by the Ford Motor Company. It must be with some irony then, flashing forward a little over a century to present day, that Ford has its own electric car on the market, and four partially electric cars, or hybrids. Ford's adoption speaks volumes about the growing trend, even among industry stalwarts, of getting in on the electric car movement now fully in swing. A combination of factors brought electric cars out of history books and back on the road, including advances in battery technology, increasing oil prices, and greater environmental awareness about climate change and air pollution.

In 2015, the best-selling all-electric car in the United States was the Tesla Model S, made by Tesla Motors, a company notable for producing electric cars exclusively, and also the first to introduce an electric sports car and luxury sedan, widening the electric car market to a new type of buyer.[2] Tesla is set to claim an even greater share of the market with their more affordable Tesla Model 3, scheduled to begin production at the end of 2017. With the number of Model 3 preorders already over 400,000, Tesla will double the current number of electric cars on the road with just one model – not bad for a company that produced its first car in 2008.[3] Although the market share of all electric cars is under 2 percent, as Tesla demonstrates, interest in electric cars continues to grow at a rapid pace and sales continue to increase.[4]

Notes

1. Clean Technica, "Electric Car History," accessed May 14, 2016, http://cleantechnica.com/2015/04/26/electric-car-history/.
2. Statista, "Best-selling All-electric Cars in the United States in 2015, Based on Sales (in units)," accessed May 15, 2016, http://www.statista.com/statistics/257966/best-selling-electric-cars-in-the-united-states/.
3. Brooke Crothers, "With Tesla Model 3 Orders Nearing 400,000, Chevy Bolt Feels Heat Of Tesla Brand," *Forbes,* April 15, 2016, accessed May 15, 2016, http://www.forbes.com/sites/brookecrothers/2016/04/15/with-tesla-model-3-orders-nearing-400000-chevy-bolt-feels-heat-of-tesla-brand/#106f06f85349.
4. Statista, "Statistics and Facts About Electric Mobility," accessed May 15, 2016, http://www.statista.com/topics/1010/electric-mobility/.

the ideal way to reduce your impact from driving is to drive less. Because this may not be very practical where you live, there are other tips to adopt when it comes to lessening the environmental impact of driving.[3]

Don't let your parked vehicle idle. For every ten minutes your engine is off, you'll prevent one pound of carbon dioxide from being released.[4] Cars only need a few seconds of idling time before driving so turn your key and go, and try to get into the habit of turning your engine off as soon as you park.

Wash the car less frequently and more efficiently. To minimize water use, cut down on washing your car, and when you do wash it, be mindful of water use. Be sure to not let the hose run when it's not being used. If you wash your car at home, park your car in grassy areas if you can in order to avoid soap

Box 9.2 Solar Roads

Roads are necessary to get us where we need to go, but what if they could generate solar energy too? The concept is not as far-fetched as you'd think: different strategies on how to actually do it are emerging around the world with two promising efforts taking place in Europe. In 2015, a public-private partnership in the Netherlands piloted the first energy-generating road for bikes, SolaRoad. Over 200,000 bikers have now ridden over the 3-millimeter, glass-covered, solar panels. Although the road is humble in size at less than a quarter of a mile, in its first six months it generated more energy than expected.[1] In 2016, another solar road technology developed through a French public-private partnership made headlines, not only because France has already committed to installing over 600 miles by 2021, but because of its versatility and durability.[2] The French technology, Wattway, glues solar cells in layers onto already existing roads and can handle the impact of cars and trucks. Although new technologies face a number of barriers and generally take time before they are cost-effective and widely deployed, solar roads have the potential to provide electricity for local needs including powering streetlights, businesses, homes, and charging stations for electric cars. Solar roadways are another example of the innovation taking place in countries around the world to rethink existing infrastructure and get more energy from clean sources.

Notes

1. Solaroad, "Solaroad," accessed May 21, 2016, http://en.solaroad.nl/.
2. Wattway by Colas, accessed May 17, 2016, http://www.wattwaybycolas.com/en/.

ending up in storm drains or sewers, and empty out buckets of soapy water in the sink instead of on the street. Self-service or hand-wash car washes are generally more efficient than drive-in, machine-operated car washes. If you go to a car wash, try to find out if they capture and recycle the water, which is more common with newer car wash facilities.

ADJUSTMENTS, REPAIRS, AND REPLACEMENTS

Going to the mechanic is often a chore we try to avoid at all costs. However, in addition to ensuring the longevity of your car, there are also some environmental reasons to give your car some attention. Taking into account the following tips can help you reduce your car's negative environmental impact and your car will thank you too.

Get tune-ups regularly. Tune-ups ensure your car is running as efficiently as possible and helps extend its life. According to the U.S. Department of Energy, fixing a car that is noticeably out of tune or has failed an emissions test can improve its gas mileage by an average of 4 percent (results will vary depending on the kind of repair and how well it's done).[5]

Check your tire pressure regularly. Underinflated and overinflated tires reduce your car's gas mileage costing you money on gas and releasing unnecessary GHG emissions. Proper pressure is defined in pounds per square inch (PSI) and you should be able to find this information in the owner's manual. Underinflated tires can lower gas mileage by 0.3 percent for every 1 PSI drop in the pressure of all four tires.[6] You can improve your gas mileage by up to 3 percent by keeping your tires inflated to the proper pressure.

Make sure your air conditioner isn't leaking. The chemical used as a refrigerant in your car's air conditioner is a type of HFC, a potent GHG. If your air conditioner is leaking it's releasing HFCs into the atmosphere, so it's important to confirm with your mechanic that this isn't the case for your car.

ALTERNATIVE MODES

Although in some cities or towns it may be difficult to get around by public transportation, it may be worth a shot to explore the options you may have to commute to work, school, or for a weekend adventure. Trying new modes of transportation can even give you a new perspective of where you live. In addition, just by switching to carpooling or busing once a week to get to work or school, you can cut down on your total GHG emissions.

Carpooling. Carpooling is great for many reasons: it reduces your contribution to climate change by not driving alone in a personal vehicle (while still commuting within the comfort and ease of a vehicle), you get to drive in the carpool lane, you may be eligible for priority parking, and you may even qualify for reimbursement programs depending on where you live and work. If you've never looked them up before, you may be surprised at how many carpooling and vanpooling services exist. Take the time to see what's out there, or you may find that setting up your own carpool with coworkers, friends, or family members is the way to go.

Public transportation. Overall, public transportation options such as metros, trains, buses, and ferries are a more sustainable choice than driving. The

Box 9.3 Walkable Suburbs: Arlington, Virginia

In the suburbs, driving is usually a necessity and walking tends to be limited to a stroll around the neighborhood. But this is changing. Policymakers, town planners, and citizens alike are calling for better infrastructure that caters to pedestrians. Arlington, Virginia, is a great example of this desire to change, as evidenced by its recognition in 2015 as the "Most Walkable Suburb" by Mother Earth News, and as one of the 15 best "Walk Friendly" communities in America by the Walk Friendly Communities project. Arlington plans to further redevelop their community, creating more downtown-like "mixed-use" developments with 75 percent of new development set to take place within walking distance of public transit.[1] Arlington County has 36 miles of multiuse trails and another 50 miles of connecting bikeways that provide stress-free routes for commuting and recreation. The county actively encourages citizens to walk and bike through its WalkArlington and BikeArlington initiatives.[2] Although the town has more work to do, such as improving pedestrian crossings at major roads, compared to other suburban areas it has proven itself exemplary and has shown commitment to creating a more sustainable community.

Notes

1. Luke Mullins, "The Audacious Plan to Turn a Sprawling D.C. Suburb Into a Big City," *The Washingtonian*, March 29, 2015, accessed May 31, 2016, http://cleantechnica.com/2014/11/29/november-transit-savings-803/.
2. BikeArlington, "Maps & Rides," accessed June 1, 2016, http://www.bikearlington.com/pages/maps-rides/.

accessibility, reliability, and cleanliness of public transportation varies significantly by city, but don't be too quick to write it off or afraid you'll make a mistake and go the wrong direction. It takes a little proactiveness and getting used to, but using public transportation can be rewarding. Not having to worry about finding a parking space or paying for parking are pluses too.

Biking or walking. Why not get some healthy exercise while also doing the environment a favor? Biking or walking to where you need to go gets your blood flowing and reduces your environmental impact. Cities across the United States are investing in making their cities more bikeable and walkable. Over 50 cities for example, including New York City, Washington D.C., and Chicago, have bike-sharing programs which make biking possible even without owning your own bike. Sustainable infrastructure like sidewalks and bike lanes are getting more attention, but residents must also continue to advocate for these changes. We know that in most cities it isn't realistic (yet) to bike or walk everywhere, but if the opportunity does arise, take it.

ACTIVITIES

Beyond your mode of transportation, try picking up some other sustainable habits when you are out-and-about. The following tips are helpful to keep in mind when planning for the day or for your next outing.

Box 9.4 The Most Bikeable City in the U.S.: Minneapolis

There are several cities vying for the top spot on rankings of the United States' most bike-friendly cities, but Minneapolis, Minnesota, is consistently ranked at or near the top. Irrespective of the metric, whether it's miles of bike lanes, bike route connectivity, percentage of bike commuters, or access to bikes through its city-run bike share program, the Twin City is leading the country and even ranks globally as well, a true novelty for an American city. Minneapolis' bikeability is no accident, but rather due to consistent investment in biking infrastructure which has resulted in about 200 miles of bikeways, half of which are "off-street," bike-only routes and trails that are inaccessible to cars. Minneapolis, as an early adopter of the bike share system in 2010, has improved and expanded its Nice Ride Minnesota program over the years. A lot of the program's success has been attributed to the shear bike-saturation of the area, which provides a bike for every 265 residents. By comparison, Citi Bikes in New York City, the United States' largest bike share program, provides a bike for every 1,400 residents. The good news is, regardless of where you live, studies show that all cities are improving their bikeability scores across the board.

Choose the stairs instead of the elevator. When presented with the option to take the stairs or the elevator, take the stairs if you can. Taking the stairs avoids the energy use needed to power the elevator, and also lets you get some exercise.

Remember your reusable water bottle, coffee mug, or bag. Bringing your own water bottle when you are out-and-about is not only cheaper than buying bottled water, but it's also convenient and helps you reduce your use of plastic. A to-go coffee mug is great too, and sometimes coffee shops will even give you a discount. Either way, you won't be contributing to increased waste. Keeping a reusable bag (cloth, paper, or plastic) in the car or in a larger personal bag, backpack, or purse, is also a simple way to avoid extra plastic bags from an unexpected stop at the store or for a container of leftovers from a restaurant.

Avoid single-use plastic. It can be easy to rely on single-use plastic items such as water bottles, cutlery, plates, and cups, but it creates a lot of waste that will most likely end up in a landfill. Similarly, try to use reusable containers to transport your food or snacks instead of ziplock bags or aluminum foil. When planning your next picnic or camping trip, think about bringing reusable cups and silverware and encourage others to do so as well.

Pack it in, pack it out. Whether it's at the beach, river, hiking, camping, or a picnic, whenever you enjoy the outdoors, be sure to leave everything you came with, especially food wrappers or other packaging, to be disposed of properly once you get back. Although this may sound simple, the amount of trash we leave behind on our trips to the outdoors can be staggering. When volunteers all over the world helped to pick up litter from their beaches for Ocean Conservancy's 2013 International Coastal Cleanup, in total they collected over two million cigarette butts; 1,140,222 food wrappers and containers; 1,065,171 plastic bottles; and 1,019,902 plastic bags.[7] Proper disposal of the things you bring with you ensures that you are not contributing to water pollution, and keeping the land and waterways free of trash helps nature retain the beauty that we go there to enjoy in the first place.

Group activities. Don't hesitate to talk about the ways you are reducing your environmental impact with the groups you take part in, such as sports teams, walking groups, book clubs, game/paint night or any other groups of friends or peers. Not only can you help your friends and networks learn about sustainability, but this also offers a way to hear about other sustainable habits or tips. Starting sustainability initiatives in your groups or clubs is one of the best ways to raise awareness and spread information on sustainability.

Box 9.5 Plastic Water Bottle Bans

Although bottled water is generally no better for your health than tap water and 25 percent of bottled water is actually just bottled-up tap water, Americans still seem to prefer bottled water.[1] Banning the sale of plastic water bottles is an attempt to reduce the number of bottles that end up in landfills or polluting land and waterways. By incentivizing individuals to rely on their own reusable bottles, bans on plastic water bottles reduce overall waste pollution.

Concord, Massachusetts, was one of the first communities in the United States to ban plastic water bottles. The ban, which took effect in 2013, targets vendors and prohibits any sale of single-use plastic water bottles within the town limits. The town encourages citizens to carry reusable water bottles and has also built water fountains for refilling them.[2]

In 2016, San Francisco became the first major city in the United States to ban the sale of plastic water bottles on city-owned property with the scope of the ban increasing over time. Although less comprehensive than Concord's, the plastic water bottle ban in San Francisco will also include outdoor events on public property, and by January 2018 will include large-scale events of 250,000 people or more.[3]

Notes

1. Andrew Postman, "The Truth About Tap, " Natural Resources Defense Council (NRDC), January 5, 2016, accessed June 1, 2016, https://www.nrdc.org/stories/truth-about-tap.
2. Elizabeth Ross, "Here's a Small Town's Advice for Cities Considering a Plastic Bottle Ban," *Public Radio International*, February 23, 2016, accessed June 8, 2016, http://www.pri.org/stories/2016-02-23/heres-small-towns-advice-cities-considering-plastic-water-bottle-ban.
3. San Francisco Public Utilities Commission, "Event Water – How to Comply with the Bottled Water Ban," accessed June 8, 2016, http://www.sfwater.org/index.aspx?page=912.

· 10 ·

At School or Work

Sustainability at school or work can consist of a variety of things, including integrating habits to reduce the use of energy and paper products and being responsible when it comes to the disposal of electronics. It also presents an opportunity to engage with peers and colleagues while supporting sustainable actions on an organizational level. As covered in chapter 3, all types of companies and other organizations are making changes to be more sustainable simply because it's good business. Yet organizations do need support in making these changes. By participating in sustainability programs that your work or school may have in place (e.g., waste diversion, reducing energy use, volunteer cleanups), you can help your company or organization transition to a sustainable culture and multiply your positive impact.

ENERGY USE

Most of us use multiple electronic items in a day, with each one consuming a fair amount of energy that easily adds up. There are some simple habits you can pick up to reduce energy use without affecting you or your device's performance.

Unplug cell phones, tablets, and laptops after charged. These are energy vampires that consume electricity when plugged in, even if not in use. The amount of energy the device draws after it's 100 percent charged varies significantly by the type of device and model. As an example, an Apple

MacBook drew 27 W of power when it was plugged in and fully charged, compared to 48 W of power when plugged in and charging.[1]

Use a power strip. Plugging electronics (e.g., computers, printers) and small appliances (e.g., coffee makers, microwaves) into a power strip and turning the power strip off when items are not in use is a simple way to eliminate unnecessary standby power. This is especially true for turning on and off multiple electronic items at once, such as when you leave work for the day, or for outlets that are difficult to reach. Using a power strip helps you minimize energy use and reduce greenhouse gas (GHG) emissions.

Buy ENERGY STAR-certified, EPEAT-registered electronics, or do your own research. If you are in the market for a new electronic device, check to see if the product has an ENERGY STAR or EPEAT label, or check the applicable websites to see if the model you are interested in is listed.[2] ENERGY STAR-certified products meet energy efficiency criteria and EPEAT goes a step further by requiring products to meet other environmental standards related to environmentally sensitive material, packaging, and what happens to it when it comes to the end of its life cycle. You can also do your own research on the manufacturer to see what they are doing when it comes to sustainability. Supporting companies that are reducing the negative environmental impact of their products and using energy-efficient electronics are two great ways to incorporate sustainability into school or work.

E-WASTE

An important aspect of reducing our environmental footprint at school or work is reducing the waste we create and disposing of it properly. Reducing the generation of waste in the first place is always the best option. Just because something can be recycled, like most electronics, doesn't mean that it will be recycled, or alternatively, it may be recycled in less than ideal conditions such as in developing countries without strict health protections for workers.[3] If you don't see any guidance or resources at your organization to help you properly dispose of items such as used electronics or batteries, research and ask around to find the best option, and then think about effective ways you may be able to share this information with others.

Ignore the urge for the newest gadget. Doesn't it feel like there are better cell phones, tablets, TVs, and computers coming out every few months? We are upgrading our current devices faster than ever, using raw material such as tin, cobalt, lithium, gold, silver, and copper and creating a lot of electronic waste or e-waste. Overall, the less frequently we replace our gadgets, the less strain we put on natural resources used to make them, and the less e-waste we create.

Recycle electronics and other large items. When you buy a new electronic device, make sure your old item is properly recycled instead of thrown out with other trash. Items may be able to be recycled through your organization, a local recycling facility, or a manufacturer/retailer take-back program that often includes a drop-off or mail-in option. The Earth911 website can also provide you with information on the most convenient proper disposal option in your area. Recycling electronics keeps them out of the landfill, reduces the need for new virgin material, and saves energy. Recycling a million laptops saves the same amount of energy used by more than 3,500 U.S. homes per year.[4] The recycling rate for computers in the United States is estimated to be around 40 percent, while the other 60 percent unfortunately goes mostly to the landfill.[5] Recycling rates for other electronics such as cell phones, TVs, and keyboards are even lower. Although recycling rates have increased over the years, we are going through electronics (such as computers and phones)

Box 10.1 What Does It Take to Make a Smartphone?

Cell phones, and in particular smartphones, are composed of tin, cobalt, lithium, gold, silver, and copper, which are all rare earth elements that are in finite supply and drive the global extractive (mining) industry. Tin mining, specifically for the pieces in our smartphones and tablets, can result in deforestation, soil degradation, the destruction of freshwater supplies as well as coral reef ecosystems, and have negative effects on the livelihoods of the local communities where the mines are located.[1] Toxic mine drainage is a serious environmental concern associated with gold mining. This drainage (which pollutes water and land with mercury and cyanide) can displace communities, contaminate drinking water, hurt workers, and destroy pristine environments, endangering the health of people and ecosystems. Unfortunately, the extraction of most metals and minerals exhibits similar environmental impacts and there are currently no effective metal substitutes for producing cell phones, but there is a lot of potential for companies to make better products by redesigning them so that fewer natural resources are needed to produce them.

Note

1. Friend of the Earth, "Mining for Smartphones: The True Cost of Tin," accessed June 4, 2016, https://www.foe.co.uk/sites/default/files/downloads/tin_mining.pdf.

quicker than ever. You can do your part to keep toxic chemicals out of the landfill and give products and materials another life, simply by making sure you're recycling them.

Recycle batteries. Batteries are made from materials such as zinc, manganese, potassium, and steel that can be recycled. Many organizations have battery drop-offs to take used batteries to a local recycling facility in bulk. Batteries may be able to be dropped off at one of your local retailers, and might even be accepted by your local recycling facility. The website, Earth911, is a great resource to see where you can drop off batteries for recycling.

Invest in reusable, rechargeable batteries. Rechargeable batteries have gone down in price over the years. They also eliminate the waste associated with regular batteries and are more convenient than having to buy new batteries and recycling old ones.

ENCOURAGE A SUSTAINABLE WORKPLACE OR CAMPUS

Another aspect of making school or workplaces more sustainable is helping others see the value in adopting sustainable habits. Employees and students are increasingly concerned with engaging in sustainability, not just in their personal or domestic lives, but in their professional and academic lives as well. These are collective issues the world is facing so it makes sense that people are looking to tackle them collectively, by starting conversations and taking action. We can do our part to make these conversations happen.

Share your sustainable habits with your peers. The acceptance that climate change is happening has increased over the years, and slowly so has the willingness to talk about environmental issues. When chatting with peers, share with them how you've made efforts to reduce your environmental impact at the workplace or on campus. They are likely to appreciate your efforts and may incorporate the tips into their own lives, if they haven't already.

Participate in your organization's sustainability programs. If your work or campus has environmental goals in place, let them know you support their efforts. Also, do your part to help meet the goals already in place; for example, if your organization has a waste diversion goal, make sure you are sorting your trash properly. If you don't know if your work or campus is committed to reducing their environmental footprint, you can inquire about it or even encourage others to start. A volunteer day with a local sustainability-related

Box 10.2 Transferring Food to Those Who Need it: Transfernation

In 2013, two New York University undergraduate students created an online app for companies in New York City to donate leftover food from corporate events and cafeterias to local shelters and soup kitchens. Through the app, small and large businesses alike register to donate their extra food. It works similar to ridesharing apps like Uber and Lyft in the sense that when food is ready to be picked up, the app sends out an alert to potential volunteers nearby, who can then accept the request to pick up the extra food and deliver it to a shelter or food pantry in the area. Because of the app's success, the two students received start-up capital to further the idea of the app, and have also since registered as a nonprofit organization with several hundred volunteers. As of 2016, Transfernation had over 50 corporate partners and had diverted over 12,500 pounds of food to those in need.[1]

Note

1. Transfernation, "About Us," accessed May 8, 2016, http://transfernation.org/about.php.

nonprofit is a great way to start thinking about impact, and it helps employees and students feel more connected to the community and to each other.

Food leftovers. As explored in chapter 6, food waste is an issue we cannot afford to ignore. To combat food waste at work or school, ask about what happens with leftover food from events such as meetings, conferences, or meals in the cafeteria/dining hall. Cafeterias and catered events can end up with a lot of leftover food that may make its way to the landfill where it will emit GHG emissions and contribute to climate change. Instead, if your workplace or campus doesn't already donate the food to those in need, find out if it's a practice they would consider implementing. It's easy to load up on food in the cafeteria, but only put food on your plate that you'll be able to finish. One way to make sure you aren't taking too much is to avoid using trays. If you do end up with leftover food, put it in a container to take with you instead of throwing it out.

PAPER AND PRINTING

With the technologies that limit our need to print anything anymore and growing efficiencies in paper recycling, we as a society must be using less paper, right? Unfortunately, this is a misconception: global paper consumption has actually increased and experts predict it will continue to increase by more than 100 percent by 2060.[6] The average American uses the paper equivalent to almost six 40-foot trees a year.[7] However, we can easily reduce how much paper we use, especially at work or school, just by paying attention to our paper use habits.

Print less. If you can read something or fill out a form on the computer, do it. It's a great way to reduce your contribution toward deforestation and it saves you or your organization money by not having to buy paper as often. Even if paper is made from recycled content, using less is still the best way to reduce your impact. Printing double sided is an easy way to cut down on paper use as well – next time you go to print, explore settings and check the box for "print double-sided" and "flip on long edge."

Recycle paper. We know recycling some other items can be a little confusing sometimes, but paper is pretty straightforward. Paper should always be recycled, and by doing so, we maximize its economic value and keep landfill space open for items that can't be recycled.

Buy paper with 100 percent recycled content. Paper made from recycled material is easy to find and is usually comparable in price to paper made from virgin material. Recycled paper not only leaves forests in place, but it also requires less energy and water to create than paper made from virgin material. If your paper is less than 100 percent recycled content, look for the FSC label to ensure that the nonrecycled percentage at least came from a forest that is managed responsibly.

Rethink textbooks. Instead of buying paper textbooks, look into buying or renting e-textbooks. By using digital textbooks, you can avoid paper use. Plus, digital books are easier to carry around on your laptop or tablet, and save you space in your dorm or apartment. If you can't go digital, try to buy used books, look into services that rent by the semester or quarter, and/or be sure to sell back your books when you are done with them so that others can use them. All of these options are cheaper than buying new hardcover textbooks.

ADJUSTMENTS, REPAIRS, AND REPLACEMENTS

Little tweaks in our work and school lives can help us minimize the energy we consume and the stress we put on precious minerals and other natural

Box 10.3 Paper Versus e-Books

According to the Green Press Initiative, approximately 30 million trees are used each year to make paper for books and newspapers that are sold in the United States. The same industry consumes 153 gallons of water annually.[1] As a Greenpeace campaign in 2006 revealed, illegal logging of ancient forests in Finland and Canada was often a result of our demand for paper, specifically our demand for books.[2] Enter the e-reader and e-books, and we should have a way to read that doesn't leave a negative impact on the environment, right? It's complicated – although e-readers do reduce deforestation and GHG emissions (for instance, the lifetime carbon footprint of an Amazon Kindle is equivalent to 42 paperback books), there are various other factors including supply chain considerations such as mining, shipping, and manufacturing, as well as energy consumption that actually prevent the e-reader from being the hands-down best substitute for books.[3, 4] Digital books are also stored in data centers connected to the electricity grid, which in the United States are usually powered by unsustainable energy sources.

Avid readers that are likely to read over 60 to 70 books on their e-readers (over the lifetime of the e-reader) can rest assured that they are offsetting the environmental impacts of their e-readers. But if you're not planning on reading that much, look for books that are either printed on 100 percent postconsumer waste recycled or Forest Stewardship Council (FSC)-certified paper, or for those that were produced by a publisher that signed the Book Industry Treatise on Environmentally Responsible Publishing. Better yet, renew your library card or start a book-sharing club with friends.

Notes

1. The Green Press Initiative, "Book sector," accessed May 11, 2016, http://greenpressinitiative.org/about/bookSector.htm.
2. Greenpeace, "Greenpeace Book Campaign," accessed May 11, 2016, http://www.greenpeace.org/international/en/campaigns/forests/greenpeace-book-campaign/.
3. The Green Press Initiative, "Environmental Impact of E-books," accessed May 11, 2016, http://www.greenpressinitiative.org/documents/ebooks.pdf.
4. Lucy Siegle, "Should I Stop Buying Paper Books and Use an e-reader Instead?" *The Guardian,* January 6, 2013, accessed May 11, 2016, http://www.theguardian.com/environment/2013/jan/06/should-i-buy-an-e-reader.

resources. These tips are simple and can go a long way in reducing our individual environmental footprint in the places where we often spend much of our time.

Optimize your computer settings. Many computers have energy management features where you can set your computer to go to sleep or hibernate when not in use. Turning your screensaver off and fully exiting programs are two other ways you can help conserve your computer's battery life, and thus, reduce the amount of energy it uses. For latops and tablets, the less you let your device get down to 0% battery, the better.

Take advantage of natural light. Have your own workspace in the office or at home? Move your desk around to capture the most natural light. Also, look into light dimmers or desk lamps to make sure you're only using the amount of light you need.

Fix instead of buy new. Although it may be easier to simply buy a new TV, smartphone, or computer when a problem arises with one that you already own, you should first do your due diligence to see if it can be fixed. Smartphone and other similar electronic repair stores (or someone you know) may be able to fix it cheaper and easier than you think.

Switch to virtual meetings. With WebEx, Skype, and other programs for virtual meetings, flying and traveling for meetings has become less necessary. Though virtual meetings can't always replace in-person interactions, they are certainly an attractive alternative in many cases, especially since you can avoid the environmental and financial costs associated with transportation.

11

At the Store

The environmental footprint of the food and material goods we consume is often difficult to observe due to complex global supply chains. Although it's easy to feel disconnected from the deforestation, air and water pollution, and GHG emissions often associated with our products, we as consumers have the ability to decrease this negative impact. We can reward companies that are doing things more sustainably, such as using natural resources more responsibly, reducing their GHG emissions, and paying workers a living wage, by choosing their products over companies that are not committing to taking on these issues.

Many individuals are already using their power as consumers to reward companies that are doing things more sustainably, and they are doing so even if it costs a little more. A survey showed that on average, 66 percent of Americans and 70 percent of millennials are willing to pay more to have a positive impact on issues they care about.[1] By supporting companies that are committed to doing things better, we signal our desire for change and help make it the norm for all companies to consider the sustainability of their products and operations. Thinking about the impact of our purchases is the main way to be sustainable at the store, but picking up other small habits can also directly minimize our environmental footprint.

PLAN AHEAD

Before leaving for the store, there are a few things we can take into account to reduce the amount of waste created and to help us save money by only buying the things we need.

Bring reusable bags. Using reusable bags (cloth, paper, or plastic) or hand-carrying items (if you're only picking up a few things) both are ways to cut down on plastic waste. Many cities have banned plastic bags altogether, and some stores now charge for bags that just a few years ago were free. Even if your city hasn't made the move on plastic bags yet, you can take matters into your own hands by remembering your reusable bags.

Make a list and try to stick to it. Around 20 percent of the food we buy never gets eaten.[2] Meal planning can help make sure you aren't buying extra food that will go bad before you have time to eat it. Making a list is not only

Box 11.1 Sea Turtles, Seabirds, and Our Plastic Bags

As explored in part 1, when our plastic ends up in the ocean, it can wreak havoc on ecosystems and contaminate the seafood we eat. This is particularly true of plastic bags that often get washed or blown away, and end up in waterways or the ocean. Plastic in the ocean kills over 100 million marine animals each year, and many of these are sea turtles.[1] Because plastic bags and other plastic debris in the ocean can be indistinguishable from jellyfish to sea turtles, they eat the plastic material, mistaking them for food. Sadly, plastic bags are often found in the stomach of sea turtles that are killed by eating plastic debris. Seabirds are another victim of our plastic: one study estimates that 90 percent of all seabird species worldwide have ingested some form of plastic from the ocean.[2] Researchers also predict that by 2050, 99 percent of seabird species will be affected by plastic ingestion.

Notes

1. Sea Turtle Conservancy, "Information About Sea Turtles: Threats from Marine Debris," accessed May 11, 2016, http://www.conserveturtles.org/seaturtle-information.php?page=marine_debris.
2. Chris Wilcox et al., "Threat of Plastic Pollution to Seabirds is Global, Pervasive, and Increasing," *Proceedings of the National Academy of Sciences of the United States of America* 112 (2015), accessed May 11, 2016, doi:10.1073/pnas.1513514112.

applicable to the grocery store, but can also be applied when visiting any other store as well. Thinking about and rationalizing your planned purchases before you go to the store can help you avoid buying unnecessary items, which take energy, water, and other resources to produce.

PRODUCT PACKAGING

Between households and businesses, packaging and containers made up 30 percent of the waste Americans sent to the landfill in 2013, and only 50 percent of recyclable packaging and containers were actually recycled.[3] Packaging is usually made from plastic, which is made from fossil fuels and may not be recyclable. Worse than that, oftentimes this packaging is unnecessary and can be avoided altogether. A number of companies are rethinking packaging and we can encourage sustainable packaging through our purchasing decisions. This is one aspect that has immense potential to minimize the pressure society puts on natural resources, and can help companies and individuals alike be more sustainable.

Go for the bulk bins. Grocery store bulk bins offer commonly used items such as nuts, grains, spices, granola, and cooking basics without all the packaging. Plastic bags are usually available, but you can avoid those by bringing your own reusable containers or bags to fill up.

A handful of "package-free" stores have popped up in cities from Berlin to Austin in the last few years, which carry a wide range of local products such as produce, nuts, grains, and eggs – all in bulk. Although package-free stores are far from being accessible to most people, it's exciting to see and know what's possible.

Look for products that minimize packaging or ones that you can reuse. Of course, no packaging is the ideal option, but for a lot of items we consume, this unfortunately is not a choice. When deciding between comparable products, choose the one that uses less packaging, or packaging that you can reuse at home, like glass jars and containers.

Paper-based before plastic. Paperboard is generally preferred over plastic because it can be recycled or composted. It's even better if the paper-based packaging is made from recycled and/or FSC-certified paper. In the United States, paper and paperboard are recycled the most, at around 75 percent, while plastics are recycled the least at under 15 percent.[4] Most cities offer the option to recycle paperboard, which decreases the need for virgin material, but

Box 11.2 The Circular Economy

The Circular Economy is a movement taking shape around the world that calls for widespread rethinking of products and packaging. The idea behind the Circular Economy is that products and packaging can be designed from the very beginning of their life cycle to be restorative and regenerative. This means that a product and its packaging can either be composted back into the soil or can be returned to the company that made it to be dismantled (with all the pieces being reused to create something new). One stipulation of the Circular Economy is that the energy used to dismantle and re-create should come from renewable energy, thus eliminating any dependence on fossil fuels.

The Circular Economy is designed as a significant contrast to the current, linear approach to products and packaging. Currently, a company makes a product and sells it without much consideration of what happens after it's no longer wanted. The consumer then uses and eventually discards the product, which may or may not be recyclable. Without due consideration of what happens after a product is used, we are faced with our current situation where only basic items such as glass, aluminum, and paper are widely recycled.[1] Other products and packaging have the potential to be recycled or reused, but many local recycling facilities don't have the capabilities or incentives to support such systems, and take-back programs can only do so much. The Circular Economy has brought to light the fact that environmental impact shouldn't solely rest with the consumer, and shouldn't kick in only at the end of a product's lifespan.

Note

1. Ellen MacArthur Foundation, "The Circular Economy," accessed May 21, 2016, https://www.ellenmacarthurfoundation.org/circular-economy/overview/concept.

even if you can't access somewhere to recycle it, paperboard will biodegrade in the compost.

Know your plastics and be careful with bioplastics. As illustrated in chapter 6, most plastics have a number between 1 and 7 on them, identifying what type of plastic they are made from. However, these numbers don't actually tell us if the packaging is recyclable or not. Although finding out the recyclability of an item really depends on where you live, you can count on rigid plastics being accepted more often than thin plastic film, even if they have the same number. Bioplastics, or plastics made from some plant-based material, may also have a number 7 and "PLA" on them, but these items are

Box 11.3 100% Compostable Packaging Materials

Some companies are beginning to use 100 percent compostable material for product packaging. The material is compostable because it is made completely from plant material such as corn, potato starch, cellulose, and so on, or from rapidly renewable materials such as hemp or bamboo. Packaging from tropical roots such as tapioca and cassava, which are grown in Asia, Africa, and Latin America, are also being explored. If done right, these tropical roots present a viable option to develop an industry that is sustainable for both the people involved and the environment. The use of compostable packaging materials is not widespread yet, and the sustainable packaging industry is still working to achieve buy-in and cost-effectiveness at scale, but it's a great sign to see some 100 percent compostable material packaged products already popping up on the shelves of our grocery stores.

not recyclable, and can even damage recycling equipment if they make it that far. There are also different types of bioplastics, which makes things even trickier. Only items that explicitly say "compostable" are compostable, otherwise they go to the landfill.

Think twice about coffee pods. Although coffee pods are convenient, they usually end up in the landfill. If you're making coffee with a machine that uses coffee pods, take advantage of any drop-off or mail-in pod recycling or composting programs available. Another option is to use the refillable and reusable pods that are widely available as an alternative.

Avoid Styrofoam. Styrofoam, or expanded polystyrene, has long been known as one of the most harmful packaging materials for the environment. Made from fossil fuels, the manufacturing process of Styrofoam releases 57 chemical by-products, including hydrofluorocarbons (HCFCs), a potent GHG. Unfortunately, most recycling facilities do not recycle Styrofoam, so it will typically sit in the landfill for hundreds of years (or even worse, it gets blown away due to its light weight where it then contaminates land and waterways). Look for egg containers made from paperboard and try to avoid single-use products in general.

BUYING FOOD

Besides packaging, there are a number of other things to look for at the grocery store to help you decipher if a product is sustainable or not. As examined in chapter 6, the production of food can have a huge impact on the environment

Box 11.4 The Environmental Impact of Coffee

The process of growing and producing coffee is plagued with negative consequences on the environment, most notably intensive water use (it takes an estimated 37 gallons of water to produce a cup of coffee), water pollution, and deforestation.[1] Large volumes of wastewater are generated when separating the coffee bean from the cherry, an essential process in coffee production. Although no chemicals are used in this process, the wastewater is a main source of water contamination in coffee-producing communities when it's not treated. This affects the entire community whose livelihoods are frequently dependent on coffee production. In addition, coffee wastewater generates a considerable amount of greenhouse gases, particularly methane, if the organic matter in the wastewater is untreated and left to decompose.[2]

In order to minimize the negative impact that our beloved cup of coffee may have on the environment, look for coffee that has either a Rainforest Alliance, Fair Trade, or Organic label on it to ensure your next coffee purchase goes toward reducing your footprint and supporting sustainable production processes. For the most environmentally friendly option, look for shade-grown coffee. Shade-grown systems, where coffee is grown under the forest canopy, are highly beneficial to biodiversity conservation in tropical forest ecosystems, have a lower carbon footprint as they store more CO_2, and use lower chemical inputs than conventional coffee because the natural vegetation reduces plants' susceptibility to pests. Shade-grown coffee can also often be associated with reforestation efforts and provide communities incentives to not cut down trees.[3] To find shade-grown coffee keep an eye out for packaging that specifically states shade-grown, or look for the Bird-Friendly certification label.[4]

Notes

1. A. K. Chapagain and A. Y. Hoekstra, *The Water Needed to Have the Dutch Drink Coffee*, The Netherlands: UNESCO-IHE (2003), accessed May 20, 2016, http://waterfootprint.org/media/downloads/Report14.pdf.
2. The Business Association of Latin American Studies, "Carbon Footprint Across the Coffee Supply Chain: The Case of Costa Rican Coffee," November 2012, accessed May 19, 2016, http://www.balas.org/BALAS_2013_proceedings_data/data/documents/p639212.pdf.
3. United Nations Development Programme (UNDP), "Haiti: Exporting Coffee While Protecting Biodiversity," accessed June 9, 2016, http://www.undp.org/content/undp/en/home/ourwork/ourstories/haiti---le-cafe--s-exporte-tout-en-protegeant-la-biodiversite.html.

before it's ever even packaged and consumed. Luckily, there are several certification labels, as well as GoodGuide and the product labels themselves that can help signal how sustainable certain products are.

Read product labels. As outlined in chapter 4, certification labels (e.g., Organic, Fair Trade) are helpful in identifying products that meet a specific standard of environmental impact. Choosing these products is a great way to purchase sustainably, but it is still worthwhile to take the time and read product labels and packaging to help you make even more informed decisions. The certification label system was invented in part because product labels and packaging can be confusing and not so forthcoming with the information you may be looking for. However, the absence of a certification label doesn't automatically mean it's an unsustainable product, and this is when diving into the details of the product label can be useful. Also, when studying up on a specific product, be conscious of greenwashing.

Beware of ingredients that may come from unsustainable sources. Some of the ingredients in foods may come from unsustainable sources, and because of the complicated and nontransparent nature of supply chains, it is often difficult to determine which ones are harmful and which ones are not. For instance, some of the ingredients you may find in your food are associated with deforestation, including palm oil (as illustrated in chapter 2), cocoa, and soybeans. It's hard to completely avoid these ingredients as palm oil in particular is used in about 50 percent of all packaged food products in supermarkets today and can also be found in your personal care products. However, you can keep an eye out for companies or products that have reputable certifications like Rainforest Alliance Certified or Roundtable on Sustainable Palm Oil (RSPO) certified, which lets you know they source responsibly.[5] You can also check to see if your preferred food brand signed onto a zero-deforestation policy, and how they are faring in achieving this goal with Greenpeace's Company-Scorecard guide.[6]

BUYING CLOTHES

How clothes are made is something we may think little about, yet the processes used to make them are known to have harmful effects not only on the environment but also on the people who make the clothes. There are a number of companies and industry organizations that have signed on to combat and regularly raise awareness about the widespread environmental and social concerns of the textile (clothes) industry. This is a great start, but there's still

4. The Bird-Friendly certification system was created by ecologists at the Smithsonian Migratory Bird Center. Bird-Friendly certified coffee must be organic and there are stringent requirements on what is considered "shade-grown" to ensure a healthy ecosystem that not only supports wildlife but also the surrounding community.

a lot to be done. We as consumers can leverage our dollars to reduce the harmful impacts of the industry, while ultimately trying to consume less.

Decide whether you really need it. It's common to see clothes at a good price and be tempted to buy them, even if you don't need them. But in thinking about the environmental costs associated with producing that shirt or pair of pants, it is likely that this low price does not reflect the price of the natural resources that were exploited to make it. Environmental factors associated with the textile industry include the use of large amounts of water, pesticides for cotton farming, toxic dyes and cleaning chemicals that pollute waterways, the generation of a lot of waste, and extraction of natural resources. All these factors negatively impact our ecosystem services.[7]

Beware of fast fashion. New styles are constantly coming in, as old styles are just as quickly fading away. Style crazes are often exacerbated by the cheap prices you can find at major retailers, and with just a small investment, you too can be walking around with threads from the latest trend. It's not even too upsetting if an item doesn't last that long – due to its cheap price tag, we can easily go out and buy a new replacement. This scenario is known as fast fashion, a culprit of the "throw-away" culture, which prompts individuals to buy more and more clothes. In turn, a lot of virgin natural resources are extracted and used to produce these clothes, and a lot of waste is created from quickly discarded clothing.

Support sustainable cotton. Growing cotton is energy and water intensive; according to the World Wildlife Fund, it can take 2,700 liters of water to produce enough cotton for a single t-shirt.[8] To put that into perspective, that same amount of water could supply one person with drinking water for 900 days. In addition, cotton is considered one of the dirtiest crops due to its reliance on insecticides and other chemicals that decrease biodiversity and contaminate local water sources. Organic cotton is currently the most sustainable cotton available because it doesn't rely on insecticides, soil nutrients and biodiversity are preserved, and it allows the soil to retain more water, thus needing less irrigated water. By choosing clothing made with organic cotton, you're signaling that you value efforts to make the production of clothes

Box 11.5 Footprint of Our Footprints: The Impact of Athletic Shoes

As we hit the trails, courts, or gym, we may not think about the natural resources used to make our shoes. Yet athletic shoes are composed of 65 different parts that come from various resources requiring different manufacturing processes.[1] These resources include cotton, polyester, nylon, and rubber – the latter of which is sometimes synthetic rubber (made in a laboratory from petroleum-based products). The production of synthetic rubber is an industrial process that results in more waste than actual product, while also releasing volatile organic compounds (VOCs). The alternative to synthetic rubber, natural rubber made from latex of the rubber tree, can actually have a smaller environmental impact when collected without harming the tree.[2]

Polyester and nylon are also petroleum-based synthetic products that are not biodegradable and require large amounts of water and energy to be produced. Nitrous oxide, a GHG 298 times more potent than CO_2, is emitted when producing nylon.[3] In terms of GHG emissions, according to researchers at the Massachusetts Institute of Technology (MIT), a typical pair of running shoes generates 30 pounds of CO_2 emissions, which is equivalent to keeping a 100-W light bulb on for a week.[4] The majority of these emissions come from the manufacturing process, specifically from coal-powered manufacturing plants in China. While companies are trying to clean up their supply chains, the negative impact of athletic shoes is greater than we'd like to think.

Notes

1. Jennifer Chu, "Footwear's (carbon) footprint," *MIT News*, May 22, 2013, accessed February 2, 2016, http://news.mit.edu/2013/footwear-carbon-footprint-0522.
2. World Wildlife Fund (WFF). *Going Wild for Rubber, Sourcing wild rubber from the Amazon: why you should and how you can* (2014), accessed February 2, 2016, http://assets.wwf.org.uk/downloads/wwf_a4_report_wild_rubber_web__2_.pdf.
3. U.S. Environmental Protection Agency, "Overview of Greenhouse Gases," accessed February 2, 2016, http://www3.epa.gov/climatechange/ghgemissions/gases/n2o.html.
4. Jennifer Chu, "Footwear's (carbon) footprint," *MIT News*, May 22, 2013, accessed February 2, 2016, http://news.mit.edu/2013/footwear-carbon-footprint-0522.

and textiles more responsible. Also, look for brands that support The Better Cotton Initiative, which seeks to improve the social and environmental issues associated with cotton.[9] Alternatives to cotton are slowly gaining traction and include hemp, tencel, bamboo, and even recycled plastic bottles.[10]

Box 11.6 Patagonia's Repair Campaigns

The outdoor apparel company Patagonia is taking the lead in ensuring environmental sustainability of their products. They pride themselves in producing durable, high-quality goods made out of organically grown and recycled materials that have a low impact on the environment. The company promises customers they will make products that last, and in exchange customers must pledge to buy only what they need to prevent unnecessary new purchases. In a campaign to counter the overconsumption and throwaway culture, Patagonia started the "Worn Wear Tour." For the "Worn Wear Tour," Patagonia sent a biodiesel truck across the country to offer free clothing repairs and sell used Patagonia gear, while also teaching customers how to repair their own clothing. The company's efforts to fight fast fashion also allows customers to send their Patagonia clothing in when it's no longer repairable so the company can recycle it into new fabric.

Look into your favorite companies' sustainability policies. Many products we buy come from multinational companies, most of which release information on their environmental footprint, as well as information on how they're working with communities to address social issues. Although it can be tricky to gauge if efforts are "good enough" or how they compare to other companies, it's important to see which companies are taking the initiative to clean up their practices. Keep an eye out for companies that are integrating sustainability into the way they operate through sustainable purchasing policies, reducing packaging, and working to ensure their workers receive a living wage and have adequate working conditions. Other resources available for you to get familiar with companies' efforts to green their supply chains include Greenpeace's "Detox Catwalk" and the Ethical Consumer's guide to ethical shopping.[11]

The industry that makes the products we enjoy is weighed down by negative environmental and social impacts, and it'll take more than a few companies and time to change this. By expressing interest in what companies are doing, demanding more transparency, and pushing for more sustainability, we can signal to these companies that these issues are important to us and support the shift.

DISPOSAL

A key part of shopping is not only what we buy, but also how we get rid of things. Extending the life of our stuff is key to reducing our negative impact,

Box 11.7 Ben & Jerry's, B Corps, and B Corp Certifications

Ben & Jerry's cares about more than just making your favorite late-night ice cream flavors, they are also a benefit corporation, or "b corp" for short, which puts them square in the middle of a growing movement to redefine the social and environmental roles that for-profit companies can play in being forces for good. A company that is either registered, certified, or both registered and certified as a b corp strives to create value for society, not just its shareholders. Registration as a b corp is now possible in 31 states – an impressive number considering the first state to pass b corp legislation was Maryland in 2010. Certification as a b corp on the other hand is available to any company, anywhere, that has completed a certification process through B Lab, the international nonprofit organization that oversees and sets standards for the transparency, accountability, sustainability, and performance of b corps, and is also responsible for the recent wave of b corp legislation in the United States.

With over 1,700 certified b corps across 130 industries in 50 countries, it's likely that you know of or regularly buy products from a b corp or certified b corp like Ben & Jerry's. Some other b corps include Comet Skateboards, Etsy, Method Products, New Belgium Brewing, Patagonia, and Seventh Generation.

but when we're ready to let something go, some options are more sustainable than others.

Receipts in the right spot. If you don't need a receipt or can have one emailed to you, it's a small way to reduce paper that can add up. If you do get a receipt, the kind that looks like actual paper is recyclable or compostable, but if a receipt is shiny, that means it has a chemical coating. Shiny receipts are not recyclable and have to go in the trash bin.

Donate or swap. Instead of sending items you don't want any more to the landfill, give them to someone you know, sell them, or donate them. Swapping clothes with friends, siblings, or coworkers is another great way to share and get "new" clothes without actually purchasing anything. Donating extends the life of each item and prevents it from going down the sad road that leads to the landfill. Some retailers such as H&M and Levi's have launched take-back programs to recycle your old clothes. This is an area of sustainability where momentum is growing.

12

Holidays and Parties

Holidays and other special occasions – even if you're throwing a party just because it's Friday – are a great time to see family and friends, and do things that are out of the ordinary. However, most parties result in a lot of waste due to gifts and the amount of delicious food we get to enjoy. One statistic captured the extent of the waste created from the holidays: overall waste from American households increases about 25 percent between Thanksgiving and New Year's Day.[1] The good news is that reducing our environmental footprint during the holidays, or at any other type of special event, is simple.

FOOD AND DRINKS

A big part of most events is the food and the drinks, which have a large environmental footprint. Yet it's easy to integrate small considerations to reduce that footprint and still offer delicious and impressive fare. Many of the tips in chapter 6, "In the Kitchen and at the Dinner Table," and chapter 11, "At the Store," come into play here as well, but we have selected a few to focus on when you go into party mode.

Less meat, more veggies. Incorporating vegetarian dishes helps reduce the GHG emissions associated with your food. It's also almost always less expensive which is great since food costs will probably be one of your largest expenses if you're hosting. Veggies are a great opportunity to go local, seasonal, and/or organic.

No-packaging appetizers. Bring your own containers to the store to turn fresh produce and items from the bulk bin into party appetizers. Swapping out the packaged food when it comes to appetizers helps you reduce waste at the source. It also means less packaging to deal with as part of clean up.

Less is more. We tend to make too much food for parties. This is especially true during the holidays since it's usually part of the holiday culture to make sure everyone has all the food and beverage they can handle, and then some. This excess is ultimately bad for the environment. However, tracking your RSVPs closely and keeping a headcount should help you avoid making this classic mistake that ultimately contributes to food waste. Of course, some extra food is not disastrous (everyone loves leftovers), but it is something to be mindful of.

Box 12.1 Sustainable Wineries and Breweries

Making wine and beer is water intensive, but exactly how water intensive is highly dependent on how productive the crop yields are for the main ingredients (grapes for wine and hops, wheat, or barley for beer). Regardless of where the winery or brewery is located, efforts to be more sustainable almost always include reducing water use. Water efficiency can be incorporated into the cultivation of ingredients and throughout the production process. Some companies are also reusing waste and water in creative ways.

In 2016, Fetzer Vineyards in Hopland, California, announced they'll be the first U.S. winery to use a Chilean wastewater treatment system that only uses earthworms (no electricity) and creates only a small amount of waste that can be applied to fields as fertilizer. Other sustainable methods being deployed in the making of beer and wine include the use of organic ingredients, preservation of soil fertility, and the use of renewable energy to reduce GHG emissions. Some companies are even looking beyond their own operations to promote sustainability. In 2015, 25 breweries including Guinness, New Belgium Brewing, and Sierra Nevada Brewing signed a Brewery Climate Declaration calling attention to the risks of climate change and signaling support for action.[1]

Note

1. Ceres, "Beer Companies Join Call for Action on Climate Change," March 10, 2015, accessed May 21, 2016, http://www.ceres.org/press/press-releases/beer-companies-join-call-for-action-on-climate-change.

GIFTS

A large part of the special occasions we celebrate are the gifts we buy and share. We can make these special occasions even more meaningful by factoring in the consideration of environmental and social impacts into our gift choices.

Activities and memories rather than things. Rather than purchasing something material, how about experiencing something new? Giving unique gifts, such as tickets to a concert or comedy show, cooking lessons, or planning a trip to go camping or some other outdoor adventure are all thoughtful presents that don't put significant stress on natural resources. Not only will you avoid unnecessary consuming, but giving the gift of an activity is extra motivation to do something out of the ordinary. And it doesn't have to be an out-of-town adventure either, check out what local options are available first. Sharing a new experience is said to strengthen relationships, and recent studies also confirm our theory that buying experiences brings us more lasting happiness than buying material things.[2]

Support the local economy. Purchasing items from a local store or craft event helps your local economy by contributing to the job and tax base that supports local needs such as education, infrastructure improvements, and so on. Locally owned businesses often purchase supplies from other local ventures, which helps to avoid the extra GHG emissions associated with long-distance transportation. However, local stores do not necessarily sell local goods, so use your best judgment.

Box 12.2 Opt Outside and Giving Tuesday in Lieu of Black Friday

In the past few years, social media has erupted with calls to participate in alternatives to Black Friday (the day after Thanksgiving), which is considered the biggest shopping day of the year. Opt Outside, initially a campaign by the outdoor gear company REI, advocates for people to spend the day in nature, not in stores, as the name suggests. Some state and national parks have even gotten on board by offering free admission on Opt Outside day. Another alternative to Black Friday is Giving Tuesday, which occurs on the Tuesday after Black Friday (and Cyber Monday). On Giving Tuesday, individuals are encouraged to donate to causes, groups, or organizations they believe in and want to support. These donations aren't necessarily a large financial sum; individuals simply give what they can or give by volunteering their time.

Who needs wrapping paper? Grocery store paper bags, newspapers, boxes, packaging from a previous present, and other types of packaging you might have lying around the house are all great alternatives to wrapping paper. Most wrapping paper is not recyclable or compostable, so it'll inevitably end up in the landfill. Going for one of these wrapping paper alternatives saves you money, and if you can pull it off, should help you impress others with your creative and personalized approach.

DECORATIONS AND FESTIVITIES

Another key aspect of holidays and other get-togethers is the decorations we use to make our homes more festive. Try to add some sustainability into the way you decorate and celebrate by thinking about where certain items come from and where they'll go after they're used.

Choose beeswax candles. If you're thinking about using decorative candles, go with beeswax instead of paraffin wax. Paraffin is a by-product of fossil fuels and is made with toxic chemicals that are released when it's burned. Beeswax uses no harmful chemicals, doesn't drip as much, and burns longer than paraffin.

Try sustainable flowers. Flower arrangements sold for events are sometimes grown in Central or South America using pesticides that may be banned in the United States. Make your flower arrangements more sustainable by looking for Certified Organic or Fair Trade flowers, picking them up from local florists or farmers who use native and seasonal flowers, or by making your own from flowers you have in the garden or backyard. Another alternative to using cut flowers as decor is using potted flowers or plants that can be kept or planted after the event is over.

Real vs. artificial Christmas trees. Although it sounds counterintuitive, the stronger environmental argument is actually for real Christmas trees. Most real trees are grown and harvested on farms specifically for the purpose of being a Christmas tree. Although real trees are associated with some pesticide or fertilizer use, the land these trees are grown on does get preserved and remains green, thus avoiding its conversion to agricultural land or for development. This forested space also provides other benefits such as generating oxygen, providing habitat, and protecting the soil. In addition, real trees can be recycled after and are biodegradable. The best option is to get a real Christmas tree from a local farm and make sure to recycle it after the holidays.

Table 12.1 Common Items and How to Dispose of Them Properly

Item	*Disposal*
Holiday string lights	Check the Earth911 website to see if these are accepted for recycling in your area
Christmas trees, mistletoe, natural wreaths	Often picked up through local programs for composting
Wrapping paper, balloons	Landfill
Paper plates, napkins	Compost
Plastic cups, cutlery	Check your local recycling facility to see if they are accepted for recycling, otherwise landfill
Food waste	Try to send leftovers with guests and reduce as much as possible, otherwise, compost
Cupcake or muffin liners	If they are paper-based, then compost or landfill; if they are metallic, then landfill

If you do decide on an artificial Christmas tree, keep in mind that it should be used for at least 10 to 20 years in order to offset the impact of producing it. Moreover, artificial trees are usually made of PVC or petroleum-derived plastic that produces carcinogens during manufacturing and disposal, which also don't biodegrade and will sit in a landfill for a long time after being thrown out.

Avoid releasing balloons. What goes up must come down, and unfortunately, when balloons come back down they are often mistaken by animals for food. In 2015, after more than a hundred balloons were collected at a cleanup of the Edwin B. Forsythe National Wildlife Refuge located along the Atlantic coast of southern New Jersey, the U.S. Fish and Wildlife Service (FWS) made a public request for people to stop releasing balloons. More than just a beautification project, the FWS made it clear that many animals in the wildlife refuge had died due to ingesting the balloons.[3]

PARTYWARE AND DISPOSAL

Using materials that are reusable and don't create waste is the best way to keep our environmental footprint low when hosting parties. Yet sometimes this may not be practical or feasible, in which case, proper disposal of post-party waste is essential.

Use reusable plates, utensils, and glasses. While it may not be as easy as paper or plastic, using the dishes you already have in your cabinet or borrowing some will cut down on the waste you create. Single-use products, in general, are not compatible with sustainable living. If you can't commit to using reusable plates, using 100 percent recycled or compostable paper plates is the next best option.

Go with cloth napkins. Although paper napkins are convenient and cheap, using cloth napkins when hosting is the way to go to avoid unnecessary trash.

Box 12.3 Landfills in the United States

Landfills are one of those "out of sight, out of mind" things that we really can't afford to ignore any longer. In 2012, a study conducted by Yale University discovered that we were severely underestimating how much waste goes to landfills since some small facilities are not required to report the waste they accept. The EPA was estimating that 122 million metric tons were getting sent to landfills, while the researchers found that the real number may be closer to double the EPA's estimate, at around 262 million metric tons.[1]

Landfill leachate and methane are the two main negative effects landfills have on the environment. Leachate, defined as a "liquid that passes through a landfill and has extracted the dissolved and suspended matter from it," can leak into the ground, contaminating surface and groundwater.[2] Another issue is methane, which is emitted from the organic waste as a consequence of its decomposition process. Landfills are considered one of the largest sources of human-produced methane emissions, accounting for 18 percent of U.S. methane emissions. Landfills can and should minimize emissions by further utilizing technologies that capture landfill methane and use it to generate electricity.

However, we can also address methane emissions in the way we separate and dispose of our waste. The same organic matter that emits methane in landfills creates nutrient-rich fertilizer in composts. By properly diverting organic waste from landfills and composting it instead, methane emissions from landfills are avoided.

Notes

1. Jon T. Powell et al., "Estimates of Solid Waste Disposal Rates and Reduction Targets for Landfill Gas Emissions," *Nature Climate Change* 6 (2016), accessed May 18, 2016, doi:10.1038/nclimate2804.
2. Safaa M. Raghab et al., "Treatment of Leachate from Municipal Solid Waste Landfill," *Housing and Building National Research Center Journal* 9 (2013), accessed May 21, 2016, doi:10.1016/j.hbrcj.2013.05.007.

Although washing them means water and energy use, washing cloth napkins instead of throwing out disposable napkins is still the sustainable choice. To be even more sustainable, hang-dry your cloth napkins instead of putting them in the dryer.

Make recycling obvious. Setting up clearly labeled bins for landfill, recycling, and/or compost helps keep your items separate for proper disposal. It helps your guests be more sustainable too and is much easier than sorting it later. Placing the bins all together in one "sorting station" is a great strategy to maximize effectiveness.

13

Traveling

Being sustainable doesn't have to (and shouldn't) stop when you're traveling. Sustainable traveling means thinking about where you're staying, supporting places that make an effort to be environmentally friendly, and keeping up with the sustainable habits presented elsewhere in this book.

It's also particularly important to think about sustainability when traveling abroad. Many of the most exotic and appealing places to visit tend to be in countries struggling with issues such as poverty, inequality, and poor infrastructure, or are economies that are often dependent on exporting raw materials. Tourism can contribute to the alleviation of some of these issues by helping to grow economies and build infrastructure. In both the United States and abroad, local businesses and communities do often see benefits from tourism through increased demand for their products and services, as well as jobs and other new opportunities.

However, these benefits do not necessarily reach all local residents and an influx of tourists can have a negative impact on the environment, putting a strain on natural resources, increasing waste, and leading to environmental degradation. This takes place even in developed countries, when a hidden gem evolves into a tourist destination. For these reasons, we as travelers must do our part to be responsible and encourage sustainability, preserving unique destinations around the world and even close by.

TRIP PREPARATION

There are a number of things you should keep in mind while you're getting ready for a trip to make it easier to be more sustainable once you're at your destination. These are easy tips that should also be shared with your travel partners.

Reuse your travel size personal care products from your previous trip. Hopefully you saved your travel size toiletry containers (e.g., shampoo, soap) from your previous trip, but if not, you can always start with the trip you're about to go on. These little travel size toiletry containers are great to keep on hand to refill with the products you use at home when packing for the next adventure. This is a simple way to cut down on purchases and reduce waste.

Go for nontoxic ingredients. Use natural, biodegradable shampoo and soap, especially if you are going to a region that lacks water treatment facilities. Your local health food store probably sells all these items: just look for plant-based, raw, or organic ingredients. Many developing countries, and especially the more rural areas, have poor infrastructure and sewage systems, meaning wastewater may go straight into the ocean or the ground. Soaps that contain phosphates can reduce the oxygen available in bodies of water, which then can kill plants and fish through a process of eutrophication. Toxins like this

Box 13.1 Coral Reefs and Sunscreen

Coral reefs are some of the most dynamic and diverse ecosystems in the world, providing habitat for up to nine million species.[1] They are also vulnerable ecosystems highly sensitive to pollutants, including oxybenzone, which is commonly found in sunscreen. According to a 2015 study, all it takes is one drop for this chemical to begin bleaching, damaging, and eventually killing a coral reef.[2] About 14,000 tons of sunscreen end up in coral reefs around the world each year, and most contain oxybenzone. Researchers have even found an uptick in the amount of oxybenzone in areas known to be frequented by tourists, specifically in coral reefs around Hawaii and in the Caribbean.[3] Coral reefs face many other challenges to their survival that are not exclusively related to sunscreen, but are related to human activity, such as a warming and acidifying ocean due to climate change and other harmful substances that end up in ocean.

President Obama made great strides during his time as president in his efforts to protect coral reefs and marine biodiversity. In August 2016, in celebrating the 100th anniversary of the U.S. National Park Service, he created the world's largest marine protected area (and actually the world's largest ecologically protected area in general) by expanding the

Papahanaumokuakea Marine National Monument off the Hawaiian Islands to include more than half a million square miles.[4] Yet these measures only go so far: coral reefs can be affected by the products that we wear in the water, even if we may not be swimming that close to them. You can also do your part in protecting these fragile ecosystems no matter where you swim or snorkel by avoiding sunscreen with oxybenzone in it. Look for sunscreens that have zinc oxide or titanium oxide instead. These alternatives are just as protective from the sun as oxybenzone. For example, Badger, a healthy body care company, offers zinc oxide sunscreens that are produced with the goal of being safe for coral reefs and other vital ecosystems.

Notes

1. Microdocs, "Species on Coral Reefs," accessed May 22, 2016, http://web.stanford.edu/group/microdocs/species.html.
2. C. A. Downs et al.,"Toxicopathological Effects of the Sunscreen UV Filter, Oxybenzone (Benzophenone-3), on Coral Planulae and Cultured Primary Cells and Its Environmental Contamination in Hawaii and the U.S. Virgin Islands," *Environmental Contamination and Toxicology* 70 (2016), accessed May 18, 2016, doi:10.1007/s00244-015-0227-7.
3. Ibid.
4. The White House Office of the Press Secretary,"Fact Sheet: President Obama to Create the World's Largest Marine Protected Area," August 26, 2016, accessed September 5, 2016, https://www.whitehouse.gov/the-press-office/2016/08/26/fact-sheet-president-obama-create-worlds-largest-marine-protected-area.

can accumulate, so to make sure you are traveling in a sustainable manner, ingredients like these should be avoided.

Learn about and respect your destination. Read up on the social and environmental issues, history, and any other characteristics pertaining to the place you are visiting. The understanding gained from a little research will support your ability to interact with the environment and locals in a positive way, and can also guide you toward ongoing, local sustainability efforts. For example, in your research you may find that your destination is prone to droughts, which would make you pay closer attention to water use, or you may read about illegal logging of rare trees, which would make you more aware of what to avoid at the souvenir market.

ACCOMMODATIONS

Because where we stay shapes our entire trip, sustainability should also be factored into our accommodations. There are a number of ways to do this and it's becoming easier and easier as more hotels are realizing the importance of minimizing negative environmental impact and communicating these efforts to their guests.

Support eco-friendly accommodations. Even big hotels are making efforts to reduce water use by giving you the option to reuse towels and sheets. Make sure you take advantage of these programs or simply use your "Do Not Disturb" sign so your sheets and towels aren't changed out. Keep an eye out for the Green Seal label, which signals that your hotel meets their sustainability standard. If there isn't enough information to tell if your accommodations minimize their negative environmental impact, ask them about their efforts to be more sustainable; guests showing they care may be the spark the place needs to begin looking at the impact of their operations.

Support local. Choosing locally owned and operated accommodations as well as restaurants and activities can help keep funds in the area you are visiting, contributing to the local economy. Local accommodations that are smaller in size also tend to have a smaller environmental footprint and purchase goods and services from other local businesses.

Think outside of the (hotel) box. Although it is tricky to say which type of accommodation is the most environmentally friendly, there are all different types of accommodations these days with less built infrastructure than hotels and that allow you to interact with your surroundings in different ways. Look into camping, or renting a local room, apartment, or house.

FLIGHTS

Planes require a lot of fuel to fly, which means a lot of GHG emissions. The aviation sector accounts for around 2 percent of global GHG emissions[1] and air travel is usually an individual's biggest contribution to climate change. One transatlantic flight can "add as much to your carbon footprint as a typical year's worth of driving."[2] Headway is being made at the international as well as at the national level to reduce the impact of flying, and although it is difficult to cut down on flights, we can still help to make flying more sustainable.

See what your airline is doing for sustainability. Many airlines are now offering passengers the option to purchase carbon offsets when booking a flight, which means you can pay extra to fund a project that reduces GHG emissions, "neutralizing" your flight. Carbon offset projects include supporting forest conservation in California, capturing GHG emissions from landfills in South Carolina, or renewable energy in Texas. Airlines are also taking measures to reduce their own environmental impact such as making planes and fleets more energy efficient and looking for alternative sources of energy.

Box 13.2 Planes Powered by Renewable Energy

The aviation sector is under increasing pressure to reduce GHG emissions associated with flying, and major emitting countries are introducing new measures and pledging support for a new deal by the International Civil Aviation Organization (ICAO) to curb carbon dioxide emissions from the aviation sector.[1] In July 2016, the Obama Administration announced that the EPA will begin to regulate carbon emissions from aviation through the Clean Air Act, particularly through energy efficiency.[2] Another key way to reducing these emissions is by using cleaner energy sources. Biofuels, or fuels made from plant material or animal waste, are beginning to be deployed as an alternative energy source. Although aviation biofuels are not deployed at scale yet, suppliers already exist and there are many groups working to support the use of biofuels in the industry. Many are also working to ensure that as the market for aviation biofuels develops, biofuels remain sustainable. According to a Natural Resources Defense Council survey, since 2008 when Virgin Atlantic became the first airline to fly a plane that partially used biofuel, more than 40 airlines have tested flights fueled by biofuels.[3] In 2016, United began using 30 percent biofuel on their flights between Los Angeles and San Francisco. Not bad considering airlines only received official approval to use biofuels on commercial flights in 2011.

The aviation industry has also been looking at incorporating solar energy as an alternative in powering airplanes. In 2015, a solar-powered plane called the Solar Impulse broke records for the longest time spent in the air and the longest distance traveled by a solar plane. Its record-breaking flight was a five-day trip from Japan to Hawaii. This flight was one of the many legs of the Solar Impulse journey that continued into 2016 and enabled it to become the first solar plane to make it around the world.[4,i]

Notes

1. Reuters, "China, U.S. Pledge Support for Global Aviation Emissions Pact," September 3, 2016, accessed September 5, 2016, http://www.reuters.com/article/us-china-aviation-idUSKCN1190B3.

2. U.S. Environmental Protection Agency, *EPA Finalizes First Steps to Address Greenhouse Gas Emissions from Aircraft Engines*, Office of Transportation and Air Quality, July 2016, accessed September 5, 2016, https://www3.epa.gov/otaq/documents/aviation/420f16036.pdf.

3. Debblie Hammel, *Aviation Biofuel Sustainability Scorecards*. Natural Resources Defense Council (NRDC) (2015), accessed May 21, 2016, https://www.nrdc.org/sites/default/files/aviation-biofuel-sustainabilitysurvey-2014.pdf.

Chelsea Harvey, "United Airlines Is Flying on Biofuels. Here's Why That's a Really Big Deal," *Washington Post*, March 11, 2016, accessed August 29, 2016, https://www.washingtonpost.com/news/energy-environment/wp/2016/03/11/united-airlines-is-flying-on-biofuels-heres-why-thats-a-really-big-deal/?utm_term=.8f9e9c24f246.

4. SolarImpulse, "SolarImpulse," accessed May 21, 2016, http://www.solarimpulse.com.

CHOOSING YOUR ADVENTURE

There are a number of travel options that provide a unique way to experience the place you are visiting and also spend your money and time supporting sustainability.

Visit a state or national park. The United States is home to some of the world's most beautiful wilderness, most of which is very accessible. These parks are special places because they conserve plants, wildlife, and waterways that we need for sustainability, but also because they give visitors a chance to feel a connection with the environment. Not only will a trip to one of these parks inspire awe and give you a new appreciation for nature, but your visit signals that you value the parks and support keeping these areas protected. The visitor fees also help with park efforts. Americans are catching on to how these parks contribute to enjoyment and well-being: More than 305 million people visited national parks in 2015, the highest number of visitors ever recorded.[3] 2016 was also the 100th anniversary of the U.S. National Park Service, so it's a great time to show some thanks.

Support sustainable businesses and organizations. If you see restaurants, stores, or other types of companies that are incorporating sustainability, consider choosing these options and make your support for sustainability known. It encourages other businesses to become sustainable as well. You may also come across a nonprofit or community organization that you believe is doing valuable work. Why not donate or reach out to see how you can support their efforts? You can consider volunteering, even if it's only for one day, to give back to the local area you're visiting.

Learn about and consider ecotourism. Ecotourism continues to grow in popularity and is defined by The International Ecotourism Society as "responsible travel to natural areas that conserves the environment, sustains the well-being of the local people, and involves interpretation and education." Similar to sustainability, the definition is broad and is implemented in many different ways, from simple accommodations that minimize environmental footprint to organized hikes and outings that explore unique ecosystems. Be careful of greenwashing, as some groups take advantage of the popularity of

Box 13.3 Ecotourism in Haiti

Haiti is usually known for being the poorest country in the western hemisphere or for the tragic earthquake that devastated the country in 2010. Few think about the Caribbean beaches or the majestic mountains that can be found on the island. Yet Haiti has begun to promote these traits through ecotourism in an attempt to attract visitors, as well as demonstrate that the country isn't simply the impoverished country we usually hear about in the news.

One such ecotourism adventure is a hike from the capital Port-au-Prince to a lodging called Auberge La Visite in Seguin, a small mountain village. Along the 12-mile hike to the lodging, hikers get an amazing view of Haiti's mountains. Auberge La Visite, which shares the mountain with Haiti's La Visite National Park, is self-sufficient; the lodge is powered by solar panels and offers visitors meals made with fresh eggs and vegetables from its garden. Visitors can either camp in the yard with provided tents (though at more than 6,500 feet high the temperature does drop at night), or stay inside in one of three rooms. The following day the hikers decide whether to stay an extra day and explore forests and waterfalls in the region, continue the hike down the mountain to the ocean and visit the beach, or return back to the city as they came.

The lodging is associated with Fondation Seguin, which besides encouraging ecotourism in the Seguin area to promote sustainability, also works to reforest and rehabilitate the La Visite National Park. This is an area that has been largely deforested, and the foundation provides direct funding for reforestation and conservation. In addition, the foundation works to build environmental awareness in the local community while also supporting other social services.

the "ecotourism" label. In addition, increased tourism to fragile natural areas can threaten ecosystems if not managed properly, so try to do a little research before you book an eco-trip to be sure of its credibility. To make sure that your trip has a low impact on the environment, learn how conservation is being promoted in the area and what ecotourism companies are doing to counter the effects of increased visitors.[4]

An Ending Note

Individuals play a pivotal role in making the structural changes for sustainability possible and when we make conscious and informed decisions, we contribute to the shift toward a healthy planet. Various organizations are addressing big issues and taking new and holistic approaches to the way we do things, but they can do more with our help. Beyond incorporating sustainability into our regular routines, we as individuals can take other steps to help our communities be more sustainable, signal to policymakers what we value, and spread sustainable habits to others. Sustainability not only offers a vital opportunity for us to change the way we interact with the environment but to also protect and enhance our own lives and communities.

Notes

CHAPTER 1

1. Will Steffen et al., "The Anthropocene: Conceptual and historical perspectives," *Philosophical Transactions of the Royal Society* (2011), accessed June 9, 2016, doi: 10.1098/rsta.2010.0327.

2. Daniel Tencer, "Number of Cars Worldwide Surpasses 1 Billion; Can the World Handle This Many Wheels?" *Huffington Post*, August 23, 2011, accessed June 9, 2016, http://www.huffingtonpost.ca/2011/08/23/car-population_n_934291.html.

3. IPCC, "2013: Summary for Policymakers." In: Climate Change 2013: The Physical Science Basis. Contribution of Working Group I to the Fifth Assessment Report of the Intergovernmental Panel on Climate Change [Stocker, T. F., D. Qin, G.-K. Plattner, M. Tignor, S. K. Allen, J. Boschung, A. Nauels, Y. Xia, V. Bex, and P. M. Midgley (eds.)]. Cambridge University Press, Cambridge, United Kingdom and New York, NY, USA, accessed January 9, 2016, http://www.ipcc.ch/report/ar5/wg1/.

4. Millennium Ecosystem Assessment, *Ecosystems and Human Well-Being: A Framework for Assessment* (2005), 56–60, accessed February 28, 2016, http://www.millenniumassessment.org/en/Framework.html#download.

5. National Human Genome Research Institute, "A Brief History of the Human Genome Project," accessed June 9, 2016, https://www.genome.gov/12011239/a-brief-history-of-the-human-genome-project/.

6. Movements include rights for minority groups, women, lesbian, gay, bisexual, or transgender individuals, and the environment. Rachel Carson's 1962 book *The Silent Spring* spurred the beginning of the environmental movement in the 1960s by highlighting the detrimental effects of pesticide use, questioning the impact of humans on nature. See *Natural Resources Defense Council, "The Story of Silent Spring."*

7. U.S. Environmental Protection Agency, "What is Sustainability," accessed June 5, 2016, https://www.epa.gov/sustainability/learn-about-sustainability#what.

8. Ecological Society of America, "Water Purification: An Essential Ecosystem Service," accessed June 9, 2016, http://www.esa.org/ecoservices/comm/body.comm.fact.wate.html.

9. Millennium Ecosystem Assessment, *Ecosystems and Human Well-Being: A Framework for Assessment.*

10. Numerous communities in the Amazon rainforest have been devastated by the impacts of oil drilling, as was the case in the Peruvian Amazon at the beginning of 2016 when 3,000 barrels of oil leaked in the forest, polluting several rivers, making people sick, and destroying ecosystems. In the United States, mountaintop removal mining for coal in the Appalachian Mountains has polluted an estimated 2,000 miles of waterways. It has also resulted in the injection of toxic chemicals into the ground, contaminating the drinking water of surrounding communities. See *Rodríguez* and *Holzman.*

11. Ecological Society of America, "Water Purification: An Essential ecosystem service."

12. Ibid.

13. The United Nations Sustainable Development Goals, which were agreed upon by the world's countries in 2015, are composed of 17 global goals to be achieved by 2030 by all countries, developed and developing, to transform our future into "the world we want." The goals include social, environmental, and economic objectives, such as, among others, the goal to ensure responsible consumption and production patterns, act to combat climate change, conserve and sustainably use the ocean and marine resources, make cities sustainable, protect and promote sustainable use of land, and ensure access to clean energy for all. See *Sustainable Development Knowledge Platform.*

CHAPTER 2

1. Prüss-Ustün, A., Wolf, J., Corvalán, C., Bos, R., and Neira, M. *Preventing Disease Through Healthy Environments: A Global Assessment of the Burden of Disease from Environmental Risks,* World Health Organization (WHO) (March 2016), accessed September 10, 2016, http://apps.who.int/iris/bitstream/10665/204585/1/9789241565196_eng.pdf?ua=1.

2. Ibid.

3. Yale Environmental Performance Index, "Key Findings: EPI 2016," accessed January 25, 2016, http://epi.yale.edu/chapter/key-findings.

4. American Lung Association, "The State of the Air 2016," accessed May 20, 2016, http://www.lung.org/assets/documents/healthy-air/state-of-the-air/sota-2016-full.pdf.

5. Ibid.

6. World Health Organization (WHO), "Ambient (outdoor) Air Quality and Health" (March 2014), accessed January 21, 2016, http://www.who.int/mediacentre/factsheets/ fs313/en/.

7. Yale Environmental Performance Index, "Environmental Performance Index Reveals Dire State of Fisheries, Worsening Air Pollution," accessed February 12, 2016, http://epi.yale.edu/chapter/key-findings.

8. Natural Resources Defense Council (NRDC), "Asthma and Air Pollution," accessed March 25, 2016, http://www.nrdc.org/health/effects/fasthma.asp.

9. NYU Langone Medical Center, "Press Release: Yearly Cost of U.S. Premature Births Linked to Air Pollution: $4.33 Billion" (March 29, 2016), accessed March 29, 2016, http://nyulangone.org/press-releases/yearly-cost-of-us-premature-births-linked-to-air-pollution-4-33-billion.

10. This study was done as natural experiment on rats in Beijing. See *Yongjie Wei et al.*

11. Anke Hüls et al., "Traffic-Related Air Pollution Contributes to Development of Facial Lentigines: Further Epidemiological Evidence from Caucasians and Asians," *Journal of Investigative Dermatology* 136(5) (March 21 2016), accessed September 10, 2016, doi: 10.1016/j.jid.2015.12.045.

12. Joshua Graff Zivin and Matthew Neidell, "The Impact of Pollution on Worker Productivity," *American Economic Review* 102(7), (2012), accessed February 16, 2016, doi: 10.1257/aer.102.7.3652.

13. Jennifer Burney and V. Ramanathan, "Recent Climate and Air Pollution Impacts on Indian Agriculture," *Proceedings of the National Academy of Sciences of the United States of America* 111(46), (2014), accessed February 16, 2016, doi: 10.1073/pnas.1317275111.

14. U.S. National Park Service, "Great Smoky Mountains Air Quality," accessed February 1, 2016, https://www.nps.gov/grsm/learn/nature/air-quality.htm.

15. Natural Resources Defense Council (NRDC), "Summary of Information concerning the Ecological and Economic Impacts of the BP Deepwater Horizon Oil Spill Disaster," accessed March 5, 2016, http://www.nrdc.org/energy/gulfspill/files/gulfspill-impacts-summary-IP.pdf.

16. Peter J. Etnoyer et al., "Decline in Condition of Gorgonian Octocorals on Mesophotic Reefs in the Northern Gulf of Mexico: Before and After the Deepwater Horizon Oil Spill," *Coral Reefs* 35 (2015): 77–90, accessed March 5, 2016, doi:10.1007/ s00338-015-1363-2.

17. World Health Organization (WHO), "The Top 10 Causes of Death by Income Group" (2012), accessed March 9, 2016, http://www.who.int/mediacentre/factsheets/fs310/en/index1.html.

18. State of New Jersey Department of Environmental Protection, "A Homeowner's Guide to Arsenic in Drinking Water," accessed March 13, 2016, http://www.state.nj.us/dep/dsr/arsenic/guide.htm.

19. Sonia Moghe, "Six charged in West Virginia water contamination," *CNN* (December 18, 2014), accessed March 13, 2016, http://edition.cnn.com/2014/12/17/justice/west-virginia-water-contamination/.

20. Michael Wines and John Schwartz, "Unsafe Lead Levels in Tap Water Not Limited to Flint," *The New York Times* (February 8, 2016), accessed March 13, 2016, http://www.nytimes.com/2016/02/09/us/regulatory-gaps-leave-unsafe-lead-levels-in-water-nationwide.html?_r=1.

21. Natural Resources Defense Council (NRDC), "Water Pollution," accessed March 6, 2016, http://www.nrdc.org/water/pollution/storm/chap3.asp.

22. United Nations Educational, Scientific and Cultural Organization (UNESCO), "Facts and Figures on Marine Pollution," accessed March 5, 2016, http://www.unesco.org/new/en/natural-sciences/ioc-oceans/priority-areas/rio-20-ocean/blueprint-for-the-future-we-want/marine-pollution/ facts-and-figures-on-marine-pollution/.

23. Ocean Conservancy, "Gulf of Mexico," accessed March 6, 2016, http://www.oceanconservancy.org/places/gulf-of-mexico/.

24. Cheslea M. Rochman, Eunha Hoh, Tomofumi Kurobe, and Swee J. Teh, "Ingested Plastic Transfers Hazardous Chemicals to Fish and Induces Hepatic Stress," *Scientific Reports* 3 (2013), accessed March 6, 2016, doi:10.1038/srep03263.

25. Jeff Fair, "A Journey to Alaska's Tongass, Where Our Last Old-Growth Temperate Forest Meets the Sea," (Audubon 2014), accessed June 9, 2016, http://www.audubon.org/magazine/march-april-2014/a-journey-alaskas-tongass-where-our-last-old.

26. Larry Edwards, "America's Largest National Forest—And Its Wolves—Need Your Help by February 22," *Greenpeace*, accessed June 9, 2016, http://www.greenpeace.org/usa/campaign-updates/americas-largest-national-forest-and-its-wolves-need-your-help-by-february-22/.

27. Yale Environmental Performance Index, "Forests," accessed February 12, 2016, http://epi.yale.edu/chapter/forests.

28. United Nations News Centre, "Forests Expand in Europe and North America, but Still Vulnerable to Climate Change" (March 11, 2011), accessed June 8, 2016, http://www. un.org/apps/news/story.asp?NewsID=37845#.V1hd3bsrLIU.

29. International Society for Reef Studies, "Briefing Paper: The Effects of Terrestrial Runoff Sediment, Nutrients, and Other Pollutants on Coral Reefs," accessed February 2, 2016, http://coralreefs.org/wp-content/uploads/2014/05/ISRS-Briefing-Paper-3-Water-Quality.pdf.

30. Eric Chivian M. D., and Aaron Bernstein M. D., M. P. H., "How our Health Depends on Biodiversity" Harvard Medical School (Boston: Center for Health and the Global Environment at Harvard Medical School, 2010), accessed March 5, 2016.

31. Montira J. Pongsiri et al., "Biodiversity Loss Affects Global Disease Ecology," *BioScience* 59(11) (2009): 945–954, accessed March 5, 2016, doi: 10.1525/bio.2009.59.11.6.

32. Edward Maltby, *Science for Environmental Policy, Promoting Natural Water Retention-An Ecosystem Approach,* European Commission (2012), accessed February 2, 2016, http://ec.europa.eu/environment/integration/research/newsalert/pdf/32si_en.pdf.

33. Louis Verchot, "The Science is Clear: Forest Loss Behind Brazil's Drought," *Forest News* (January 29, 2015), accessed February 2, 2016, http://blog.cifor.org/26559/ the-science-is-clear-forest-loss-behind-brazils-drought?fnl=en.

34. Gregory N. Bratman, J. Paul Hamilton, Kevin S. Hahn, Gretchen C. Daily, James J. Gross, "Nature Experience Reduces Rumination and Subgenual Prefrontal Cortex Activation," *Proceedings of the National Academy of Sciences of the United States of America* 112(28), accessed March 6, 2016, doi: 10.1073/pnas.1510459112.

35. Katy Reckdahl, "Losing Louisiana," *The Weather Channel*, accessed April 16, 2016, http://stories.weather.com/story/5931.

36. National Oceanic and Atmospheric Administration (NOAA), "Climate Change Increased Chances of Record Rains in Louisiana by At Least 40 Percent" (September 7, 2016), accessed September 10, 2016, http://www.noaa.gov/media-release/climate-change-increased-chances-of-record-rains-in-louisiana-by-at-least-40-percent.

37. United Nations Framework Convention on Climate Change (UNFCCC), *Draft decision-/CP.15 Proposal by the President Copenhagen Accord* (Copenhagen, 2009), accessed February 3, 2016, http://unfccc.int/resource/docs/2009/cop15/eng/l07.pdf.

38. Instead of tracking global temperatures, two academics from University of California, San Diego, David G. Victor and Charles F. Kennel, suggest to track a range of vital signs or "more scientifically meaningful goals," such as concentrations of CO_2 and changes in the ocean heat content. According to their argument, human stresses on the climate are rising faster even as global surface temperatures stay flat. Moreover, the world will inevitably eventually pass the two-degree limit. Victor and Kennel insist that a set of science-based indicators is needed to "gauge the varied stresses that humans are placing on the climate system and their possible impacts" and allow policy-makers to better implement effective goals with roadmaps that target specific indicators. See *Victor, David and Charles Kennel.*

39. *The States at Risk: America's Preparedness Report Card* is the "first-ever quantitative assessment" that summarizes and assesses how prepared each U.S. state is in regard to climate-related threats. See *Climate Central and ICF International.*

40. National Aeronautics and Space Administration (NASA), "July 2016 Was the Hottest Month on Record" (August 21, 2016), accessed September, 10 2016, http://earthobservatory.nasa.gov/IOTD/view. php?id=88607.

41. National Oceanic and Atmospheric Administration (NOAA), "Global Summary Information – December 2015," accessed February 4, 2016, http://www.ncdc.noaa. gov/sotc/summary-info/global/201512.

42. National Aeronautics and Space Administration (NASA), "NASA, NOAA Analyses Reveal Record-Shattering Global Warm Temperatures in 2016" (January 20, 2016), accessed February 4, 2016, http://www.nasa.gov/press-release/nasa-noaa-analyses-reveal-record-shattering-global-warm-temperatures-in-2015/.

43. Gordon McGranahan, Deborah Balk and Bridget Anderson, "The Rising Tide: Assessing the Risks of Climate Change and Human Settlements in Low Elevation Coastal Zones," *Environment and Urbanization* 19(1) (April 2007): 17–37, accessed January 25, 2016, doi: 10.1177/0956247807076960.

44. Robert M. DeConto and David Pollard, "Contribution of Antarctica to past and Future Sea-Level Rise," *Nature* 531 (2016), accessed May 22, 2016, doi:10.1038/nature17145.

45. J. A. Church, et al. "2013: Sea Level Change." In: Climate Change 2013: The Physical Science Basis. Contribution of Working Group I to the Fifth Assessment Report of the Intergovernmental Panel on Climate Change [Stocker, T.F., D. Qin, G.-K. Plattner, M. Tignor, S.K. Allen, J. Boschung, A. Nauels, Y. Xia, V. Bex and P.M. Midgley (eds.)]. Cambridge University Press, Cambridge, United Kingdom and New York, NY, USA.

46. CNN Staff, "Typhoon Haiyan Death Toll Tops 6,000 in the Philippines," *CNN* (December 13, 2013), accessed February 4, 2016, http://edition.cnn.com/2013/12/13/world/asia/philippines-typhoon-haiyan/.

47. Chaitanya Mallapur, "61% Rise in Heat-Stroke Deaths Over Decade," *India Spend* (May 27, 2015), accessed May 23, 2016, http://www.indiaspend.com/cover-story/61-rise-in-heat-stroke-deaths-over-decade-60404.

48. Jia Coco Liu et al, "Particulate Air Pollution from Wildfires in the Western Us Under Climate Change," *Climactic Change* (July 30, 2015), accessed September 11, 2016, doi: 10.1007/s10584-016-1762-6.

49. World Bank, *High and Dry: Climate Change, Water, and the Economy* (Washington D.C.: International Bank for Reconstruction and Development / The World Bank, 2016), accessed May 29, 2016, http://www.worldbank.org/en/topic/water/publication/high-and-dry-climate-change-water-and-the-economy?CID=WAT_TT_ Water_EN_EXT.

50. Stephane Hallegatte et al., *Shock Waves: Managing the Impacts of Climate Change on Poverty,* World Bank (Washington, D.C.: International Bank for Reconstruction and Development / The World Bank, 2016), accessed June 9, 2016, https://openknowledge.worldbank.org/bitstream/handle/10986/22787/9781464806735.pdf.

51. Seth Kovar and Steve Almasy, "Thousands of Birds Found Dead Along Alaskan Shoreline," *CNN* (January 22, 2016), accessed February 4, 2016, http://edition.cnn.com/2016/01/21/us/alaska-bird-die-off/.

52. The Nature Conservancy, "Climate Change Impacts – Wildlife at Risk," accessed February 2, 2016, http://www.nature.org/ourinitiatives/urgentissues/global-warming-climate-change/threats-impacts/wildlife-at-risk.xml.

53. U.S. Department of Agriculture, Forest Service. "Insect Disturbance," accessed January 25, 2016, http://www.fs.usda.gov/ccrc/topics/insect-disturbance.

54. Sarah Yang, "Climate Change Leading to Major Vegetation Shifts Around the World," *University of California, Berkeley News* (June 4, 2010), accessed January 25, 2016, http://news.berkeley.edu/2010/06/04/climate/.

55. Marshall Burke et al., "Global Non-Linear Effect of Temperature on Economic Production," *Nature* (2015), accessed March 1, 2016, doi:10.1038/nature15725.

56. Another study done by the NextGen Climate, an advocacy group, found that climate change will particularly hit the millennial generation hard: A 21-year-old graduating from college in 2015 would lose $126,000 in lifetime income due to climate change, if no action is taken. This is more than other losses due to other lifetime economic challenges (such as student debt, which costs the average individual $113,000 in lost wealth over a lifetime), and even more than the losses from the Great Recession. See *NextGen Climate.*

57. U.S. Environmental Protection Agency, *Climate Change in the United States: Benefits of Global Action* (U.S. Environmental Protection Agency, Office of Atmospheric Programs, 2015), accessed March 1, 2016, http://www.epa.gov/sites/production/files/2015-06/documents/frontmatter.pdf.

58. Elizabeth Martin Perera and Todd Sanford, "Climate Change and Your Health, Rising Temperatures, Worsening Ozone Pollution," Union of Concerned Scientists (2011), accessed March 2, 2016, http://www. ucsusa.org/sites/default/files/legacy/assets/documents/global_warming/climate-change-and-ozone-pollution.pdf.

59. Umair Irfan, "Climate Change Expands Allergy Risk," *Scientific American* (2012), accessed March 2, 2016, http://www.scientificamerican.com/article/climate-change-expands-allergy-risk/.

60. Sean Poulter, "Price of your Coffee to Rise: Cost Rises by a Fifth in a Week after Drought Hits Bean Crops in Brazil," *Daily Mail,* accessed March 2, 2016, http://www.dailymail.co.uk/news/article-2553570/Price-coffee-rise-Cost-rises-fifth-week-drought-hits-bean-crops-Brazil.html.

61. Corey Lesk et al., "Influence of Extreme Weather Disasters on Global Crop Production," *Nature* (2016), accessed March 3, 2016, doi:10.1038/nature16467.

62. Sean Breslin, "Yosemite's Waterfalls Have Returned, Thanks To Much-Needed Rain," *The Weather Channel* (December 24, 2014), accessed March 2, 2016, https://weather.com/science/nature/news/yosemite-waterfalls-return.

63. Bianca Seidman, "Poison Ivy, Poison Oak Becoming Stronger Over Time," *CBS News* (June 9, 2015), accessed March 2, 2016, http://www.cbsnews.com/news/poison-ivy-poison-oak-becoming-stronger-over-time/.

64. Simpson, M. C., Gössling, S., Scott, D., Hall, C. M. and Gladin, E., *Climate Change Adaptation and Mitigation in the Tourism Sector: Frameworks, Tools and Practices.* UNEP, University of Oxford, UNWTO, WMO: Paris, France (2008), accessed March 5, 2016, http://sdt.unwto.org/sites/all/files/docpdf/ccoxford.pdf.

65. Matt Siegel, "Australian Scientists Alarmed at New Great Barrier Reef Coral Bleaching," *Reuters* (March 21, 2016), accessed March 22, 2016, http://www.businessinsider.com/r-australia-scientists-alarmed-at-new-great-barrier-reef-coral-bleaching-2016-3.

66. Kiley Kroh, "Endless Summer: How Climate Change Could Wipe Out Surfing," *Climate Progress* (August 1, 2013), accessed March 3, 2016, http://thinkprogress.org/climate/2013/08/01/2164691/endless-summer-how-climate-change-could-wipe-out-surfing/.

67. Chris Mooney, "Global Warming is Now Slowing Down the Circulation of the Oceans – with Potentially Dire Consequences," *The Washington Post* (March 23, 2015), accessed March 3, 2016, https://www.washingtonpost.com/news/energy-environment/wp/2015/03/23/global-warming-is-now-slowing-down-the-circulation-of-the-oceans-with-potentially-dire-consequences/.

68. U.S. Environmental Protection Agency, "Inventory of U.S. Greenhouse Gas Emissions and Sinks" (Washington, D.C.: U.S. Environmental Protection Agency, 2015), accessed January 27, 2016, http://www3.epa.gov/climatechange/Downloads/ghgemissions/US-GHG-Inventory-2015-Main-Text.pdf.

69. Bruckner T., Bashmakov, I. A., Mulugetta, Y., Chum, H., de la Vega Navarro, A., Edmonds, J., et al., "2014: Energy Systems." In: Climate Change 2014: Mitigation of Climate Change. Contribution of Working Group III to the Fifth Assessment Report of the Intergovernmental Panel on Climate Change [Edenhofer, O., R. Pichs-Madruga, Y. Sokona, E. Farahani, S. Kadner, K. Seyboth, A. Adler, I. Baum, S. Brunner, P. Eickemeier, B. Kriemann, J. Savolainen, S. Schlömer, C. von Stechow, T. Zwickel and J.C. Minx (eds.)]. Cambridge University Press, Cambridge, United Kingdom and New York, NY, USA. https://www.ipcc.ch/pdf/assessment-report/ar5/wg3/ ipcc_wg3_ar5_chapter7.pdf.

70. Waterworld, "World Water Day 2016: Water from Coal Operations Could Sustain 1 Billion People, Finds Study," accessed March 22, 2016, http://www.waterworld.com/articles/wwi/2016/03/world-water-day-2016-water-from-coal-operations-could-sustain-1-billion-people-finds-study.html.

71. International Energy Agency (IEA), "Coal," accessed March 5, 2016, http://www.iea.org/aboutus/faqs/coal/.

72. Waterworld, "World Water Day 2016: Water from Coal Operations Could Sustain 1 Billion People, Finds Study."

73. U.S. Energy Information Administration, "What is U.S. electricity generation by energy source?" accessed May 22, 2016, https://www.eia.gov/tools/faqs/faq.cfm?id=427&t=3.

74. International Energy Agency (IEA), "Frequently Asked Questions," accessed March 5, 2016, https://www.eia.gov/tools/faqs/faq.cfm?id=69&t=2.

75. Sims R., R. Schaeffer, F. Creutzig, X. Cruz-Núñez, M. D'Agosto, D. Dimitriu, M. J. et al., "2014: Transport." In: Climate Change 2014: Mitigation of Climate Change. Contribution of Working Group III to the Fifth Assessment Report of the Intergovernmental Panel on Climate Change [Edenhofer, O., R. Pichs-Madruga, Y. Sokona, E. Farahani, S. Kadner, K. Seyboth, A. Adler, I. Baum, S. Brunner, P. Eickemeier, B. Kriemann, J. Savolainen, S. Schlömer, C. von Stechow, T. Zwickel and J.C. Minx (eds.)]. Cambridge University Press, Cambridge, United Kingdom and New York, NY, USA, accessed January 28, 2016, https://www.ipcc.ch/pdf/assessment-report/ar5/wg3/ipcc_wg3_ar5_chapter8. Pdf.

76. U.S. Environmental Protection Agency, "Inventory of U.S. Greenhouse Gas Emissions and Sinks."

77. Ibid.

78. Camille von Kaenel, "Americans Are Driving More Than Ever," *Scientific American* (February 22, 2016), accessed March 5, 2016, http://www.scientificamerican.com/article/americans-are-driving-more-than-ever1/?utm_content=buffer5831e&utm_medium=social&utm_source=twitter.com&utm_campaign=buffer.

79. U.S. Department of Transportation, "2016 Traffic Volume Trends," accessed September 11, 2016, https://www.fhwa.dot.gov/policyinformation/travel_monitoring/16juntvt/page2.cfm.

80. World Economic Forum, "The Number of Cars Worldwide is Set to Double By 2040" (April 22, 2016), accessed May 15, 2016, http://bit.ly/1VXVIIa.

81. Sims R., et al., "Transport." In: Climate Change 2014: Mitigation of Climate Change.

82. U.S. Environmental Protection Agency, "Inventory of U.S. Greenhouse Gas Emissions and Sinks."

83. Smith P., M. Bustamante, H. Ahammad, H. Clark, H. Dong, E. A. Elsiddig, et al., 2014: Agriculture, Forestry and Other Land Use (AFOLU). In: Climate Change 2014: Mitigation of Climate Change. Contribution of Working Group III to the Fifth Assessment Report of the Intergovernmental Panel on Climate Change [Edenhofer, O., R. Pichs-Madruga, Y. Sokona, E. Farahani, S. Kadner, K. Seyboth, A. Adler, I. Baum, S. Brunner, P. Eickemeier, B. Kriemann, J. Savolainen, S. Schlömer, C. von Stechow, T. Zwickel and J.C. Minx (eds.)]. Cambridge University Press, Cambridge, United Kingdom and New York, NY, USA, accessed January 27, 2016. https://www.ipcc.ch/pdf/assessment-report/ar5/wg3/ipcc_wg3_ar5_chapter11.pdf.

84. U.S. Environmental Protection Agency, "Inventory of U.S. Greenhouse Gas Emissions and Sinks."

85. Ibid.

86. Gabrielle Kissinger et al., *Drivers of Deforestation and Forest Degradation: A Synthesis Report for REDD+ Policymakers* (Vancouver Canada: Lexeme Consulting, 2012), accessed January 24, 2016, https://www.gov.uk/government/uploads/system/uploads/attachment_data/file/65505/6316-drivers-deforestation-report.pdf.

87. Global Forest Coalition, *REDD+ and the Underlying Causes of Deforestation and Forest Degradation* (2013), accessed January 25, 2016, http://globalforestcoalition.org/wp-content/uploads/2013/11/REDD-and-UC-report-final.pdf.

88. Smith P., M. Bustamante, H. Ahammad, H. Clark, H. Dong, E. A. Elsiddig, et al., "2014: Agriculture, Forestry and Other Land Use (AFOLU)." In: Climate Change 2014: Mitigation of Climate Change. Contribution of Working Group III to the Fifth Assessment Report of the Intergovernmental Panel on Climate Change [Edenhofer, O., R. Pichs-Madruga, Y. Sokona, E. Farahani, S. Kadner, K. Seyboth, A. Adler, I. Baum, S. Brunner, P. Eickemeier, B. Kriemann, J. Savolainen, S. Schlömer, C. von Stechow, T. Zwickel and J. C. Minx (eds.)]. Cambridge University Press, Cambridge, United Kingdom and New York, NY, USA. (2000): 827, accessed January 27, 2016. https://www.ipcc.ch/pdf/assessment-report/ar5/wg3/ipcc_wg3_ar5_chapter11.pdf.

89. M.A. Palmer et al., "Mountaintop Mining Consequences," *Science* 327 (2010): 148–149, accessed January 17, 2016, doi: 10.1126/science.1180543.

90. A lack of data still exists as to the leading causes of oil and gas spills. See *Pearen, Holly*.

91. UV rays are linked to skin cancer, genetic damage, a poor immune system, and even low agricultural productivity. See Clancy, S., World Health Organization (WHO). "Health Effects of UV Radiation;" and Food and Agriculture Organization (FAO). "Adverse Effects of Elevated Levels of Ultraviolet (UV)-B Radiation and Ozone (O_3) on Crop Growth and Productivity."

92. Perinaz Bhada-Tata and Daniel A. Hoornweg, "What a Waste?: A Global Review of Solid Waste Management. Urban Development Series Knowledge Papers; No. 15," World Bank (2012), accessed March 7, 2016, http://documents.worldbank.org/curated/en/2012/03/20213522/waste-global-review-solid-waste-management.

93. Ocean Conservancy, "The World's Only Snapshot of Trash in the Ocean and Its Hazardous Effects on Ocean Life," accessed March 13, 2016, http://act.oceanconservancy.org/site/DocServer/ICC_Presskit.pdf?docID=3761.

94. Dominick A. DellaSal, "The Tongass Rainforest as Alaska's Fist Line of Climate Change Defense and Importance to the Paris Climate Change Agreements," *Geos Institut* (2016) accessed June, 9, 2016, http://forestlegacies.org/images/projects/tongass-report-emissions-2016-01.pdf.

95. Eliminating the billions in federal subsidies that oil and gas companies receive is cited as an easy way to even the playing field between renewables and fossil fuels. See Bast, Elizabeth, et al.

CHAPTER 3

1. World Bank, "Green Bond Issuances to Date," accessed May 14, 2016, http://treasury.worldbank.org/cmd/htm/GreenBondIssuancesToDate.html.

2. Mission Innovation, "Member Participation – United States," accessed June 4, 2016, http://www.mission-innovation.net/participating-countries/#UnitedStates.

3. Public Broadcasting Service (PBS), "Running on renewable energy, Burlington, Vermont powers green movement forward," *PBS NewsHour* (January 31, 2015), accessed June 2, 2016, http://www.pbs.org/newshour/bb/vermont-city-come-rely-100-percent-renewable-energy/.

4. Matt Richtel, "San Diego Vows to Move Entirely to Renewable Energy in 20 Years," *The New York Times* (December 15, 2015), accessed June 2, 2016, http://www. nytimes.com/2015/12/16/science/san-diego-vows-to-move-entirely-to-renewable-energy-in-20-years.html?_r=1.

5. Earth Policy Institute, "Plastic Bags Factsheet," accessed June 5, 2016, http://www.earth-policy.org/press_room/C68/plastic_bags_fact_sheet.

6. Microsoft, "Environmental Sustainability at Microsoft," accessed June 4, 2016, https://www.microsoft.com/about/csr/environment/.

7. Frankfurt School of Finance & Management, "Global Trends in Renewable Energy Investment 2016" (Frankfurt School-UNEP Centre/BNEF, 2016), accessed May 16, 2016, http://fs-unep-centre.org/sites/default/files/publications/globaltrendsinrenewableenergyinvestment2016lowres_0.pdf.

8. Ceres, *Shareholders Spur Action On Climate Change: Company Commitments From the 2014 & 2015 Proxy Seasons* (Ceres, The Investor Network on Climate Risk, 2015), accessed June 5, 2016, https://www.ceres.org/resources/reports/shareholders-spur-action-on-climate-change-company-commitments-from-the-2014-2015 -proxy-seasons.

9. Ceres, "Shareholder Resolutions," accessed June 5, 2016, http://www.ceres.org/press/press-releases/shareholders-achieve-major-corporate-sustainability-improvementshttp://www.ceres.org/investor-network/resolutions.

10. Matt McGrath, "Exxon Mobil Faces 'change or die' Moment on Climate," *BBC* (May 24, 2016), accessed May 26, 2016, http://www.bbc.com/news/science-environment-36332076.

11. Fossil Free, "Divestment Commitments," accessed September 3, 2016, http://gofossilfree.org/commitments/.

12. Another interesting argument against the divestment movement is that by selling shares, shareholders don't hurt the company, but rather transfer ownership of shares to others that may care even less about the issue.

13. The Vatican, "Encyclical Letter Laudato SI' of The Holy Father Francis on Care for our Common Home," (2015), accessed February 22, 2016, http://w2.vatican. va/content/francesco/en/encyclicals/documents/papa-francesco_20150524_enciclica-laudato-si.html.

14. Ecobuddhism, "A Buddhist Declaration on Climate Change," accessed June 8, 2016, http://www.ecobuddhism.org/bcp/all_content/buddhist_declaration/.

15. United Nations Framework Convention on Climate Change (UNFCCC), "Islamic Declaration on Climate Change Calls For 1.6 billion Muslims to Support Strong Paris Agreement," accessed June 8, 2016, http://newsroom.unfccc.int/unfccc-newsroom/islamic-declaration-on-climate-change/.

16. Fossil Free, "Divestment Commitments."

17. Brian Clark Howard, "India Plants 50 Million Trees in One Day, Smashing World Record," *National Geographic* (July 18, 2016), accessed September 11,

2016, http://news.nationalgeographic.com/2016/07/india-plants-50-million-trees-uttar -pradesh-reforestation/.

18. Steve Mollman, "Santiago's Subway System Will Soon be Powered Mostly by Solar and Wind Energy," *Quartz* (May 24, 2016), accessed June 1, 2016, http://qz.com/691078/santiagos-subway-system-will-soon-be-powered-mostly-by-solar-and-wind-energy/.

19. Paris, France, "Paris réaménage ses grandes places" (March 3, 2016), accessed June 1, 2016, http://www.paris.fr/grandesplaces.

20. Michael Porter and Mark Kramer, "Creating Shared Value," *Harvard Business Review* (January-February, 2011), accessed June 9, 2016, https://hbr.org/2011/01/the-big-idea-creating-shared-value.

21. Social Progress Index, socialprogressimperative.org.

CHAPTER 4

1. Diana Ivanova, et al., "Environmental Impact Assessment of Household Consumption," *Journal of Industrial Ecology* (2015), accessed February 28, 2016, doi 10.1111/jiec.12371.

2. Lydia Saad and Jeffrey M. Jones, "U.S. Concern About Global Warming at Eight-Year High" *Gallup Polls* (March 16, 2016), accessed September 10, 2016, http://www.gallup.com/poll/190010/concern-global-warming-eight-year-high.aspx.

3. To get a better picture of consumption in the United States, think about this: The planet has about 4.7 acres of land available per person on earth to supply us with resources and absorb our waste, yet the average American uses almost 24 acres worth. See Worldwatch Institute, "The State of Consumption Today," accessed March 16, 2016, http://worldwatch.org/node/810.

4. Global Footprint Network, "Earth Overshoot Day – Pledge 3: Is Your Country an Ecological Creditor or Debtor?" accessed September 5, 2016, http://www.overshootday.org/portfolio/creditor-debtor/.

5. Diana Ivanova, et al., "Environmental Impact Assessment of Household Consumption."

6. Good Guide, goodguide.com.

7. "Consumer Guides," Environmental Working Group, ewg.org/consumer-guides and "Healthy Living App," Environmental Working Group, http://www.ewg.org/apps/.

8. "Skin Deep Database," Environmental Working Group, ewg.org/skindeep.

9. Think Dirty, thinkdirtyapp.com.

10. In a survey by the Pew Research Center in 2015, the majority (an average of 54 percent) of people in 40 countries said climate change was a serious problem. In the same poll, 45 percent of Americans saw climate change as a problem, compared to almost 75 percent of people in Latin America. See *Stokes, Bruce, Richard Wike, and Jill Carle.*

11. Nathaniel Geiger and Janet Swim, "Climate of Silence: Pluralistic Ignorance as a Barrier to Climate Change Discussion," *Journal of Environmental Psychology* in press (2016), accessed May 13, 2016, doi:10.1016/j.jenvp.2016.05.002.

12. National Aeronautics and Space Administration (NASA), "Scientific consensus: Earth's climate is warming," accessed May 13, 2016, http://climate.nasa.gov/ scientific-consensus/.

CHAPTER 5

1. U.S. Environmental Protection Agency, *Advancing Sustainable Materials Management: 2013 Fact Sheet* (Washington, D.C.: United States Environmental Protection Agency Solid Waste and Emergency Response, 2015), accessed April 24, 2016, https://www.epa.gov/sites/production/files/2015-09/documents/2013_advncng_smm_fs.pdf.

2. Earth 911, earth911.com.

3. The U.S. Environmental Protection Agency has a fun and interactive tool that demonstrates the energy saved when different products are recycled, see *U.S. Environmental Protection Agency, "Reduce, Reuse, Recycle."*

4. The How2Recycle initiative from the Sustainable Packaging Coalition has developed standardized product labels that communicate helpful information on how to dispose of items properly. Member companies adopt the standardized labels for their products and include large companies such as Wal-Mart, Nestle, and Target. How2Recycle, how2recycle.info

5. Elizah Leigh, "What Aluminum Extraction Really Does to the Environment," *Recycle Nation* (November 9, 2010), accessed May 11, 2016, http://recyclenation.com/2010/11/aluminum-extraction-recycling-environment.

6. Earth Day Network, "About Junk Mail," accessed April 23, 2016, http://www.earthday.org/take-action/about-junk-mail/.

7. Websites include DMA Choice, www.dmachoice.org and Catalog Choice, www.catalogchoice.org.

8. Opt Out Prescreen, www.optoutprescreen.com.

9. U.S. Department of Energy, "Air Conditioning," accessed February 2, 2016, http://energy.gov/energysaver/air-conditioning.

10. U.S. Department of Energy, "Heating and Cooling," accessed March 6, 2016, http://energy.gov/public-services/homes/heating-cooling.

11. Michael Vandenbergh and Anne Steinemann, "The Carbon Neutral Individual," *New York Law Review* 82(6) (2007), accessed May 9, 2016, http://www. nyulawreview.org/issues/volume-82-number-6/carbon-neutral-individual.

12. Duke Energy, "100 Ways to Save Energy at Home," accessed March 8, 2016, https://www.progress-energy.com/florida/home/save-energy-money/energy-saving-tips-calculators/100-tips.page?

13. B. C. Wolverton, Anne Johnson, and Keith Bounds, *Interior Landscape Plants for Indoor Air Pollution Abatement,* National Aeronautics and Space Administration (NASA) Office of Commercial Program – Technology Utilization Division and the Associated Landscape Contractors of America, 1989, accessed March 6, 2016, http://ntrs.nasa.gov/archive/nasa/casi.ntrs.nasa.gov/19930073077.pdf.

14. There are many ingredients that should be avoided including petroleum-based ingredients ("nonylphenol ethoxylate" or "ethylene"), chlorine, or phosphates. Also, ingredients with bronopol (often written as "2-bromo-2-nitropropane-1,3-diol") release formaldehyde. Quaternary ammonium compounds (written as "alkyl dimethyl benzyl ammonium chlorides (C-12-16)" and "benzyl-C8-18-alkyldimethyl chlorides") aggravate allergies and asthma, are toxic to aquatic life and breed antibiotic-resistant bacteria. "Guide to Healthy Cleaning," Environmental Working Group, www.ewg.org/guides/cleaners.

15. "Guide to Healthy Cleaning," Environmental Working Group, www.ewg.org/guides/cleaners.

16. U.S. Energy Information Administration. "How much electricity is used for lighting in the United States?" accessed March 13, 2016, http://www.eia.gov/tools/faqs/faq.cfm?id=99&t=3

17. Heather E. Dillon and Michael J. Scholand, *Life-Cycle Assessment of Energy and Environmental Impacts of LED Lighting Products Part 2: LED Manufacturing and Performance,* U.S. Department of Energy (Solid-State Lighting Program Building Technologies Program Office of Energy Efficiency and Renewable Energy U.S. Department of Energy, 2012), accessed March 14, 2016, http://apps1.eere.energy.gov/buildings/publications/pdfs/ssl/2012_led_lca-pt2.pdf.

18. It is commonly thought that CFLs require a lot of energy to turn on and off and that we should limit how often we switch a light on and off because of this energy consumption. But the 15-minute rule of thumb associated with the use of CFLs is actually due to the fact that the lifespan of CFLs is affected by the number of times they are switched on and off – not necessarily with the energy consumed in turning them on or off. By limiting the frequency that we switch CFL light bulbs on and off, we can extended the life of the bulb. "When to Turn off Your Lights," U.S. Department of Energy, http://energy. gov/energysaver/when-turn-your-lights.

19. National Renewable Energy Laboratory (NREL), "Saving Power Through Advanced Power Strips," accessed April 9, 2016, http://www.nrel.gov/docs/fy14o-sti/60461. Pdf.

20. National Geographic, "Water Conservation Tips," accessed March 17, 2016, http://environment.nationalgeographic.com/environment/freshwater/water-conservation-tips/.

21. ENERGY STAR, "Clothes Washers," accessed March 17, 2016, https://www.energystar.gov/products/appliances/clothes_washers.

22. U.S. Environmental Protection Agency, "Save Water and Energy by Showering Better," accessed April 22, 2016, https://www3.epa.gov/watersense/docs/ws_shower_better_learning_resource_508.pdf.

23. ENERGY STAR, "Clothes Washers."

24. U.S. Department of Energy, "15 Ways to Save on Your Water Heating Bill," accessed February 20, 2016, http://energy.gov/energysaver/articles/15-ways-save-your-water-heating-bill.

25. National Oceanic and Atmospheric Administration (NOAA), "Study Supports EPA to Control Both Nitrogen and Phosphorus in Freshwaters" (December 8, 2015),

accessed June 9, 2016, https://coastalscience.noaa.gov/news/coastal-pollution/study-lends-scientific-support -epa-control-nitrogen-phosphorus-freshwaters/.

26. Procter & Gamble, which makes Tide detergent has been working to remove phosphates from their laundry detergents since 2014 and in 2016, Wal-Mart announced plan to work with suppliers to remove right chemicals from their products.

27. U.S. Department of Energy, "Savings Project: Lower Water Heater Temperature," accessed March 6, 2016, http://energy.gov/energysaver/projects/savings-project-lower-water-heating-temperature.

28. U.S. Department of Energy, "Maintaining Your Air Conditioner," accessed September 8, 2016, http://energy.gov/energysaver/maintaining-your-air-conditioner.

29. Database of State Incentives for Renewables & Efficiency (DSIRE) website aggregates information on rebates and incentives available in the United Sates. It's helpful to search by zip code and then filter by the type of technology you plan to purchase. DSIRE, www.dsireusa.org

CHAPTER 6

1. Food and Agriculture Organization (FAO), *Food Wastage Footprint Impacts on Natural Resources Summary Report* (2013), accessed May 11, 2016, http://www.fao.org/docrep/018/i3347e/i3347e.pdf.

2. Kari Hamerschlag and Kumar Venkat, *Meat Eaters Guide to Climate Change + Health Methodology*, Environmental Working Group (2011), accessed March 8, 2016, http://static.ewg.org/reports/2011/meateaters/pdf/methodology_ewg_meat_eaters_guide_to_health_and_climate_2011.pdf.

3. John Hopkins Bloomberg School of Public Health, Center for a Livable Future, "Health & Environmental Implications of U.S. Meat Consumption & Production," accessed May 9, 2016, https://www.jhsph.edu/research/centers-and-institutes/johns-hopkins-center-for-a-livable-future/projects/meatless_monday/resources/meat_consumption.html.

4. Kyle Kim, et al., "Water Leaves a 'Footprint' in our Food; Here's How it Works," *The Los Angeles Times* (April 17, 2015), accessed April 17, 2016, http://www. latimes.com/visuals/graphics/la-g-food-water-footprint-20150410-html-story.html.

5. Research on food miles is still limited. The 2001 research by Rich Pirog at the Leopold Center for Sustainable Agriculture, which looked at the miles fruit and vegetables traveled to Chicago has its limitations but is still the most commonly cited statistic to illustrate food transport in the United States.

6. Sarah DeWeerdt, "Is Local Food Better?" *World Watch,* accessed March 12, 2016, http://www.worldwatch.org/node/6064.

7. Epicurious offers an interactive map to look at what's in season in your state by month: http://www.epicurious.com/archive/seasonalcooking/farmtotable/seasonalingredientmap or try "Seasonal Food Guide," Sustainable Table, http://gracelinks.org/seasonalfoodguide/.

8. U.S. Department of Agriculture, "Number of U.S. Farmers' Markets Continues to Rise," accessed May 13, 2016, http://www.ers.usda.gov/data-products/chart-gallery/ detail.aspx?chartId=48561&ref=collection&embed=True

9. Daniel Pauly and Dirk Zeller, "Catch Reconstructions Reveal that Global Marine Fisheries Catches are Higher than Reported and Declining," *Nature Communications* 7 (2016), accessed April 17, 2016, doi: 10.1038/ncomms10244l.

10. The Seafood Watch Guide outlines the "Best Choices," "Good Alternatives," and types of fish to avoid and thus to ensure that the seafood that you eat is not at risk of being overfished. According to the guide, for instance, seafood consumers in Florida should avoid wild conch, spiny lobster from Belize, Brazil, Honduras, and Nicaragua, imported swordfish, and yellowfin Atlantic tuna. "Consumer Guides," Monterey Bay Aquarium Seafood Watch, https://www.seafoodwatch.org/seafood-recommendations/consumer-guides.

11. Dana Gunders, *Wasted: How America Is Losing Up to 40 Percent of Its Food from Farm to Fork to Landfill*, Natural Resources Defense Council (2012), accessed September 10, 2016, https://www.nrdc.org/sites/default/files/wasted-food-IP.pdf.

12. U.S. Department of Agriculture Economic Research Service, "Food Security in the U.S. Key Statistics and Graphics 2014," accessed April 25, 2016, http://www.ers.usda.gov/topics/food-nutrition-assistance/food-security-in-the-us/ key-statistics-graphics.aspx.

13. Natural Resources Defense Council and Ad Council, "Save the Food," accessed May 15, 2016, http://savethefood.com/.

14. There are several websites that provide more detailed guidance on how to reduce food waste. Our favorite is Save The Food, savethefood.com, which is based on *The Waste Free Kitchen Handbook* by Natural Resources Defense Council's Dana Gunders.

15. U.S. Environmental Protection Agency, *Advancing Sustainable Materials Management: 2013 Fact Sheet,* (Washington, D.C.: United States Environmental Protection Agency Solid Waste and Emergency Response, 2015), accessed May 11, 2016, https:// www3.epa.gov/epawaste/nonhaz/municipal/pubs/2012_msw_fs.pdf.

16. See Find A Composter, findacomposter.com to see if a composting facility exists in your area or ask around in your community.

17. U.S. Department of Energy, "Tips: Kitchen Appliances," accessed April 5, 2016, http://energy.gov/energysaver/tips-kitchen-appliances.

18. David Carini, "The Best Way to Boil Water: Nitty-Gritty," *Stanford Magazine* (2010), accessed March 13, 2016, https://alumni.stanford.edu/get/page/magazine/article/?article_id=29243.

19. U.S. Department of Energy, "Are Energy Vampires Sucking You Dry?" (October 29, 2015), accessed April 24, 2016, http://energy.gov/articles/are-energy-vampires-sucking-you-dry.

CHAPTER 7

1. U.S. Geological Survey, "Water Questions and Answers," accessed March 12, 2016, http://water.usgs.gov/edu/qa-home-percapita.html.

2. Environmental Working Group's Skin Deep Cosmetics Database, "Exposures add up – Survey results," accessed May 10, 2016, http://www.ewg.org/skindeep/2004/06/15/exposures-add-up-survey-results/.

3. WaterSense, "Showerheads," accessed March 17, 2016, https://www3.epa.gov/watersense/products/showerheads.html

4. U.S. Geological Survey, "Water Questions and Answers," accessed March 12, 2016, http://water.usgs.gov/edu/qa-home-percapita.html.

5. A. R. Carrico et al., "The Environmental Cost of Misinformation: Why the Recommendation to Use Warm Water for Handwashing is Problematic," *International Journal of Consumer Studies* (2013), accessed May 12, 2016, doi: 10.1111/ ijcs.12012.

6. U.S. Geological Survey, "Water Questions and Answers," accessed March 12, 2016, http://water.usgs.gov/edu/qa-home-percapita.html.

7. Siemens, "11 Surprising Facts that will Change Your Water Usage," *Mother Nature Network,* accessed May 19, 2016, http://www.mnn.com/money/sustainable-business-practices/sponsorstory/11-surprising-facts-that-will-change-your-water.

8. See the Frank R. Lautenberg, Chemical Safety for the 21st Century Act, https://www.epa.gov/assessing-and-managing-chemicals-under-tsca/frank-r-lautenberg-chemical-safety-21st-century-act.

9. The banned chemicals are commonly found in antiseptic or antibacterial soap and include triclosan.

10. U.S. Geological Survey, "Water Questions and Answers," accessed March 12, 2016, http://water.usgs.gov/edu/qa-home-percapita.html.

CHAPTER 8

1. See "Four Easy Do-It-Yourself Soil Tests," organicgardening.about.com, http://organicgardening. about.com/od/soil/a/easysoiltests.htm.

2. Lady Bird Johnson Wildflower Center, "Native Plant Database," accessed May 13, 2016, http://www.wildflower.org/plants/.

3. EarthBox and GrowBoxes (by The Garden Patch) make vegetable gardening accessible to anyone, even those that live in small apartments or with no backyard. These convenient boxes require little maintenance yet yield beautiful vegetables.

4. U.S.DepartmentofEnergy,"EnergySaver101Infographic:Landscaping,"accessed May 12, 2016, http://energy.gov/articles/energy-saver-101-infographic-landscaping.

5. U.S. Department of Energy. "Energy Saver 101 Infographic: Landscaping."

6. Ibid.

7. For a good breakdown on plant and vegetable arrangements, see Israel, Sarah.

CHAPTER 9

1. Camille von Kaenel, "Americans Are Driving More Than Ever," *Scientific American* (2016), accessed May 12, 2016, http://www.scientificamerican.com/article/americans-are-driving-more-than-ever1/.

2. Elliot Martin and Susan Shaheen, *Impacts of Car2go on Vehicle Ownership, Modal Shift, Vehicle Miles Traveled, and Greenhouse Gas Emissions; An Analysis of Five North American Cities,* Transportation Sustainability Research Center (2016), accessed September 10, 2016, http://innovativemobility.org/wp-content/uploads/2016/07/Impactsofcar2go_FiveCities_2016.pdf.

3. U.S. Environmental Protection Agency, "Greenhouse Gas Emissions from a Typical Passenger Vehicle," accessed March 18, 2016, https://www3.epa.gov/otaq/climate/documents/420f14040a.pdf.

4. Environmental Defense Fund, "Attention Drivers! Turn off Your Idling Engines," accessed February 2, 2016, https://www.edf.org/climate/reports/idling.

5. U.S. Department of Energy, "Keeping Your Vehicle in Shape," accessed May 9, 2016, https://www.fueleconomy.gov/feg/maintain.jsp.

6. Ibid.

7. Ocean Conservancy, "International Coastal Cleanup: Top 10 Items Found," accessed June 8, 2016, http://www.oceanconservancy.org/our-work/international-coastal-cleanup/top-10-items-found-1.html.

CHAPTER 10

1. Tatiana Schlossberg, "Just How Much Power Do Your Electronics Use When They Are 'Off'?" *New York Times* (May 7, 2016), accessed May 10, 2016, http://www.nytimes.com/2016/05/08/science/just-how-much-power-do-your-electronics-use-when-they-are-off.html?_r=0.

2. ENERGY STAR, energystar.gov and EPEAT, epeat.net

3. Katie Campbell, "Where Does America's e-waste End Up? GPS Tracker Tells All," *PBS Newshour* (May 10, 2016), accessed May 13, 2016, http://www.pbs.org/newshour/updates/america-e-waste-gps-tracker-tells-all-earthfix/.

4. U.S. Environmental Protection Agency, "Electronics Donation and Recycling," accessed May 10, 2016, https://www.epa.gov/recycle/electronics-donation-and-recycling.

5. U.S. Environmental Protection Agency, *Electronics Waste Management in the United States through 2009* (U.S. Environmental Protection Agency Office of Resources Conservation and Recovery, 2011), accessed May 11, 2016, http://1.usa.gov/1TQTaYU.

6. Pipa Elias and Doug Boucher, *Planting for the Future: How Demand for Wood Products Could Be Friendly to Tropical Forests,* Union of Concerned Scientists, Tropical Forest and Climate Initiative (TFCI) of the Union of Concerned Scientists (UCS), (2014), accessed May 13, 2016, http://www.ucsusa.org/our-work/global-warming/stop-deforestation/planting-future-demand-wood-products#.VzW4cY-cE2w.

7. The Economist, "How Much Paper Does a Person Use on Average in a Year?" April 3, 2012, accessed May 13, 2016, http://www.economist.com/blogs/graphicdetail/2012/04/daily-chart-0.

CHAPTER 11

1. Cone Communications, *2015 Cone Communications Millennial CSR Study* (2015), accessed May 13, 2016, http://www.conecomm.com/2015-cone-communications-millennial-csr-study.

2. Natural Resources Defense Council and Ad Council, "Save the Food, Home," accessed May 15, 2016, http://savethefood.com/.

3. U.S. Environmental Protection Agency, "Advancing Sustainable Materials Management: 2013 Fact Sheet," Washington, D.C.: United States Environmental Protection Agency Solid Waste and Emergency Response (2013), accessed April 24, 2016, https://www.epa.gov/sites/production/files/2015-09/documents/2013_advncng_smm_fs.pdf.

4. U.S. Environmental Protection Agency, "Advancing Sustainable Materials Management: 2013 Fact Sheet," Washington, D.C.: United States Environmental Protection Agency Solid Waste and Emergency Response (2013), accessed April 24, 2016, https://www.epa.gov/sites/production/files/2015-09/documents/2013_advncng_smm_fs.pdf.

5. World Wildlife Fund (WWF), "Palm Oil," accessed May 20, 2016, http://wwf.panda.org/what_we_do/footprint/agriculture/palm_oil/.

6. Greenpeace's "Cutting Deforestation Out of the Palm Oil Supply Chain: Company Scorecard" 2016 guide evaluates companies who committed to zero-deforestation on their progress to fulfilling this commitment. Companies that Greenpeace scored as "strong" in achieving this included Ferrero (producer of Ferrero Rocher and Nutella) and Nestle. The companies that were "failing" in their commitment to zero-deforestation included PepsiCo, Colgate-Palmolive, and Johnson & Johnson. The companies scored as doing a "decent" job were Danon, General Mills, Ikea, Kellogg, Mars, Modelez (producer of Cadbury, Nabisco and Oreo food-brands), Orkla, P&G and Unilever, http://www.greenpeace.org/international/Global/international/publications/forests/2016/gp_IND_PalmScorecard_FINAL.pdf.

7. Sarah Murray, "Fixing the Fashion Industry," Natural Resources Defense Council (NRDC) (June 15, 2016), accessed June 9. 2016, https://www.nrdc.org/stories/fixing-fashion-industry.

8. World Wildlife Fund (WWF), "The Impact of a Cotton T-Shirt," accessed February2,2016,http://www.worldwildlife.org/stories/the-impact-of-a-cotton-t-shirt.

9. Better Cotton Initiative, bettercotton.org.

10. Natural Resources Defense Council (NRDC), "Clean by Design Fiber Selection," accessed June 9, 2016, https://www.nrdc.org/sites/default/files/CBD-Fiber-Selection-FS.pdf.

11. Greenpeace's the Detox Catwalk ranks companies on their efforts to deliver toxic-free fashion. Greenpeace ranks Adidas, Burberry, ESPRIT, H&M, Levi's, Benetton group, and Puma, among others, as leaders in this field, while Gap, Versace, and D&G (among others) rank in as "losers." The Ethical Consumer website, ethicalconsumer.org is a useful site that provides insight into which companies are doing what.

CHAPTER 12

1. U.S. Environmental Protection Agency, "Reduce, Recycle, Reuse: Greening the Season," accessed April 20, 2016, https://www3.epa.gov/region9/waste/recycling/index.html.
2. Amit Kumar et al., "Waiting for Merlot Anticipatory Consumption of Experiential and Material Purchases," *Psychological Science* 25(10) (2014), accessed May 21, 2016, doi: 10.1177/0956797614546556.
3. U.S. Fish and Wildlife Service, "Balloons and Wildlife: Please Don't Release Your Balloons," accessed May 21, 2016, https://www.fws.gov/news/blog/index.cfm/2015/8/5/Balloons-and-Wildlife-Please-Dont-Release-Your-Balloons.

CHAPTER 13

1. International Civil Aviation Organization, *ICAO Environmental Report 2013* (Montreal: Environmental Branch of the ICAO, 2013), accessed May 16, 2016, http://cfapp.icao.int/Environmental-Report-2013/#212/z.
2. Duncan Clark, "The Surprisingly Complex Truth About Planes and Climate Change," *The Guardian* (September 9, 2010), accessed May 22, 2016, http://www.theguardian.com/environment/blog/2010/sep/09/carbon-emissions-planes-shipping.
3. U.S. National Park Service, "America's National Parks: Record Number of Visitors in 2015," *National Park Service Press Release* (January 27, 2016), accessed September 11, 2016. https://www.nps.gov/aboutus/news/release.htm?id=1775.
4. The Nature Conservancy, "What is Ecotourism?" accessed May 22, 2016, http://www.nature.org/greenliving/what-is-ecotourism.xml.

Bibliography

A. K. Chapagain and A. Y. Hoekstra. *The Water Needed to Have the Dutch Drink Coffee.* The Netherlands: UNESCO-IHE (2003). Accessed May 20, 2016. http://waterfootprint.org/media/downloads/Report14.pdf.

American Chemistry Council. "Plastic Packaging Resins." Accessed September 5, 2016. https://plastics.americanchemistry.com/Plastic-Resin-Codes-PDF/.

American Lung Association. "The State of the Air 2016." Accessed May 20, 2016. http://www.lung.org/assets/documents/healthy-air/state-of-the-air/sota-2016-full.pdf.

Apple. "Climate Change." Accessed June 4, 2016. http://www.apple.com/environment/climate-change/.

Bast, Elizabeth, et al. *Empty Promises: G20 Subsidies to Oil, Gas, and Coal Production.* Overseas Development Institute and Oil Change International (2015). Accessed March 3, 2016. http://priceofoil.org/content/uploads/2015/11/Empty-promises_main-report.2015.pdf.

Berghage, Robert D., et al. *Green Roofs for Stormwater Runoff Control.* U.S. Environmental Protection Agency. Cincinnati: National Risk Management Research Laboratory Office of Research and Development (2009). Accessed May 19, 2016. http://nepis.epa.gov/Exe/ZyPDF.cgi/P1003704.PDF?Dockey=P1003704.PDF.

Bethencourt, Daniel. "Snyder: Flint Has Seen Spike in Legionnaires' Disease." *Detroit Free Press,* January 15, 2016. Accessed September 10, 2016. http://www.freep.com/story/news/local/michigan/2016/01/13/snyder-flint-area-has-seen-spike-legionnaires/78750610/.

B Corporations. www.bcorporation.net.

Better Cotton Initiative. bettercotton.org.

Bhada-Tata, Perinaz and Daniel A. Hoornweg. "What a Waste?: A Global Review of Solid Waste Management. Urban Development Series Knowledge Papers; no. 15." World Bank (2012). Accessed March 7, 2016. http://documents.worldbank.org/curated/en/2012/03/20213522/waste-global-review-solid-waste-management.

BikeArlington. Maps & Rides. Accessed June 1, 2016. http://www.bikearlington.com/pages/maps-rides/.

Bratman, Gregory N., J. Paul Hamilton, Kevin S. Hahn, Gretchen C. Daily, and James J. Gross. "Nature Experience Reduces Rumination and Subgenual Prefrontal Cortex Activation." *Proceedings of the National Academy of Sciences of the United States of America* 1122, no. 28. Accessed March 6, 2016. doi: 10.1073/pnas.1510459112.

Breslin, Sean. "Yosemite's Waterfalls Have Returned, Thanks To Much-Needed Rain." *The Weather Channel*, December 24, 2014. Accessed March 2, 2016. https://weather.com/science/nature/news/yosemite-waterfalls-return.

Bruckner, T., Bashmakov, I. A., Mulugetta, Y., Chum, H., de la Vega Navarro, A., Edmonds, J. et al. 2014: Energy Systems. In: *Climate Change 2014: Mitigation of Climate Change*. Contribution of Working Group III to the Fifth Assessment Report of the Intergovernmental Panel on Climate Change [Edenhofer, O., R. Pichs-Madruga, Y. Sokona, E. Farahani, S. Kadner, K. Seyboth, A. Adler, I. Baum, S. Brunner, P. Eickemeier, B. Kriemann, J. Savolainen, S. Schlömer, C. von Stechow, T. Zwickel and J. C. Minx (eds.)]. Cambridge University Press, Cambridge, United Kingdom and New York, NY, USA. https://www.ipcc.ch/pdf/assessment-report/ar5/wg3/ipcc_wg3_ar5_chapter7.pdf.

Burke, Marshall, et al. "Global Non-linear Effect of Temperature on Economic Production." *Nature* (2015). Accessed March 1, 2016. doi:10.1038/nature15725.

Burney, Jennifer and V. Ramanathan. "Recent Climate and Air Pollution Impacts on Indian Agriculture." *Proceedings of the National Academy of Sciences of the United States of America* 111, no. 46 (2014). Accessed February 16, 2016. doi: 10.1073/pnas.1317275111.

The Business Association of Latin American Studies. "Carbon Footprint Across the Coffee Supply Chain: The Case of Costa Rican Coffee," November 2012. Accessed May 19, 2016. http://www.balas.org/BALAS_2013_proceedings_data/data/documents/p639212.pdf.

California Department of Food and Agriculture. "California Agriculture Production Statistics." Accessed May 12, 2016. https://www.cdfa.ca.gov/statistics/.

California Environmental Protection State Water Resources Control Board. "Adopted text of the Emergency Regulation (adopted 5/18/16)." Accessed May 21, 2016. http://www.waterboards.ca.gov/water_issues/programs/conservation_portal/docs/emergency_reg/051816_10_final%20adopted%20regs.pdf.

Campbell, Katie. "Where Does America's E-waste End Up? GPS Tracker Tells All." *PBS Newshour*, May 10, 2016. Accessed May 13, 2016. http://www.pbs.org/newshour/updates/america-e-waste-gps-tracker-tells-all-earthfix/.

Carini, David. "The Best Way to Boil Water: Nitty-Gritty." *Stanford Magazine* (2010). Accessed March 13, 2016. https://alumni.stanford.edu/get/page/magazine/article/?article_id=29243.

Carrico, R., et al. "The Environmental Cost of Misinformation: Why the Recommendation to Use Warm Water for Handwashing Is Problematic." *International Journal of Consumer Studies* (2013). Accessed May 12, 2016. doi: 10.1111/ijcs.12012.

Catalog Choice. www.catalogchoice.org.

Ceres. "Beer Companies Join Call for Action on Climate Change." March 10, 2015. Accessed May 21, 2016. http://www.ceres.org/press/press-releases/beer-companies-join-call-for-action-on-climate-change.

Ceres. "Shareholder Resolutions." Accessed June 5, 2016. http://www.ceres.org/press/press-releases/shareholders-achieve-major-corporate-sustainability-improvement-shttp://www.ceres.org/investor-network/resolutions.

Ceres. *Shareholders Spur Action On Climate Change: Company Commitments from the 2014 & 2015 Proxy Seasons.* Ceres, The Investor Network on Climate Risk, 2015. Accessed June 5, 2016. http://www.ceres.org/resources/reports/shareholders-spur-action-on-climate-change-company-committments-from-the-2014-2015-proxy-season

Chaitanya Mallapur. "61% Rise in Heat-Stroke Deaths Over Decade." *India Spend*, May 27, 2015. Accessed May 23, 2016. http://www.indiaspend.com/cover-story/61-rise-in-heat-stroke-deaths-over-decade-60404.

Chivian, Eric MD, and Aaron Bernstein MD, MPH. "How our Health Depends on Biodiversity." Harvard Medical School (Boston: Center for Health and the Global Environment at Harvard Medical School, 2010). Accessed March 2, 2016. http://www.chgeharvard.org/sites/default/files/resources/182945%20HMS%20Biodiversity%20booklet.pdf

Chu, Jennifer. "Footwear's (carbon) Footprint." *MIT News*, May 22, 2013. Accessed February 2, 2016. http://news.mit.edu/2013/footwear-carbon-footprint-0522.

Church, J. A., et al. 2013: Sea Level Change. In: *Climate Change 2013: The Physical Science Basis*. Contribution of Working Group I to the Fifth Assessment Report of the Intergovernmental Panel on Climate Change [Stocker, T. F., D. Qin, G.-K. Plattner, M. Tignor, S. K. Allen, J. Boschung, A. Nauels, Y. Xia, V. Bex and P. M. Midgley (eds.)]. Cambridge University Press, Cambridge, United Kingdom and New York, NY, USA.

City of Chicago. "Chicago Green Roofs." Accessed May 19, 2016. http://www.cityofchicago.org/city/en/depts/dcd/supp_info/chicago_green_roofs.html.

Climate Central and ICF International. "States at Risk." Accessed January 25, 2016. www.statesatrisk.org.

Clancy, S. "DNA Damage & Repair: Mechanisms for Maintaining DNA Integrity." *Nature Education* 1, no.1 (2008):103. Accessed March 3, 2016. http://www.nature.com/scitable/topicpage/DNA-Damage-Repair-Mechanisms-for-Maintaining-DNA-344.

Clark, Duncan. "The Surprisingly Complex Truth about Planes and Climate Change." *The Guardian,* September 9, 2010. Accessed May 22, 2016. http://www.theguardian.com/environment/blog/2010/sep/09/carbon-emissions-planes-shipping.

Clean Technica. "Electric Car History." Accessed May 14, 2016. http://cleantechnica.com/2015/04/26/electric-car-history/.

CNN. "Flint Water Crisis Fast Facts." Accessed September 10, 2016. http://www.cnn.com/2016/03/04/us/flint-water-crisis-fast-facts/.

CNN Staff. "Typhoon Haiyan Death Toll Tops 6,000 in the Philippines." *CNN*, December 13,2013. Accessed February 4,2016. http://edition.cnn.com/2013/12/13/world/asia/philippines-typhoon-haiyan/.

Cone Communications. *2015 Cone Communications Millennial CSR Study* (2015). Accessed May 13, 2016. http://www.conecomm.com/2015-cone-communications-millennial-csr-study.

Conley, S., et al. "Methane Emissions from the 2015 Aliso Canyon Blowout in Los Angeles, CA." *Science,* February 25, 2016. Accessed March 5, 2016. doi: 10.1126/science.aaf2348.

Crothers, Brooke. "With Tesla Model 3 Orders Nearing 400,000, Chevy Bolt Feels Heat of Tesla Brand." *Forbes*, April 15, 2016. Accessed May 15, 2016. http://www.forbes.com/sites/brookecrothers/2016/04/15/with-tesla-model-3-orders-nearing-400000-chevy-bolt-feels-heat-of-tesla-brand/#106f06f85349.

Database of State Incentives for Renewables & Efficiency (DSIRE). http://www.dsireusa.org/.

DeConto, Robert M., and David Pollard. "Contribution of Antarctica to past and Future Sea-level Rise." *Nature* 531 (2016). Accessed May 22, 2016. doi:10.1038/nature17145.

DellaSal, Dominick A. "The Tongass Rainforest as Alaska's Fist Line of Climate Change Defense and Importance to the Paris Climate Change Agreements." *Geos Institut* (2016). Accessed June 9, 2016. http://forestlegacies.org/images/projects/tongass-report-emissions-2016-01.pdf.

DeWeerdt, Sarah. "Is Local Food Better?" *World Watch.* Accessed March 12, 2016. http://www.worldwatch.org/node/6064.

Dickinson, Tamara, Timothy Male, and Ali Zaidi. "Incorporating Natural Infrastructure and Ecosystem Services in Federal Decision-Making." The White House, October 7, 2015. Accessed September 5, 2016.

Dillon, Heather E., and Michael J. Scholand. *Life-Cycle Assessment of Energy and Environmental Impacts of LED Lighting Products Part 2: LED Manufacturing and Performance.* U.S. Department of Energy. Solid-State Lighting Program Building Technologies Program Office of Energy Efficiency and Renewable Energy (2012). Accessed March 14, 2016. http://apps1.eere.energy.gov/buildings/publications/pdfs/ssl/2012_led_lca-pt2.pdf.

DMA Choice, www.dmachoice.org.

Downs, C. A., et al. "Toxicopathological Effects of the Sunscreen UV Filter, Oxybenzone (Benzophenone-3), on Coral Planulae and Cultured Primary Cells and Its Environmental Contamination in Hawaii and the U.S. Virgin Islands." *Environmental Contamination and Toxicology* 70, no.2 (2016). Accessed May 18, 2016. doi:10.1007/s00244-015-0227-7.

Duke Energy. "100 Ways to Save Energy at Home." Accessed March 8, 2016. https://www.progress-energy.com/florida/home/save-energy-money/energy-saving-tips-calculators/100-tips.page?

Earth 911, earth911.com.

Earth Day Network. "About Junk Mail." Accessed April 23, 2016. http://www.earthday.org/take-action/about-junk-mail/.

Earth Policy Institute. "Plastic Bags Factsheet." Accessed June 5, 2016. http://www.earth-policy.org/press_room/C68/plastic_bags_fact_sheet.

Ecobuddhism. "A Buddhist Declaration on Climate Change." Accessed June 8, 2016. http://www.ecobuddhism.org/bcp/all_content/buddhist_declaration/.

Ecological Society of America. "Water Purification: An Essential Ecosystem Service." Accessed June 9, 2016. http://www.esa.org/ecoservices/comm/body.comm.fact.wate.html.

The Economist. "How Much Paper Does a Person Use on Average in a Year?" April 3, 2012. Accessed May 13, 2016. http://www.economist.com/blogs/graphicdetail/2012/04/daily-chart-0.

Edwards, Larry. "America's Largest National Forest—And Its Wolves—Need Your Help by February 22," Greenpeace. Accessed June 9, 2016. http://www.greenpeace.org/usa/campaign-updates/americas-largest-national-forest-and-its-wolves-need-your-help-by-february-22/.

Elias, Pipa and Doug Boucher. *Planting for the Future: How Demand for Wood Products Could Be Friendly to Tropical Forests (2014).* Union of Concerned Scientists, Tropical Forest and Climate Initiative (2014). Accessed May 13, 2016. http://www.ucsusa.org/our-work/global-warming/stop-deforestation/planting-future-demand-wood-products#.VzW4cY-cE2w.

Ellen MacArthur Foundation. "The Circular Economy." Accessed May 21, 2016. https://www.ellenmacarthurfoundation.org/circular-economy/overview/concept.

Embrapa. "Embrapa e Inpe apresentam dados sobre o uso da terra na Amazônia." May 9, 2016. Accessed May 13, 2016. https://www.embrapa.br/busca-de-noticias/-/noticia/12355787/embrapa-e-inpe-apresentam-dados-sobre-o-uso-da-terra-na-amazonia.

ENERGY STAR. energystar.gov.

———. "Clothes Washers." Accessed March 17, 2016. https://www.energystar.gov/products/appliances/clothes_washers.

Environmental Defense Fund. "Attention Drivers! Turn off Your Idling Engines." Accessed February 2, 2016. https://www.edf.org/climate/reports/idling.

Environmental Working Group. "2016 Shopper's Guide to Pesticides in Produce." Accessed April 20, 2016. https://www.ewg.org/foodnews/summary.php.

———. "Consumer Guides." ewg.org/consumer-guides.

———. "Exposures Add Up-Survey Results." Skin Deep Cosmetics Database. Accessed May 10, 2016. http://www.ewg.org/skindeep/2004/06/15/exposures-add-up-survey-results/

———. "Guide to Healthy Cleaning." www.ewg.org/guides/cleaners.

———. "Healthy Living App." http://www.ewg.org/apps/.

———. "Skin Deep Database." ewg.org/skindeep.

———. "Top Tips for Safer Products." Accessed May 12, 2016. http://www.ewg.org/skindeep/top-tips-for-safer-products/.

EPEAT. epeat.net.

Epicurious. "Seasonal Cooking." http://www.epicurious.com/archive/seasonalcooking/farmtotable/seasonalingredientmap.

Ethical Consumer. http://www.ethicalconsumer.org/buyersguides/clothing/.

Etnoyer, Peter J., et al. "Decline in Condition of Gorgonian Octocorals on Mesophotic Reefs in the Northern Gulf of Mexico: Before and after the Deepwater Horizon Oil Spill." *Coral Reefs* 35 (2015): 77–90. Accessed March 5, 2016. doi:10.1007/s00338-015-1363-2.

Fair, Jeff. "A Journey to Alaska's Tongass, Where Our Last Old-Growth Temperate Forest Meets the Sea." Audubon (2014). Accessed June 9, 2016. http://www.

audubon.org/magazine/march-april-2014/a-journey-alaskas-tongass-where-our-last-old.

Fears, Darryl. "The Monarch Massacre: Nearly a Billion Butterflies Have Vanished." *The Washington Post*, February 9, 2015. Accessed May 13, 2016. https://www.washingtonpost.com/news/energy-environment/wp/2015/02/09/the-monarch-massacre-nearly-a-billion-butterflies-have-vanished/.

Find A Composter. findacomposter.com.

Food and Agriculture Organization (FAO). "Adverse Effects of Elevated Levels of Ultraviolet (UV)-B Radiation and Ozone (O_3) on Crop Growth and Productivity." Accessed March 3, 2016. http://www.fao.org/docrep/W5183E/w5183e09.html.

———. *Food Wastage Footprint Impacts on Natural Resources Summary Report* (2013). Accessed May 11, 2016. http://www.fao.org/docrep/018/i3347e/i3347e.pdf

———. "Ground-breaking Illegal Fishing Accord Soon to Enter into Force." May 16, 2016. Accessed May 17, 2016. http://www.fao.org/news/story/en/item/414494/icode/?utm_source=twitter&utm_medium=social+media&utm_campaign=faoknowledge.

Foreman, William, et al. "Determination of (4-methylcyclohexyl)methanol isomers by heated purge-and-trap GC/MS in water samples from the 2014 Elk River, West Virginia, Chemical Spill." *Chemosphere* 131 (2015). Accessed May 29, 2016. doi:10.1016/j.chemosphere.2014.11.006.

Fossil Free. "Divestment Commitments." Accessed September 3, 2016. http://gofossilfree.org/commitments/

Frankfurt School of Finance & Management. "Global Trends in Renewable Energy Investment 2016." Frankfurt School-UNEP Centre/BNEF, 2016. Accessed May 16, 2016. http://fs-unep-centre.org/sites/default/files/publications/globaltrendsinrenewableenergyinvestment2016lowres_0.pdf

Friend of the Earth. "Mining for Smartphones: The True Cost of Tin." Accessed June 4, 2016. https://www.foe.co.uk/sites/default/files/downloads/tin_mining.pdf.

Geiger, Nathaniel and Janet Swim. "Climate of Silence: Pluralistic Ignorance as a Barrier to Climate Change Discussion." *Journal of Environmental Psychology* (2016). Accessed May 13, 2016. doi:10.1016/j.jenvp.2016.05.002.

Gibbs, H. K., Munger, J., L'Roe, J., Barreto, P., Pereira, R., Christie, M., Amaral, T., and Walker. N. "Did Ranchers and Slaughterhouses Respond to Zero-Deforestation Agreements in the Brazilian Amazon?" *Conservation Letters* 9 (2016). Accessed May 13, 2016. doi: 10.1111/conl.12175.

Gilleo, Annie, Seth Nowak, Meegan Kelly, Shruti Vaidyanathan, Mary Shoemaker, Anna Chittum, and Tyler Bailey. *The 2015 State Energy Efficiency Scorecard*. American Council for an Energy-Efficient Economy (Washington, D.C.: American Council for an Energy-Efficient Economy, 2015). Accessed June 5, 2016. http://aceee.org/state-policy/scorecard.

Global Footprint Network. "Earth Overshoot Day-pledge 3: Is Your Country an Ecological Creditor or Debtor?" Accessed September 5, 2016. http://www.overshootday.org/portfolio/creditor-debtor/.

———. "Earth Overshoot Day." Accessed September 4, 2016. www.overshootday.org.

Global Forest Coalition. *REDD+ and the Underlying Causes of Deforestation and Forest Degradation.* 2013. Accessed January 25, 2016. http://globalforestcoalition.org/wp-content/uploads/2013/11/REDD-and-UC-report-final.pdf.

Goldenberg, Suzanne. "A Single Gas Well Leak Is California's Biggest Contributor to Climate Change." *The Guardian*, January 5, 2016. Accessed March 5, 2016. http://www.theguardian.com/environment/2016/jan/05/aliso-canyon-leak-california-climate-change.

"Good Guide," goodguide.com.

The Green Press Initiative. "Book sector." Accessed May 11, 2016. http://greenpressinitiative.org/about/bookSector.htm.

———. "Environmental Impact of E-books." Accessed May 11, 2016. http://www.greenpressinitiative.org/documents/ebooks.pdf.

Greenpeace. "The Detox Catwalk 2016." http://www.greenpeace.org/international/en/campaigns/detox/fashion/detox-catwalk/.

———. "Greenpeace Book Campaign." Accessed May 11, 2016. http://www.greenpeace.org/international/en/campaigns/forests/greenpeace-book-campaign/.

Gunders, Dana. "Wasted: How America Is Losing Up to 40 Percent of Its Food from Farm to Fork to Landfill." Natural Resources Defense Council (NRDC) (2012). Accessed September 10, 2016. https://www.nrdc.org/sites/default/files/wasted-food-IP.pdf.

Hallegatte, Stephane, et al. *Shock Waves: Managing the Impacts of Climate Change on Poverty.* World Bank (Washington, D.C.: International Bank for Reconstruction and Development/The World Bank, 2016). Accessed June 9, 2016. https://openknowledge.worldbank.org/bitstream/handle/10986/22787/9781464806735.pdf.

Hamerschlag, Kari and Kumar Venkat. *Meat Eaters Guide to Climate Change + Health Methodology*. Environmental Working Group (2011). Accessed March 8, 2016. http://static.ewg.org/reports/2011/meateaters/pdf/methodology_ewg_meat_eaters_guide_to_health_and_climate_2011.pdf.

Hammel, Debbie. *Aviation Biofuel Sustainability Scorecards.* Natural Resources Defense Council (NRDC) (2015). Accessed May 21, 2016. https://www.nrdc.org/sites/default/files/aviation-biofuel-sustainability-survey-2014.pdf.

Hardin, Garett. "The Tragedy of the Commons." *Science* 162 (1968). Accessed February 24, 2016. doi: 10.1126/science.162.3859.1243.

Harding, John. "10 Million Scallops Are Dead; Qualicum Company Lays off Staff." *The Parksville Qualicum Beach News*, February 25, 2014. Accessed March 2, 2016. http://www.pqbnews.com/news/247092381.html.

Harvey, Chelsea. "United Airlines Is Flying on Biofuels. Here's Why That's a Really Big Deal." *Washington Post,* March 11, 2016. Accessed August 29, 2016. https://www.washingtonpost.com/news/energy-environment/wp/2016/03/11/united-airlines-is-flying-on-biofuels-heres-why-thats-a-really-big-deal/?utm_term=.8f9e9c24f246.

Holzman, David C. "Mountaintop Removal Mining: Digging into Community Health Concerns." *Environmental Health Perspectives* 119, no. 11 (2011): a476–83. Accessed June 9, 2016. doi: 10.1289/ehp.119-a476.

How2Recycle. http://www.how2recycle.info/.

Howard, Brian Clark. "India Plants 50 Million Trees in One Day, Smashing World Record." *National Geographic*, July 18, 2016. Accessed September 11, 2016. http://news.nationalgeographic.com/2016/07/india-plants-50-million-trees-uttar-pradesh-reforestation/.

Hüls, Anke, et al. "Traffic-Related Air Pollution Contributes to Development of Facial Lentigines: Further Epidemiological Evidence from Caucasians and Asians." *Journal of Investigative Dermatology* 136, no. 5 (March 21, 2016). Accessed September 10, 2016. doi: 10.1016/j.jid.2015.12.045.

International Civil Aviation Organization. *ICAO Environmental Report 2013* (Montreal: Environmental Branch of the ICAO, 2013). Accessed May 16, 2016. http://cfapp.icao.int/Environmental-Report- 2013/#212/z.

International Energy Agency (IEA). "Coal." Accessed March 5, 2016. http://www.iea.org/aboutus/faqs/coal/.

———. "Frequently Asked Questions." Accessed March 5, 2016. https://www.eia.gov/tools/faqs/faq.cfm?id=69&t=2.

International Society for Reef Studies. "Briefing Paper: The Effects of Terrestrial Runoff Sediment, Nutrients, and Other Pollutants on Coral Reefs." Accessed February 2, 2016. http://coralreefs.org/wp-content/uploads/2014/05/ISRS-Briefing-Paper-3-Water-Quality.pdf.

International Union for Conservation of Nature (IUCN). "Whale Sharks, Winghead Sharks and Bornean Orangutans Slide Towards Extinction." July 8, 2016. Accessed September 5, 2016. https://www.iucn.org/news/whale-sharks-winghead-sharks-and-bornean-orangutans-slide-towards-extinction.

IPCC, 2013: Summary for Policymakers. In: *Climate Change 2013: The Physical Science Basis*. Contribution of Working Group I to the Fifth Assessment Report of the Intergovernmental Panel on Climate Change [Stocker, T. F., D. Qin, G.-K. Plattner, M. Tignor, S. K. Allen, J. Boschung, A. Nauels, Y. Xia, V. Bex and P. M. Midgley (eds.)]. Cambridge University Press, Cambridge, United Kingdom and New York, NY, USA. Accessed January 9, 2016. http://www.ipcc.ch/report/ar5/wg1/.

Irfan, Umair. "Climate Change Expands Allergy Risk." *Scientific American* (2012). Accessed March 2, 2016. http://www.scientificamerican.com/article/climate-change-expands-allergy-risk/.

Israel, Sarah. "An In-Depth Companion Planting Guide." *Mother Jones* (1981). http://www.motherearthnews.com/organic-gardening/companion-planting-guide-zmaz81mjzraw.aspx.

Ivanova, Diana, et al. "Environmental Impact Assessment of Household Consumption." *Journal of Industrial Ecology* (2015). Accessed February 28, 2016. doi 10.1111/jiec.12371.

John Hopkins Bloomberg School of Public Health, Center for a Livable Future. "Health & Environmental Implications of U.S. Meat Consumption & Production." Accessed May 9, 2016. https://www.jhsph.edu/research/centers-and-institutes/johns-hopkins-center-for-a-livable-future/projects/meatless_monday/resources/meat_consumption.html.

Johnson, Bea. "Zero Waste Home." Accessed May 15, 2016. zerowastehome.com.

Johnston, Ian. "Orangutans Face Complete Extinction Within 10 Years, Animal Rescue Charity Warns" *The Independent*, August 19, 2016. Accessed September 5, 2016. http://www.independent.co.uk/environment/orangutans-extinction-population-borneo-reasons-palm-oil-hunting-deforestation-rainforest-a7199366.html.

Kim, Kyle, et al. "Water Leaves a 'footprint' in Our Food; Here's How It Works." *The Los Angeles Times*, April 17, 2015. Accessed April 17, 2016. http://www.latimes.com/visuals/graphics/la-g-food-water-footprint-20150410-htmlstory.html.

Kissinger, Gabrielle, et al. *Drivers of Deforestation and Forest Degradation: A Synthesis Report for REDD+ Policymakers.* Vancouver Canada: Lexeme Consulting, 2012. Accessed January 24, 2016. https://www.gov.uk/government/uploads/system/uploads/attachment_data/file/65505/6316-drivers-deforestation-report.pdf.

Kovar, Seth and Steve Almasy. "Thousands of Birds Found Dead along Alaskan Shoreline." *CNN*, January 22, 2016. Accessed February 4, 2016. http://edition.cnn.com/2016/01/21/us/alaska-bird-die-off/.

Kroh, Kiley. "Endless Summer: How Climate Change Could Wipe Out Surfing." *Climate Progress*, August 1, 2013. Accessed March 3, 2016. http://thinkprogress.org/climate/2013/08/01/2164691/endless-summer-how-climate-change-could-wipe-out-surfing/

Kumar, Amit, et al. "Waiting for Merlot Anticipatory Consumption of Experiential and Material Purchases." *Psychological Science* 25, no. 10 (2014). Accessed May 21, 2016. doi: 10.1177/0956797614546556.

Lady Bird Johnson Wildflower Center. "Native Plant Database." Accessed May 13, 2016. http://www.wildflower.org/plants/.

Leigh, Elizah. "What Aluminum Extraction Really Does to the Environment." *Recycle Nation*, November 9, 2010. Accessed May 11, 2016. http://recyclenation.com/2010/11/aluminum-extraction-recycling-environment.

Lesk, Corey, et al. "Influence of Extreme Weather Disasters on Global Crop Production." *Nature* (2016). Accessed March 3, 2016. doi:10.1038/nature16467.

Liu, Jia Coco et al. "Particulate Air Pollution from Wildfires in the Western US under Climate Change." *Climactic Change*, July 30, 2015. Accessed September 11, 2016. doi: 10.1007/s10584-016-1762-6.

Maine Department of Environmental Protection Sustainability. "What Do Your Recyclables Become?"Accessed March 6, 2016.http://www.maine.gov/dep/waste/recycle/whatrecyclablesbecome.html#cardboard.

Main, Emily. "7 Plants That Purify Air." *Rodale's Organic Life*, April 2, 2015. Accessed March 6, 2016. http://www.rodalesorganiclife.com/garden/7-plants-purify-indoor-air

Maltby, Edward. *Science for Environmental Policy, Promoting Natural Water Retention-An Ecosystem Approach.* European Commission (2012). Accessed February 2, 2016. http://ec.europa.eu/environment/integration/research/newsalert/pdf/32si_en.pdf.

Margono, Belinda Arunarwati, Peter V. Potapov, Svetlana Turubanova, Fred Stolle, and Matthew C. Hansen. "Primary Forest Cover Loss in Indonesia Over 2000–2012." *Nature Climate Change* 4 (2014): 730–35. Accessed March 3, 2016. doi:10.1038/nclimate2277.

Martin, Elliot and Susan Shaheen. "Impacts of Car2go on Vehicle Ownership, Modal Shift, Vehicle Miles Traveled, and Greenhouse Gas Emissions; An Analysis of Five North American Cities." *Transportation Sustainability Research Center.* (2016). Accessed September 10, 2016. http://innovativemobility.org/wpcontent/uploads/2016/07/Impactsofcar2go_FiveCities_2016.pdf.

Martin Perera, Elizabeth and Todd Sanford. *Climate Change and Your Health, Rising Temperatures, Worsening Ozone Pollution. Union of Concerned Scientists.* (2011). Accessed March 2, 2016. http://www.ucsusa.org/sites/default/files/legacy/assets/documents/global_warming/climate-change-and-ozone-pollution.pdf.

McGranahan, Gordon, Deborah Balk, and Bridget Anderson. "The Rising Tide: Assessing the Risks of Climate Change and Human Settlements in Low Elevation Coastal Zones." *Environment and Urbanization* 19, no. 1 (April 2007): 17–37. Accessed January 25, 2016. doi: 10.1177/0956247807076960.

McGrath, Matt. "Exxon Mobil Faces 'Change or Die' Moment on Climate." *British Broadcasting Corporation*,May 24, 2016. Accessed May 26, 2016. http://www.bbc.com/news/science-environment-36332076.

McKirdy, Euan, and Mallika Kapur. "Poor Suffer as Mumbai Chokes on Garbage Dump Haze." *CNN*, February 5, 2016. Accessed March 7, 2016. http://edition.cnn.com/2016/02/05/asia/mumbai-giant-garbage-dump-fire/.

Microdocs. "Species on Coral Reefs." Accessed May 22, 2016.http://web.stanford.edu/group/microdocs/species.html.

Microsoft. "Environmental Sustainability at Microsoft." Accessed June 4, 2016. https://www.microsoft.com/about/csr/environment/.

Millennium Ecosystem Assessment. *Ecosystems and Human Well-Being: A Framework for Assessment* (2005): 56–60. Accessed February 28, 2016. http://www.millenniumassessment.org/en/Framework.html#download.

Mission Innovation. "Member Participation- United States." Accessed June 4, 2016. http://www.mission-innovation.net/participating-countries/#UnitedStates.

Moghe, Sonia. "Six Charged in West Virginia Water Contamination." *CNN*, December 18, 2014. Accessed March 13, 2016. http://edition.cnn.com/2014/12/17/justice/west-virginia-water-contamination/.

Mollman, Steve. "Santiago's Subway System will Soon be Powered Mostly by Solar and Wind Energy." *Quartz*, May 24, 2016. Accessed June 1, 2016. http://qz.com/691078/santiagos-subway-system-will-soon-be-powered-mostly-by-solar-and-wind-energy/.

Monterey Bay Aquarium Seafood Watch. "Consumer Guides." https://www.seafoodwatch.org/seafood-recommendations/consumer-guides.

Mooney, Chris. "Global Warming is now Slowing down the Circulation of the Oceans—with Potentially Dire Consequences." *The Washington Post*, March 23, 2015. Accessed March 3, 2016. https://www.washingtonpost.com/news/energy-environment/wp/2015/03/23/global-warming-is-now-slowing-down-the-circulation-of-the-oceans-with-potentially-dire-consequences/.

Mullins, Luke. "The Audacious Plan to Turn a Sprawling D.C. Suburb into a Big City." *The Washingtonian*, March 29, 2015. Accessed May 31, 2016. http://cleantechnica.com/2014/11/29/november-transit-savings-803/.

Murray, Sarah. "Fixing the Fashion Industry." *NRDC*, June 15, 2016. Accessed June 9, 2016. https://www.nrdc.org/stories/fixing-fashion-industry.

National Aeronautics and Space Administration (NASA). "July 2016 Was the Hottest Month on Record." August 21, 2016. Accessed September 10 2016. http://earthobservatory.nasa.gov/IOTD/view.php?id=88607.

National Aeronautics and Space Administration (NASA). "NASA, NOAA Analyses Reveal Record-Shattering Global Warm Temperatures in 2016." January 20, 2016. Accessed February 4, 2016. http://www.nasa.gov/press-release/nasa-noaa-analyses-reveal-record-shattering-global-warm-temperatures-in-2015.

National Aeronautics and Space Administration (NASA). "Scientific Consensus: Earth's Climate is Warming." Accessed May 13, 2016. http://climate.nasa.gov/scientific-consensus/.National Geographic. "Great Pacific Garbage Patch." Accessed March 5, 2016. http://education.nationalgeographic.org/encyclopedia/great-pacific-garbage-patch/.

National Geographic. "Water Conservation Tips." Accessed March 17, 2016. http://environment.nationalgeographic.com/environment/freshwater/water-conservation-tips/.

National Oceanic and Atmospheric Administration (NOAA). "Climate Change Increased Chances of Record Rains in Louisiana by at least 40 Percent." September 7, 2016. Accessed September 10, 2016. http://www.noaa.gov/media-release/climate-change-increased-chances-of-record-rains-in-louisiana-by-at-least-40-percent.

National Oceanic and Atmospheric Administration (NOAA). "Global Summary Information-December 2015." Accessed February 4, 2016. http://www.ncdc.noaa.gov/sotc/summary-info/global/201512.

National Oceanic and Atmospheric Administration (NOAA). "Study Supports EPA to Control Both Nitrogen and Phosphorus in Freshwaters." December 8, 2015. Accessed June 9, 2016. https://coastalscience.noaa.gov/news/coastal-pollution/study-lends-scientific-support-epa-control-nitrogen-phosphorus-freshwaters/

National Renewable Energy Laboratory (NREL). "Saving Power Through Advanced Power Strips." Accessed April 9, 2016. http://www.nrel.gov/docs/fy14osti/60461.pdf.

Natural Resources Defense Council (NRDC). "Asthma and Air Pollution." Accessed March 25, 2016. http://www.nrdc.org/health/effects/fasthma.asp.

Natural Resources Defense Council (NRDC). "Clean by Design Fiber Selection." Accessed June 9, 2016. https://www.nrdc.org/sites/default/files/CBD-Fiber-Selection-FS.pdf.

Natural Resources Defense Council (NRDC). "The Story of Silent Spring." August 13, 2015. Accessed June 9, 2016. https://www.nrdc.org/stories/story-silent-spring.

Natural Resources Defense Council (NRDC). "Summary of Information Concerning the Ecological and Economic Impacts of the BP Deepwater Horizon Oil Spill Disaster." Accessed March 5, 2016. http://www.nrdc.org/energy/gulfspill/files/gulfspill-impacts-summary-IP.pdf.

Natural Resources Defense Council (NRDC). "Water Pollution." Accessed March 6, 2016. http://www.nrdc.org/water/pollution/storm/chap3.asp.

Natural Resources Defense Council (NRDC). "Why We Need Bees." Accessed April 30, 2016. https://www.nrdc.org/sites/default/files/bees.pdf.

Natural Resources Defense Council and Ad Council. "Save the Food." Accessed May 15, 2016. http://savethefood.com/

The Nature Conservancy. "Climate Change Impacts-Wildlife at Risk." Accessed February 2, 2016. http://www.nature.org/ourinitiatives/urgentissues/global-warming-climate-change/threats-impacts/wildlife-at-risk.xml.

The Nature Conservancy. "What is Ecotourism?" Accessed May 22, 2016. http://www.nature.org/greenliving/what-is-ecotourism.xml

NextGen Climate. *The Price Tag of Being Young: Climate Change and Millennials' Economic Future*. (August 2016). Accessed September 2016. https://nextgenclimate.global.ssl.fastly.net/wp-content/uploads/2016/08/NGC-Report-The-Price-Tag-of-Being-Young-2016-0820-single-pages-1-1.pdf.

Nobel Prize. "Blue LEDs-Filling the World with New Light." Accessed March 8, 2016. https://www.nobelprize.org/nobel_prizes/physics/laureates/2014/popular-physicsprize2014.pdf.

NYU Langone Medical Center. "Press Release: Yearly Cost of U.S. Premature Births Linked to Air Pollution: $4.33 Billion." March 29, 2016. Accessed March 29, 2016. http://nyulangone.org/press- releases/yearly-cost-of-us-premature-births-linked-to-air-pollution-4-33-billion.

Ocean Conservancy. "Gulf of Mexico." Accessed March 6, 2016. http://www.oceanconservancy.org/places/gulf-of-mexico/.

Ocean Conservancy. "International Coastal Cleanup: Top 10 Items Found." Accessed June 8, 2016. http://www.oceanconservancy.org/our-work/international-coastal-cleanup/top-10-items-found-1.html.

Ocean Conservancy. "The World's Only Snapshot of Trash in the Ocean and Its Hazardous Effects on Ocean Life." Accessed March 13, 2016. http://act.oceanconservancy.org/site/DocServer/ICC_Presskit.pdf?docID=3761.Opt Out Prescreen. www.optoutprescreen.com.

Organicgardening.about.com. "Four Easy Do-It-Yourself Soil Tests." http://organicgardening. about.com/od/soil/a/easysoiltests.htm.

Osnos, Evans. "The Crisis in Flint Goes Deeper Than the Water." *The New Yorker*, January 20, 2016. Accessed June 9, 2016. http://www.newyorker.com/news/news-desk/the-crisis-in-flint-goes-deeper-than-the-water.

Palmer, M.A., et al. "Mountaintop Mining Consequences." *Science* 327 (2010): 148–49. Accessed January 17, 2016. doi: 10.1126/science.1180543.

Paris, France. "Paris réaménage ses grandes places." March 3, 2016. Accessed June 1, 2016. http://www.paris.fr/grandesplaces.

Parussini, Gabriele. "Mumbai's Vast Garbage Dump Catches Fire Again, Covering City in Smog." *The Wall Street Journal*, March 22, 2016. Accessed September 5, 2016. http://blogs.wsj.com/indiarealtime/2016/03/22/mumbais-vast-garbage-dump-catches-fire-again-covering-city-in-smog/.

Pauly, Daniel and Dirk Zeller. "Catch Reconstructions Reveal that Global Marine Fisheries Catches are Higher than Reported and Declining." *Nature Communications* 7 (2016). Accessed April 17, 2016. doi: 10.1038/ncomms10244l.

Pearen, Holly. "Want to Know the Leading Cause of Oil & Gas Spills? So Do We." Environmetnal Defesnse Fund Energy Exchange, August 31, 2016. Accessed September 20, 2016. http://blogs.edf.org/energyexchange/2016/08/31/want-to-know-the-leading-cause-of-oil-gas-spills-so-do-we/.

Phillips, Tom. "Brazilian Explorers Search 'Medicine Factory' to Save Lives and Rainforest." *The Guardian*, April 27, 2009. Accessed June 8, 2016. http://www.theguardian.com/environment/2009/apr/27/amazon-rainforest-medicine.

Pirog, Rich, et al. *Food Fuel, and Freeways: An Iowa perspective on how far Food Travels, Fuel Usage, and Greenhouse Gas Emissions.* Leopold Centre for Sustainable Agriculture (Iowa State University, 2001). Accessed September 21, 2016. http://ngfn.org/resources/ngfn-database/knowledge/food_mil.pdf.

Pongsiri, Montira J., et al. "Biodiversity Loss Affects Global Disease Ecology." *BioScience* 59, no. 11 (2009): 945–54. Accessed March 5, 2016. doi: 10.1525/bio.2009.59.11.6.

Porter, Michael, and Mark Kramer. "Creating Shared Value." *Harvard Business Review*, January–February 2011. Accessed June 9, 2016. https://hbr.org/2011/01/the-big-idea-creating-shared-valuesocialprogressimperative.org.

Postman, Andrew. "The Truth About Tap." Natural Resource Defense Council (NRDC). January 5, 2016. Accessed June 1, 2016. https://www.nrdc.org/stories/truth-about-tap.

Poulter, Sean. "Price of your Coffee to Rise: Cost Rises by a Fifth in a Week after Drought Hits Bean Crops in Brazil." *Daily Mail*, February 7, 2014. Accessed March 2, 2016. http://www.dailymail.co.uk/news/article-2553570/Price-coffee-rise-Cost-rises-fifth-week-drought-hits-bean-crops-Brazil.html.

Powell, Jon T., et al. "Estimates of Solid Waste Disposal Rates and Reduction Targets for Landfill Gas Emissions." *Nature Climate Change* 6 (2016). Accessed May 18, 2016. doi:10.1038/nclimate2804.

Raghab, Safaa M., et al. "Treatment of Leachate from Municipal Solid Waste Landfill." *Housing and Building National Research Center Journal* 9, no. 2 (2013). Accessed May 21, 2016, doi:10.1016/j.hbrcj.2013.05.007.

Reckdahl, Katy. "Losing Louisiana." *The Weather Channel.* Accessed April 16, 2016. http://stories.weather.com/story/5931.

Reuters. "China, U.S. Pledge Support for Global Aviation Emissions Pact." September 3, 2016. Accessed September 5, 2016. http://www.reuters.com/article/us-china-aviation-idUSKCN1190B3.

Richtel, Matt. "San Diego Vows to Move Entirely to Renewable Energy in 20 Years." *The New York Times*, December 15, 2015. Accessed June 2, 2016. http://www.nytimes.com/2015/12/16/science/san-diego-vows-to-move-entirely-to-renewable-energy-in-20-years.html?_r=1.

Rochman, Cheslea M., Eunha Hoh, Tomofumi Kurobe, and Swee J. Teh. "Ingested Plastic Transfers Hazardous Chemicals to Fish and Induces Hepatic Stress." *Scientific Reports* (2013). Accessed March 6, 2016. doi:10.1038/srep03263.

Rochman, Chelsea M., et al. "Scientific Evidence Supports a Ban on Microbeads." *Environmental Science & Technology* 49 (2015): 10759–0761. Accessed April 23, 2016. doi: 10.1021/acs.est.5b03909.

Rodríguez Mega, Emiliano. "Oil Spills Stain Peruvian Amazon." *Scientific American*, March 4, 2016. Accessed June 9, 2016. http://www.scientificamerican.com/article/oil-spills-stain-peruvian-amazon/.

Ross, Elizabeth. "Here's a Small Town's Advice for Cities Considering a Plastic Bottle Ban." Public Radio International, February 23, 2016. Accessed June 8, 2016. http://www.pri.org/stories/2016-02-23/heres-small-towns-advice-cities-considering-plastic-water-bottle-ban.

Prüss-Ustün, A., J. Wolf, C. Corvalán, R. Bos, and M. Neira, *Preventing Disease Through Healthy Environments: A Global Assessment of the Burden of Disease from Environmental Risks*. World Health Organization. March 2016. Accessed September 10, 2016. http://apps.who.int/iris/bitstream/10665/204585/1/9789241565196_eng.pdf?ua=1.

Public Broadcasting Service (PBS). "Running on Renewable Energy, Burlington, Vermont Powers Green Movement Forward." *PBS NewsHour*, January 31, 2015. Accessed June 2, 2016. http://www.pbs.org/newshour/bb/vermont-city-come-rely-100-percent-renewable-energy/.

Saad, Lydia and Jeffrey M. Jones. "U.S. Concern About Global Warming at Eight-Year High." Gallup Polls, March 16, 2016. Accessed September 10, 2016. http://www.gallup.com/poll/190010/concern-global-warming-eight-year-high.aspx.

San Francisco Public Utilities Commission. "Event Water-How to Comply with the Bottled Water Ban." Accessed June 8, 2016. http://www.sfwater.org/index.aspx?page=912.

Schlossberg, Tatiana. "Just How Much Power Do Your Electronics Use When They Are 'Off'?" *New York Times*, May 7, 2016. Accessed May 10, 2016. http://www.nytimes.com/2016/05/08/science/just-how-much-power-do-your-electronics-use-when-they-are-off.html?_r=0.

Sea Turtle Conservancy. "Information About Sea Turtles: Threats from Marine Debris." Accessed May 11, 2016. http://www.conserveturtles.org/seaturtleinformation.php?page=marine_debris.

Seidman, Bianca. "Poison Ivy, Poison Oak Becoming Stronger over Time." *CBS News*, June 9, 2015. Accessed March 2, 2016. http://www.cbsnews.com/news/poison-ivy-poison-oak-becoming-stronger-over-time/.

Siegel, Matt. "Australian Scientists Alarmed at New Great Barrier Reef Coral Bleaching." *Reuters*, March 21, 2016. Accessed March 22, 2016. http://www.businessinsider.com/r-australia-scientists-alarmed-at-new-great-barrier-reef-coral-bleaching-2016-3.

Siegle, Lucy. "Should I Stop Buying Paper Books and Use an e-reader Instead?" *The Guardian*, January 6, 2013. Accessed May 11, 2016. http://www.theguardian.com/environment/2013/jan/06/should-i-buy-an-e-reader.

Siemens. "11 Surprising Facts that will Change Your Water Usage." *Mother Nature Network*. Accessed May 19, 2016. http://www.mnn.com/money/sustainable-business-practices/sponsorstory/11-surprising-facts-that-will-change-your-water.

Simpson, M. C., S. Gössling, D. Scott, C. M. Hall, and E. Gladin. *Climate Change Adaptation and Mitigation in the Tourism Sector: Frameworks, Tools and Practices.*

UNEP, University of Oxford, UNWTO, WMO: Paris, France (2008). Accessed March 5, 2016. http://sdt.unwto.org/sites/all/files/docpdf/ccoxford.pdf.

Sims, R., R. Schaeffer, F. Creutzig, X. Cruz-Núñez, M. D'Agosto, D. Dimitriu, M. J. Figueroa Meza, L., Fulton, S. Kobayashi, O. Lah, A. McKinnon, P. Newman, M. Ouyang, J. J. Schauer, D. Sperling, and G. Tiwari. 2014: Transport. In: *Climate Change 2014: Mitigation of Climate Change*. Contribution of Working Group III to the Fifth Assessment Report of the Intergovernmental Panel on Climate Change [Edenhofer, O., R. Pichs-Madruga, Y. Sokona, E. Farahani, S. Kadner, K. Seyboth, A. Adler, I. Baum, S. Brunner, P. Eickemeier, B. Kriemann, J. Savolainen, S. Schlömer, C. von Stechow, T. Zwickel and J. C. Minx (eds.)]. Cambridge University Press, Cambridge, United Kingdom and New York, NY, USA. Accessed January 28, 2016. https://www.ipcc.ch/pdf/assessment-report/ar5/wg3/ipcc_wg3_ar5_chapter8.pdf.

Smith, P., M. Bustamante, H. Ahammad, H. Clark, H. Dong, E. A. Elsiddig, H. Haberl, R. Harper, J. House, M. Jafari, O. Masera, C. Mbow, N. H. Ravindranath, C. W. Rice, C. Robledo Abad, A. Romanovskaya, F. Sperling, and F. Tubiello, 2014: Agriculture, Forestry and Other Land Use (AFOLU). In: *Climate Change 2014: Mitigation of Climate Change*. Contribution of Working Group III to the Fifth Assessment Report of the Intergovernmental Panel on Climate Change [Edenhofer, O., R. Pichs-Madruga, Y. Sokona, E. Farahani, S. Kadner, K. Seyboth, A. Adler, I. Baum, S. Brunner, P. Eickemeier, B. Kriemann, J. Savolainen, S. Schlömer, C. von Stechow, T. Zwickel and J.C. Minx (eds.)]. Cambridge University Press, Cambridge, United Kingdom and New York, NY, USA. Accessed January 27, 2016. https://www.ipcc.ch/pdf/assessment-report/ar5/wg3/ipcc_wg3_ar5_chapter11.pdf.

"Social Progress Index," socialprogressimperative.org.

SolarImpulse. "SolarImpulse." Accessed May 21, 2016. http://www.solarimpulse.com.

Solaroad. "Solaroad." Accessed May 21, 2016. http://en.solaroad.nl/."Stanford and Climate Change: A Statement of the Board of Trustees." *Stanford News*, April 25, 2016. Accessed June 7, 2016. https://news.stanford.edu/2016/04/25/stanford-climate-change-statement-board-trustees/.

Stanford University Office of the President. *Letter to Laurent Fabius, President, COP21 Conference*. October 28, 2015. Accessed June 7, 2016. http://news.stanford.edu/news/2015/october/climate1_statement_102815.pdf.

State of New Jersey Department of Environmental Protection. "A Homeowner's Guide to Arsenic in Drinking Water." Accessed March 13, 2016. http://www.state.nj.us/dep/dsr/arsenic/guide.htm.

Statista. "Best-selling all-electric Cars in the United States in 2015, Based on Sales (in units)." Accessed May 15, 2016. http://www.statista.com/statistics/257966/best-selling-electric-cars-in-the-united-states/.

Statista. "Statistics and Facts about Electric Mobility." Accessed May 15, 2016. http://www.statista.com/topics/1010/electric-mobility/`.

Steffen, Will, et al. "The Anthropocene: Conceptual and Historical Perspectives." *Philosophical Transactions of the Royal Society* (2011). Accessed June 9, 2016. doi: 10.1098/rsta.2010.0327.

Stokes, Bruce, Richard Wike, and Jill Carle. "Global Concern about Climate Change, Broad Support for Limiting Emissions." *Pew Research Center Global Attitudes and Trends*, November 2, 2015. Accessed May 13, 2016. http://www.pewglobal.org/2015/11/05/global-concern-about-climate-change-broad-support-for-limiting-emissions/.

Sustainable Development Knowledge Platform. "Sustainable Development Goals." Accessed September 6, 2016. https://sustainabledevelpoment.un.org/sdgs.

Sustainable Table. "Seasonal Food Guide." http://gracelinks.org/seasonalfoodguide/.

Taub, Erica. "How Long Did You Say That Bulb Would Last?" *New York Times Bits*, February 11, 2009. Accessed August 30, 2016. http://bits.blogs.nytimes.com/2009/02/11/how-long-did-you-say-that-bulb-will-last/.

Tencer, Daniel. "Number of Cars Worldwide Surpasses 1 Billion; Can The World Handle This Many Wheels?" *Huffington Post*, August 23, 2011. Accessed June 9, 2016. http://www.huffingtonpost.ca/2011/08/23/car-population_n_934291.html.

Ter Steege, Hans, et al. "Estimating the Global Conservation Status of More than 15,000 Amazonian Tree Species." *Science Advances* 1, no. 10 (2015). Accessed January 25, 2016. doi:10.1126/sciadv.1500936.

Think Dirty. thinkdirtyapp.com.

Toxnet Toxicology Data Network. "4-Methylcyclohexanemethanol." Accessed May 29, 2016. https://toxnet.nlm.nih.gov/cgi-bin/sis/search/a?dbs+hsdb:@term+@DOCNO+8182.

Trade and Environment Database (TED). "Jamaica Bauxite Case." Accessed May 11, 2016. http://www1.american.edu/TED/bauxite.htm.

Trager Rebecca. "Investigators Find Cause of West Virginia Chemical Spill." Chemistry World, July 24, 2014. Accessed May 29, 2016. http://www.rsc.org/chemistryworld/2014/07/investigators-find-cause-west-virginia-chemical-spill.

Transfernation. "About Us." Accessed May 8, 2016. http://transfernation.org/about.php.

Trucost. "EP&L." Accessed April 9, 2016. http://www.trucost.com/environmental-profit-and-loss-accounting.

United Nations Development Programme (UNDP). "Haiti: Exporting Coffee While Protecting Biodiversity." Accessed June 9, 2016. http://www.undp.org/content/undp/en/home/ourwork/ourstories/haiti---le-cafe--s-exporte-tout-en-protegeant-la-biodiversite.html.

United Nations Educational, Scientific and Cultural Organization (UNESCO). "Facts and Figures on Marine Pollution." Accessed March 5, 2016. http://www.unesco.org/new/en/natural-sciences/ioc-oceans/priority-areas/rio-20-ocean/blueprint-for-the-future-we-want/marine-pollution/facts-and-figures-on-marine-pollution/.

United Nations Framework Convention on Climate Change (UNFCCC). *Draft decision-/CP.15 Proposal by the President Copenhagen Accord* (Copenhagen, 2009). Accessed February 3, 2016. http://unfccc.int/resource/docs/2009/cop15/eng/l07.pdf.

United Nations Framework Convention on Climate Change (UNFCCC). "Islamic Declaration on Climate Change Calls for 1.6 billion Muslims to Support Strong

Paris Agreement." Accessed June 8, 2016. http://newsroom.unfccc.int/unfccc-newsroom/islamic-declaration-on-climate-change/.

United Nations News Centre. "Forests Expand in Europe and North America, but Still Vulnerable to Climate Change." March 11, 2011. Accessed June 8, 2016. http://www.un.org/apps/news/story.asp?NewsID=37845#.V1hd3bsrLIU.

United Nations Reducing Emissions from Deforestation and Degradation (REDD+) Programme. "UN-REDD Programme Donors." Accessed June 4, 2016. http://www.un-redd.org/Donors_and_Partners/tabid/102612/Default.aspx.

U.S. Department of Agriculture. "Number of U.S. Farmers' Markets Continues to Rise." Accessed May 13, 2016. http://www.ers.usda.gov/data-products/chart-gallery/detail.aspx?chartId=48561&ref=collection&embed=True.

U.S. Department of Agriculture Economic Research Service. "Food Security in the U.S. Key Statistics and Graphics 2014." Accessed April 25, 2016. http://www.ers.usda.gov/topics/food-nutrition-assistance/food-security-in-the-us/key-statistics-graphics.aspx.

U.S. Department of Agriculture, Forest Service. "Insect Disturbance." Accessed January 25, 2016. http://www.fs.usda.gov/ccrc/topics/insect-disturbance.

U.S. Department of Energy. "15 Ways to Save on Your Water Heating Bill." Accessed February 20, 2016. http://energy.gov/energysaver/articles/15-ways-save-your-water-heating-bill.

U.S. Department of Energy. "Air Conditioning." Accessed February 2, 2016. http://energy.gov/energysaver/air-conditioning.

U.S. Department of Energy. "Are Energy Vampires Sucking You Dry?" October 29, 2015. Accessed April 24, 2016. http://energy.gov/articles/are-energy-vampires-sucking-you-dry.

U.S. Department of Energy. "Energy Saver 101 Infographic: Landscaping." Accessed May 12, 2016. http://energy.gov/articles/energy-saver-101-infographic-landscaping.

U.S. Department of Energy. "Heating and Cooling." Accessed March 6, 2016. http://energy.gov/public-services/homes/heating-cooling.

U.S. Department of Energy. "Keeping Your Vehicle in Shape." Accessed May 9, 2016. https://www.fueleconomy.gov/feg/maintain.jsp.

U.S. Department of Energy. "Maintaining Your Air Conditioner." Accessed September 8, 2016. http://energy.gov/energysaver/maintaining-your-air-conditioner.

U.S. Department of Energy. "Savings Project: Lower Water Heater Temperature." Accessed March 6, 2016. http://energy.gov/energysaver/projects/savings-project-lower-water-heating-temperature.

U.S. Department of Energy. "Tips: Kitchen Appliances." Accessed April 5, 2016. http://energy.gov/energysaver/tips-kitchen-appliances.

U.S. Department of Energy. "When to Turn off Your Lights." http://energy. gov/energysaver/when-turn-your-lights.

U.S. Department of Transportation. "2016 Traffic Volume Trends." Accessed September 11, 2016. https://www.fhwa.dot.gov/policyinformation/travel_monitoring/16juntvt/page2.cfm.

U.S. Energy Information Administration. "How much Electricity is Used for Lighting in the United States?" Accessed March 13, 2016. http://www.eia.gov/tools/faqs/faq.cfm?id=99&t=3.

U.S. Energy Information Administration. "Total Energy." Accessed May 7, 2016. http://www.eia.gov/totalenergy/

U.S. Energy Information Administration. "What is U.S. Electricity Generation by Energy source?" Accessed May 22, 2016. https://www.eia.gov/tools/faqs/faq.cfm?id=427&t=3.

U.S. Energy Information Administration. "Which States Consume and Produce the Most Natural Gas?" Accessed January 9, 2016. https://www.eia.gov/tools/faqs/faq.cfm?id=46&t=8.

U.S. Environmental Protection Agency. *Advancing Sustainable Materials Management: 2013 Fact Sheet.* Washington, D.C.: United States Environmental Protection Agency Solid Waste and Emergency Response (2015). Accessed April 24, 2016. https://www.epa.gov/sites/production/files/2015-09/documents/2013_advncng_smm_fs.pdf.

U.S. Environmental Protection Agency. *Climate Change in the United States: Benefits of Global Action.* U.S. Environmental Protection Agency, Office of Atmospheric Programs (2015). Accessed March 1, 2016. http://www.epa.gov/sites/production/files/2015-06/documents/frontmatter.pdf.

U.S. Environmental Protection Agency. "Electronics Donation and Recycling." Accessed May 10, 2016. https://www.epa.gov/recycle/electronics-donation-and-recycling.

U.S. Environmental Protection Agency. *Electronics Waste Management in the United States through 2009.* U.S. Environmental Protection Agency Office of Resources Conservation and Recovery. (2011). Accessed May 11, 2016. http://1.usa.gov/1TQTaYU.

U.S. Environmental Protection Agency. *EPA Finalizes First Steps to Address Greenhouse Gas Emissions from Aircraft Engines.* Office of Transportation and Air Quality. July 2016. Accessed September 5, 2016. https://www3.epa.gov/otaq/documents/aviation/420f16036.pdf.

U.S. Environmental Protection Agency. "Greenhouse Gas Emissions from a Typical Passenger Vehicle." Accessed March 18, 2016. https://www3.epa.gov/otaq/climate/documents/420f14040a.pdf.

U.S. Environmental Protection Agency. "Inventory of U.S. Greenhouse Gas Emissions and Sinks." Washington, D.C.: U.S. Environmental Protection Agency. (2015). Accessed January 27, 2016. http://www3.epa.gov/climatechange/Downloads/ghgemissions/US-GHG-Inventory-2015-Main-Text.pdf.

U.S. Environmental Protection Agency. "National Summary of State Information." Accessed May 19, 2016. https://ofmpub.epa.gov/waters10/attains_nation_cy.control.

U.S. Environmental Protection Agency. "Overview of Greenhouse Gases." Accessed February 2, 2016. http://www3.epa.gov/climatechange/ghgemissions/gases/n2o.html.

U.S. Environmental Protection Agency, "Reduce, Reuse, Recycle." Accessed October 30, 2016. https://www.epa.gov/recycle

U.S. Environmental Protection Agency. "Reduce, Recycle, Reuse: Greening the Season." Accessed April 20, 2016. https://www3.epa.gov/region9/waste/recycling/index.html.

U.S. Environmental Protection Agency. "Save Water and Energy by Showering Better." Accessed April 22, 2016. https://www3.epa.gov/watersense/docs/ws_shower_better_learning_resource_508.pdf.

U.S. Environmental Protection Agency. "What is Sustainability." Accessed June 5, 2016. https://www.epa.gov/sustainability/learn-about-sustainability#what.

U.S. Fish and Wildlife Service. "Balloons and Wildlife: Please Don't Release Your Balloons." Accessed May 21, 2016. https://www.fws.gov/news/blog/index.cfm/2015/8/5/Balloons-and-Wildlife-Please-Dont-Release-Your-Balloons.

U.S. Food and Drug Administration. "Cosmetics Safety Q&A: Personal Care Products." Accessed May 12, 2016. http://www.fda.gov/Cosmetics/ResourcesForYou/Consumers/ucm136560.htm.

U.S. Food and Drug Administration. "Safety and Effectiveness of Consumer Antiseptics; Topical Antimicrobial Drug Products for Over-the-Counter Human Use." Health and Human Services. Final Rule. *Federal Register.* Document Citation 81 FR 61106. September 6, 2016. Accessed September 15, 2016. https://s3.amazonaws.com/public-inspection.federalregister.gov/2016-21337.pdf.

U.S. Geological Survey. "Water Questions and Answers." Accessed March 12, 2016. http://water.usgs.gov/edu/qa-home-percapita.html.

U.S. National Park Service. "Great Smoky Mountains Air Quality." Accessed April 10, 2016. https://www.nps.gov/grsm/learn/nature/air-quality.htm.

U.S. National Park Service. "America's National Parks: Record Number of Visitors in 2015." National Service Press Release, January 27. 2016. Accessed September 11, 2016. http://www.nps.gov/aboutus/news/release.htm?id=1775.

University of Maryland. "U.S. Beekeepers Lost 40 Percent of Bees in 2014–15." *ScienceDaily*, May 13 2015. Accessed April 30, 2016. www.sciencedaily.com/releases/2015/05/150513093605.htm.

Vandenbergh, Michael, and Anne Steinemann. "The Carbon Neutral Individual." *New York Law Review* 82, no. 6 (2007). Accessed May 9, 2016. http://www.nyulawreview.org/issues/volume-82-number-6/carbon-neutral-individual.

The Vatican. "Encyclical Letter Laudato SI' of The Holy Father Francis on Care for Our Common Home." Accessed February 22, 2016. http://w2.vatican.va/content/francesco/en/encyclicals/documents/papa-francesco_20150524_enciclica-laudato-si.html.

Verchot, Louis. "The Science is Clear: Forest Loss behind Brazil's Drought." Forest News, January 29, 2015. Accessed February 2, 2016. http://blog.cifor.org/26559/the-science-is-clear-forest-loss-behind-brazils-drought?fnl=en.

Von Kaenel, Camille. "Americans Are Driving More Than Ever." *Scientific American*, February 22, 2016. Accessed March 5, 2016. http://www.scientificamerican.com/article/americans-are-driving-more-thanever1/?utm_content=buffer5831e&utm_medium=social&utm_source=twitter.com&utm_campaign=buffer.

Victor, David and Charles Kennel. "Climate Policy: Ditch the 2 °C Warming Goal." *Nature* October 1, 2014, Accessed September 20, 2016. doi:10.1038/514030a.

WaterSense. "Showerheads." Accessed March 17, 2016. https://www3.epa.gov/watersense/products/showerheads.html.

Waterworld. "World Water Day 2016: Water from Coal Operations Could Sustain 1 Billion People, Finds Study." Accessed March 22, 2016. http://www.waterworld.com/articles/wwi/2016/03/world-water-day-2016-water-from-coal-operations-could-sustain-1-billion-people-finds-study.html.

Wattway by Colas. Accessed May 17, 2016. http://www.wattwaybycolas.com/en/.

The Weather Channel. "Climate Disruption Index." Accessed April 16, 2016. http://stories.weather.com/disruptionindex.

Wei, Yongjie, et al. "Chronic Exposure to Air Pollution Particles Increases the Risk of Obesity and Metabolic Syndrome: Findings from a Natural Experiment in Beijing." *The FASEB Journal* (2016). Accessed February 23, 2016. doi: 10.1096/fj.201500142.

Welch, Catherine. "An All-Volunteer Squad of Farmers is Turning Florida Lawns into Food." *National Public Radio, All Things Considered,* May 16, 2016. Accessed May 31, 2016. http://www.npr.org/sections/thesalt/2016/05/15/477036910/an-all-volunteer-squad-of-farmers-is-turning-florida-lawns-into-food?utm_campaign=storyshare&utm_source=twitter.com&utm_medium=social.

The White House. "FACT SHEET: Federal Support for the Flint Water Crisis Response and Recovery." May 3, 2016. Accessed September 10, 2016. https://www.whitehouse.gov/the-press-office/2016/05/03/fact-sheet-federal-support-flint-water-crisis-response-and-recovery.

The White House Office of the Press Secretary. "Fact Sheet: President Obama to Create the World's Largest Marine Protected Area." August 26, 2016. Accessed September 5, 2016. https://www.whitehouse.gov/the-press-office/2016/08/26/fact-sheet-president-obama-create-worlds-largest-marine-protected-area.

Wilcox, Chris, et al. "Threat of Plastic Pollution to Seabirds is Global, Pervasive, and Increasing." *Proceedings of the National Academy of Sciences of the United States of America* 112, no. 38 (2015). Accessed May 11, 2016. doi:10.1073/pnas.1513514112.

Wilkinson, Allie. "In Brazil, Cattle Industry Begins to Help Fight Deforestation." *Science,* May 15, 2015. Accessed May 13, 2016. http://www.sciencemag.org/news/2015/05/brazil-cattle-industry-begins-help-fight-deforestation.

Williams, Geoffrey, et al. "Neonicotinoid Pesticides Severely Affect Honey Bee Queens." *Scientific Reports* 5 (2015). Accessed April 30, 2016. doi:10.1038/srep14621.

Wines, Michael, and John Schwartz. "Unsafe Lead Levels in Tap Water Not Limited to Flint." *The New York Times*, February 8, 2016. Accessed March 13, 2016. http://www.nytimes.com/2016/02/09/us/regulatory-gaps-leave-unsafe-lead-levels-in-water-nationwide.html?_r=1 =.

Wolverton, B.C., Anne Johnson, and Keith Bounds. *Interior Landscape Plants for Indoor Air Pollution Abatement.* National Aeronautics and Space Administration (NASA) Office of Commercial Program- Technology Utilization Division and the Associated Landscape Contractors of America. (1989). Accessed March 6, 2016. http://ntrs.nasa.gov/archive/nasa/casi.ntrs.nasa.gov/19930073077.pdf.

World Bank. "Green Bond Issuances to Date." Accessed May 14, 2016. http://treasury.worldbank.org/cmd/htm/GreenBondIssuancesToDate.html.

World Bank. *High and Dry: Climate Change, Water, and the Economy.* Washington, D.C.: International Bank for Reconstruction and Development/The World

Bank (2016). Accessed May 29, 2016. http://www.worldbank.org/en/topic/water/publication/high-and-dry-climate-change-water-and-the-economy?CID=WAT_TT_Water_EN_EXT.

World Bank. "Rural Population (Percent of total)." Accessed March 3, 2016. http://data.worldbank.org/indicator/SP.RUR.TOTL.ZS.

World Economic Forum. "The Number of Cars Worldwide is Set to Double by 2040." April 22, 2016. Accessed May 15, 2016. http://bit.ly/1VXVIIa.

World Health Organization (WHO). "Ambient (outdoor) Air Quality and Health." March 2014. Accessed January, 21, 2016. http://www.who.int/mediacentre/factsheets/fs313/en/.

World Health Organization (WHO). "Health Effects of UV radiation." Accessed March 3, 2016. http://www.who.int/uv/health/uv_health2/en/index3.html.

World Health Organization (WHO). "The Top 10 Causes of Death by Income Group." (2012). Accessed March 9, 2016. http://www.who.int/mediacentre/factsheets/fs310/en/index1.html.

World Resources Institute (WRI). "Aqueduct." Accessed May 12, 2016. http://www.wri.org/our-work/project/aqueduct.

World Resources Institute (WRI). "Paris Agreement Tracker." CAIT Climate Data Explorer. Accessed September 4, 2016. https://cait.wri.org/indc/#/ratification.

World Wildlife Fund (WWF). *Going Wild for Rubber, Sourcing Wild Rubber from the Amazon: Why You should and How You Can* (2014). Accessed February 2, 2016. http://assets.wwf.org.uk/downloads/wwf_a4_report_wild_rubber_web__2_.pdf.

World Wildlife Fund (WWF). "The Impact of a Cotton T-Shirt." Accessed February 2, 2016. http://www.worldwildlife.org/stories/the-impact-of-a-cotton-t-shirt.

World Wildlife Fund (WWF). "Inside the Amazon." Accessed January 25, 2016. http://wwf.panda.org/what_we_do/where_we_work/amazon/about_the_amazon/.

World Wildlife Fund (WWF). "Palm Oil." Accessed May 20, 2016. http://wwf.panda.org/what_we_do/footprint/agriculture/palm_oil/.

Worldwatch Institute. "The State of Consumption Today." Accessed March 16, 2016. http://www.worldwatch.org/node/810.

Yale Environmental Performance Index. "Climate and Energy." Accessed February 12, 2016. http://epi.yale.edu/chapter/climate-and-energy.

Yale Environmental Performance Index. "Environmental Performance Index Reveals Dire State of Fisheries, Worsening Air Pollution." Accessed February 12, 2016. http://epi.yale.edu/chapter/key-findings.

Yale Environmental Performance Index. "Forests." Accessed February 12, 2016. http://epi.yale.edu/chapter/forests.

Yang, Sarah. "Climate Change Leading to Major Vegetation Shifts around the World." *University of California, Berkeley News*, June 4, 2010. Accessed January 25, 2016. http://news.berkeley.edu/2010/06/04/climate/.

Zero Deforestation Cattle. Accessed May 13, 2016. http://www.zerodeforestation-cattle.org/ch1t2.html.

Zivin, Joshua Graff, and Matthew Neidell. "The Impact of Pollution on Worker Productivity." *American Economic Review* 102, no. 7 (2012). Accessed February 16, 2016. doi: 10.1257/aer.102.7.3652.

Index